LEARNING-DISABLED/ GIFTED CHILDREN

LEARNING-DISABLED/ GIFTED CHILDREN
Identification and Programming

edited by

Lynn H. Fox, Ph.D.
Linda Brody, M.S.
Dianne Tobin, M.S.
Education Division, Evening College
and Summer Session
The Johns Hopkins University

University Park Press
Baltimore

UNIVERSITY PARK PRESS
International Publishers in Medicine and Human Services
300 North Charles Street
Baltimore, Maryland 21201

Copyright © 1983 by University Park Press

Typeset by Maryland Composition Company, Inc.

Manufactured in the United States of America by
The Maple Press Company

This book is protected by copyright. All rights, including that of translation
into other languages, are reserved. No part of this book may be reproduced,
stored in a retrieval system, or transmitted, in any form or by any means,
electronic, mechanical, photocopying, recording, or otherwise, without the
prior written permission of the publisher.

Library of Congress Cataloging in Publicaton Data
Main entry under title:
Learning–disabled/gifted children.

Includes bibliographical references and index.
1. Gifted children—Education—Evaluation—Addresses,
essays, lectures. 2. Learning disabilities—Evaluation
—Addresses, essays, lectures. I. Fox, Lynn H.,
1944–   . II. Brody, Linda. III. Tobin, Dianne.
LC3993.2.L43   1983   371.95′2   83-5930
ISBN 0-8391-1881-3

Contents

Contributors vii
Preface ix
Dedication xi

Introduction 1
        Lynn H. Fox, Linda Brody, and Dianne Tobin

PART I   The Learning-Disabled/Gifted Child:
        Concepts and Characteristics

Chapter 1 Giftedness and Learning Disability:
           A *Paradoxical Combination* 11
           Abraham J. Tannenbaum and Lois J. Baldwin

Chapter 2 The Nature and Identification of Learning Disabilities and
           Their Relationship to the Gifted Child 37
           Gerald M. Senf

Chapter 3 Learning Disabilities as a Category of
           Underachievement 51
           Ronald A. Berk

Chapter 4 The Gifted Child with a Learning Disability:
           Clinical Evidence 77
           Stanley L. Rosner and Jeannette Seymour

PART II   Issues in Identification: *Problems and Practices*

Chapter 5 Models for Identifying Giftedness: *Issues Related to the*
           Learning-Disabled Child 101
           Lynn H. Fox and Linda Brody

Chapter 6 Gifted Students with Reading Problems:
           An Empirical Study 117
           Lynn H. Fox

Chapter 7 Diagnosis: *A Case-Typing Approach* 141
           Stanley L. Rosner

vi   *Contents*

PART III   Programming

Chapter 8   Teaching the Learning-Disabled/Gifted Child 153
              Paul R. Daniels

Chapter 9   The Adaptation of Gifted Programming for
              Learning-Disabled Students 171
              James J. Gallagher

Chapter 10   Adaptive Methods and Techniques for
              Learning-Disabled/Gifted Children 183
              Lynn H. Fox, Dianne Tobin, and
              Gilbert B. Schiffman

Chapter 11   Computer Technology for Learning-Disabled/
              Gifted Students 195
              Dianne Tobin and Gilbert B. Schiffman

Chapter 12   A Model Program for Elementary-Age
              Learning-Disabled/Gifted Youngsters 207
              Lois J. Baldwin and Denise A. Gargiulo

Chapter 13   A Pilot Program for Elementary-Age Learning-Disabled/
              Gifted Students 223
              Anne J. Udall and C. June Maker

Chapter 14   Working with Parents of Learning-Disabled/Gifted
              Children 243
              Patricia M. Bricklin

Chapter 15   Teacher Training in the Clinical Method for Learning-
              Disabled/Gifted Children 261
              M.E.B. Lewis and Paul R. Daniels

Conclusion: *Future Directions for Research and Practice* 275
              Lynn H. Fox, Linda Brody, and Dianne Tobin

Author Index 281

Subject Index 285

Contributors

Lois J. Baldwin, M.A.
Doctoral Candidate in Gifted
  Education
Teachers College
Columbia University
New York, New York;
Teacher for Gifted/Special
  Education Students
Board of Cooperative Educational
  Services
Pocantico Hills School District
North Tarrytown, New York 10591

Ronald A. Berk, Ph.D.
Associate Professor of Education
The Johns Hopkins University
Evening College and Summer
  Session
Baltimore, Maryland 21218

Patricia M. Bricklin, Ph.D.
Clinical Professor
Hahnemann University School of
  Medicine
Philadelphia, Pennsylvania;
Psychological-Educational
  Consultant
470 General Washington Road
Wayne, Pennsylvania 19087

Linda Brody, M.S.
Doctoral Candidate in Gifted
  Education;
Project Associate, Intellectually
  Gifted Child Study Group
The Johns Hopkins University
Evening College and Summer
  Session
Baltimore, Maryland 21218

Paul R. Daniels, Ed.D.
Professor of Education

The Johns Hopkins University
Evening College and Summer
  Session
Baltimore, Maryland 21218

Lynn H. Fox, Ph.D.
Professor of Education;
Coordinator of the Intellectually
  Gifted Child Study Group
The Johns Hopkins University
Evening College and Summer
  Session
Baltimore, Maryland 21218

James J. Gallagher, Ph.D.
Director, Frank Porter Graham
  Child Development Center;
Kenan Professor, School of
  Education
University of North Carolina
Chapel Hill, North Carolina 27514

Denise A. Gargiulo, M.A.
Graduate Student
Teachers College
Columbia University
New York, New York;
Resource Teacher for Learning
  Disabled Students
North Salem School District
North Salem, New York 10560

M.E.B. Lewis, Ed.D.
Principal, Kennedy School for
  Learning Disabled Children
John F. Kennedy Institute for
  Handicapped Children
707 North Broadway
Baltimore, Maryland 21205

C. June Maker, Ph.D.
Associate Professor of Special
  Education;

viii   *Contributors*

Coordinator, Graduate Programs in
    Education of the Gifted
Department of Special Education
University of Arizona
Tucson, Arizona 85721

Stanley L. Rosner, Ph.D.
Chairman, Psychology of Reading
    Department
Temple University
Philadelphia, Pennsylvania 19122

Gilbert B. Schiffman, Ed.D.
Professor of Education
The Johns Hopkins University
Evening College and Summer
    Session
Baltimore, Maryland 21218;
Senior Educational Consultant
John F. Kennedy Institute for
    Handicapped Children
Baltimore, Maryland 21205

Gerald M. Senf, Ph.D.
Editor-in-Chief
Journal of Learning Disabilities
1331 East Thunderhead Drive
Tucson, Arizona 85718

Jeannette Seymour, M.A.
Doctoral Candidate in Reading
Temple University
Philadelphia, Pennsylvania;
Cognitive Therapist
Moss Rehabilitation Center
Philadelphia, Pennsylvania 19141

Abraham J. Tannenbaum, Ph.D.
Professor of Education
Teachers College
Columbia University
New York, New York 10027

Dianne Tobin, M.S.
Doctoral Candidate in Gifted
    Education
Project Associate, Intellectually
    Gifted Child Study Group
The Johns Hopkins University
Baltimore, Maryland 21218

Anne J. Udall, M.A.
Doctoral Candidate in Gifted
    Education
University of Arizona
Tucson, Arizona;
Resource Teacher for Gifted/
    Learning Disabled Students
Tucson Unified School District
Tucson, Arizona 85717

Preface

This book is an outgrowth of a 3-year research study of learning-disabled/gifted children in the Division of Education of the Evening College and Summer Session of The Johns Hopkins University. This project was funded by the Spencer Foundation. The study developed out of concern that there are children who have great intellectual potential, but who are having difficulty in school because of learning disabilities. It was felt that these children are often overlooked by current screening methods for programs for gifted children; at the same time, they frequently are not identified as learning disabled perhaps because their high ability allows them to compensate somewhat for their deficiencies. As a result of the publicity about the study, there was an outpouring of letters and phone calls from parents and teachers about children they felt were gifted and learning disabled; this reinforced the investigators' belief in the existence of these children. The researchers hoped to gain insight into the characteristics of the learning-disabled/gifted children, to define appropriate identification measures, and to recommend relevant educational strategies for them.

As part of the project, a panel of experts convened in May, 1981 to discuss theory and practice related to the learning-disabled/gifted child. These experts, who represented both the fields of learning disabilities and the gifted, presented papers and discussed their mutual concerns. The chapters in this book are an outgrowth of the issues and concerns discussed at that colloquium.

Principal investigators on the Spencer grant were Professors Gilbert Schiffman, Paul Daniels, Lynn Fox, and Ronald Berk; they were assisted by research associates Linda Brody and Dianne Tobin. During the 3-year period of the grant, many graduate students at The Johns Hopkins University assisted in the collection of data. We wish to thank Virginia Berninger, Saralee Bernstein, Wendy Bloomberg, Deborah Dolan, Mary Ellen Lewis, Joyce Steeves, and Joanna Thomas. Deborah Loomis and Elizabeth Vaughn, two secretaries in the Division of Education, were assigned to the grant on a part-time basis. We wish to thank them for their help throughout the study. We would especially like to thank Mrs. Loomis for her patience and attention to detail in the preparation of this manuscript.

We are appreciative for the help we received from other universities, public and private elementary and middle schools, and parents. In particular, we are most grateful to Dr. Stanley Rosner, Chairman of the Psychology of Reading Department at Temple University, who provided us access to the wealth of clinical data in the files of the Temple Reading Clinic.

We are greatly indebted to the Spencer Foundation for its support of our research on learning-disabled/gifted children and for making this book possible. We hope that this book will enhance the recognition of learning-disabled/gifted children and provide guidance for educators in meeting their needs.

Dedication

This volume is dedicated to the late Professor Halbert Robinson (1925–1981) of the University of Washington whose thoughtful approach to problems of the education of special children will long be remembered, especially his research on identification of giftedness in the preschool years and his program for radical early admission to college. Hal was working on the outline of a chapter for this volume the morning of March 25, 1981 while on spring vacation in Mexico. Later that day he died while scuba diving. We mourn the loss of this leader in gifted education and regret that he was unable to fully share with us his ideas on the learning-disabled/gifted child.

Introduction

Lynn H. Fox, Linda Brody, and Dianne Tobin

Albert Einstein did not speak until he was 3 years of age. He was a poor student and his problems with spelling and writing persisted into adulthood. This contrasted sharply with his exceptional abilities in nonverbal areas. Frequently, Einstein is cited as an example of a gifted person who, as a child, very likely was learning disabled (Elkind, 1973; Patten, 1972; Thompson, 1971). Thomas Edison also had problems in school. Woodrow Wilson did not learn the alphabet until he was 9 years of age and he was 11 before he learned to read. Harvey Cushing, Auguste Rodin, and George Patton all had some degree of reading, writing, and spelling retardation in their early lives (Thompson, 1971). In their book *Cradles of Eminence*, Goertzel and Goertzel (1962) analyzed the lives of 400 eminent men and women and found that one-fourth of them overcame handicaps.

Despite biographical evidence indicating that some people can be both gifted and learning disabled, these terms are often viewed as contradictory. This phenomenon is rarely discussed in educational circles, and little research on the subject has been conducted. Educators who work with learning-disabled children frequently overlook that some of these students may be gifted, and educators who work with the gifted do not look for learning disabilities among their students. Neither group of educators is likely to investigate the possibility that some students who are considered to be average actually are gifted with learning disabilities, but their gifts mask their disabilities.

MYTHS AND STEREOTYPES

Stereotypes that resulted from early works in the areas of learning disabilities and giftedness may have led to the belief that both conditions could not coexist in the same child. This may have contributed to a lack of awareness of the learning-disabled/gifted child.

2   *Fox, Brody, and Tobin*

With the work of such people as Goldstein, Strauss and Werner, and Cruickshank, early research in learning disabilities focused on brain-damaged and mentally retarded children (Ross, 1977). This focus gradually shifted to more normal populations, but the early studies may have caused people to associate learning disabilities with mental deficiencies, which was not compatible with their idea of giftedness.

Meanwhile, in the area of gifted education, there have been two prevailing stereotypes. As Maker pointed out:

> The pre-Terman view of a gifted child in the classroom was of a puny, bespectacled little boy in a corner by himself, poring over scientific journals or working calculus problems while the other children were simply being children; he grew up to be nearly insane, weird, and ostracized by society. The post-Terman stereotype reverses this image and shows the gifted child in comparison to his average or above average peers as the epitome of everything teachers and parents would want—more physically attractive, better adjusted emotionally, larger in size, more healthy, more verbal, more popular, more sociable, highly motivated to achieve, and well-liked by his teachers—a child who grows up to be a more successful, well-adjusted, productive adult. (p. 7)

If the post-Terman stereotype of the gifted child as one who must be good at everything still prevails, it is not surprising that the learning-disabled/gifted child who is not a high achiever would be overlooked and not considered gifted. Terman identified some underachievers, but this aspect of his work was not well-publicized (Maker, 1977).

DEFINITIONS

Prior to the development of an adequate means for screening and identification, it is important to define the learning-disabled/gifted child. No clear definition is evident in the literature, however. This is partially the result of confusion over definitions and labels in the fields of learning disabilities and the gifted

In the area of learning disabilities, Cruickshank (1977) pointed to the fact that there are more than 40 terms used in professional literature, each slightly different from the others and all essentially pertaining to the same group of children. Fry (1968) developed the "Do-It-Yourself Terminology Generator," where a person selects any word from column 1 (a list of qualifiers), column 2 (a list of areas of involvement), and column 3 (a list of problems) and, in this way, can generate any one of 1,000 three-word labels to describe the learning-disabled child.

Almost as many definitions as labels apply to the learning-disabled child. Cruickshank (1977) offered a definition that describes specific

Introduction 3

symptoms, such as difficulty in discrimination and memory. The federal definition under P.L. 94-142 (1967) focused more on what learning disability is not rather than what it is. This definition is cited often, however, and its use is important in helping to determine the allocation of funds for learning-disabled populations. It reads as follows:

> Children with specific learning disabilities exhibit a disorder in one or more of the basic psychological processes involved in understanding or in using spoken or written language. These may be manifested in disorders of listening, thinking, reading, writing, spelling, or arithmetic. They include conditions which have been referred to as perceptual motor handicaps, brain injury, minimal brain dysfunction, dyslexia, developmental aphasia, etc. They do not include learning problems which are due primarily to visual, hearing, motor handicaps, to mental retardation, emotional disturbance, or to environmental disadvantage.

The concept that a learning disability is evidenced by a discrepancy between potential and achievement is implied in the federal definition, but not stressed to the extent that it is by others (Bannatyne, 1968; McCarthy and McCarthy, 1974; Ross, 1977). Ross (1977) pointed out:

> As is true of children in general, no two of these children are ever alike. They have just one thing in common—they show a discrepancy between the school performance expected of them on the basis of their potential and the performance they actually produce (p. 4).

This concept is important in order to understand learning-disabled/gifted children who may differ from average learning-disabled children only in that their potential is much greater.

Definitions of the gifted child vary as well. Following Terman's study (Terman, 1925), it was persistently believed that a single intelligence test score was usually considered sufficient to define giftedness (Gallagher, 1979). Gradually, there has been less reliance on the global intelligence test scores, and a more multi-faceted view of giftedness has evolved. The works of such people as Getzels and Jackson (1962) and Torrance (1969) alerted people to the concept of creatively gifted children, and the work of Stanley and The Study of Mathematically Precocious Youth at The Johns Hopkins University demonstrated extraordinary possibilities for the achievement of children who are gifted in a specific academic area (Stanley et al., 1974).

The federal definition of gifted children recognizes a variety of areas of giftedness. It reads as follows (Marland, 1972):

> Gifted and talented children are those identified by professionally qualified persons (and) who by virtue of outstanding abilities are capable of high performance. These are children who require differentiated edu-

4   Fox, Brody, and Tobin

cational programs and services beyond those normally provided by the regular school program in order to realize their contribution to self and society.

Children capable of high performance include those with demonstrated achievement and/or potential ability in any of the following areas: (a) general intellectual ability, (b) specific academic aptitude, (c) creative or productive thinking, (d) leadership ability, (e) visual and performing arts, (f) psychomotor ability.[1]

For the learning-disabled/gifted child, it is significant that the federal definition mentions achievement and/or potential but does not require both. As Whitmore (1980) said:

One must include as gifted those individuals who excel in only one or a few categories of ability and those who reveal on aptitude tests high potential for learning that has not been evidenced in their academic performance (p. 67).

Maker (1977) pointed out that the person who is handicapped and gifted "simply has both strengths and weaknesses that are very pronounced" (p. 7).

PURPOSES OF THIS BOOK

This book dispels some of the myths that have contributed to a lack of awareness of the learning-disabled/gifted child and also broadens the understanding of the characteristics and special needs of these children. In addition, suggestions for identification and programming are provided.

Attention will be directed to a group of children who often have been overlooked by educators, researchers, and the general public. The number of children who could be described as both learning disabled and gifted is still unknown. However, in addition to children whose gifts and deficits easily can be detected, it is possible that a staggering number of children sitting in classrooms and functioning at or slightly below grade level have learning disabilities that inhibit the realization of their true potential.

There is a tremendous need for program development for these children. Program planning for a learning-disabled/gifted child should include three aspects: 1) developmental teaching where the goals, materials, methods, and management techniques are the same for the special population as for normally developing children; 2) remedial teaching, designed to ameliorate specific disability areas; and 3) adap-

---

[1] The psychomotor category was omitted in subsequent legislation.

Introduction 5

tive teaching, where methods, materials, and management techniques are selected to circumvent specific areas of disability in order to maximize areas of ability. Hopefully, educators will be stimulated to try some of the suggested techniques and develop some of their own.

Another goal is to encourage other researchers to study learning-disabled/gifted children so that identification strategies and program models might be improved. In addition, this book intends to increase general public awareness as to the characteristics and needs of this population and thus to eventually influence policymaking, legislation, and funding.

OVERVIEW

This book is organized into three major sections: Part I—Concepts and Characteristics of the Learning-Disabled Child; Part II—Issues in Identification; and Part III—Programming for Learning-Disabled/Gifted Children. Part IV, in which future directions for research and practice are discussed, serves as a conclusion.

Part I is comprised of four chapters. Chapter 1, by Tannenbaum and Baldwin, presents arguments for defining the learning-disabled/ gifted child within the context of existing defintions of giftedness. In addition, their proposed approach to identifying gifted children involves a wide funnel at the initial screening stage so that gifted children with learning disabilities will not be excluded. In Chapter 2, Senf focuses on the concept of the learning-disabled/gifted child within the context of traditional definitions of learning disabilities. He presents a historical overview related to diagnosis and treatment. A historical overview of the development of definitions of learning disabilities is provided by Berk in Chapter 3. Here, the issues related to processing disorders and discrepancy formulas are addressed. In Chapter 4, Rosner and Seymour provide clinical evidence to support the concept of the learning-disabled/gifted child. Their concerns relate to diagnosis and remediation and case studies are included to illustrate these points.

Part II includes three chapters. In Chapter 5, Fox and Brody discuss current methods for identifying giftedness in children and how these methods relate to gifted children who have learning disabilities. In Chapter 6, Fox describes an empirical study of children who were tested at the Temple University Reading Clinic. In spite of intelligence test scores of at least 125, these children were found to have reading problems. In Chapter 7, Rosner uses one case study to explain the case-typing approach to identifying learning disabilities. This approach is used at the Temple University Reading Clinic and is being adopted by school systems throughout the state of Maryland.

6   *Fox, Brody, and Tobin*

Part III includes a variety of suggestions for facilitating learning-disabled/gifted children and for working with teachers and parents. In Chapter 8, Daniels summarizes his ideas about how program models and curricula should be modified to meet the needs of learning-disabled/gifted children. In Chapter 9, Gallagher discusses how traditional programs for gifted children can be adapted in order to include learning-disabled/gifted children. In Chapter 10, Fox, Tobin, and Schiffman deal with specific adaptive strategies that can be used to circumvent disabilities. The microcomputer is discussed as a tool for instructing and managing learning-disabled/gifted students in Chapter 11 by Tobin and Schiffman. Chapter 12 by Baldwin and Gargiulo and Chapter 13 by Udall and Maker present model programs that have worked with learning-disabled/gifted children in school systems. Chapter 14 by Bricklin describes a counseling program for parents. Chapter 15 by Lewis and Daniels describes teacher training in a clinical setting.

In Part IV, some of the major points of agreement across various chapters are summarized. In addition, the conclusion offers specific suggestions for research and practice.

Hopefully, this book will be useful to psychologists who diagnose children with special needs, to school administrators who make many of the decisions involving staffing and school organization, to legislators who make decisions that affect policy and funding for special education, and to parents of learning-disabled/gifted children. But most important, this book is for teachers and teacher educators. The learning-disabled/gifted child may be in programs for the gifted, in classes for the learning disabled, or in regular classrooms. Thus, it is important that all teachers become aware of the existence of the unique educational needs of these children.

REFERENCES

Bannatyne, A. 1968. Diagnosing learning disabilities and writing remedial prescriptions. J. Learn. Disabil. 1:242–249.

Cruickshank, W. 1977. Learning Disabilities in Home, School and Community. Syracuse, Syracuse University Press, New York.

Elkind, J. 1973. The gifted child with learning disabilities. Gifted Child Q. 17:96–97, 115.

Fry, E. 1968. Fry's do-it-yourself terminology generator. Int. Reading Assoc. Reprinted in Farnham-Diggory, S. 1978. Learning Disabilities. Harvard University Press, Boston.

Gallagher, J.J. 1979. Issues in education for the gifted. In: H. Passow, (ed.), The Gifted and the Talented: their education and development, the 78th yearbook of the Natl. Soc. for the Study of Educ. University of Chicago Press, Chicago. pp. 28–44.

Getzels, J., and Jackson, P. 1962. Creativity and Intelligence. John Wiley and Sons, Inc., New York.

Goertzel, V., and Goertzel, M. 1962. Cradles of Eminence. Little, Brown and Co., Boston.

Maker, C.J. 1977. Providing Programs for the Gifted Handicapped. Council for Exceptional Child., Reston, VA.

Marland, S.P. 1972. Education of the gifted and talented, Vol. 1. Report to the Congress of the United States by the U.S. Commissioner of Education. U.S. Government Printing Office, DC.

McCarthy, J., and McCarthy, J. 1974. Learning Disabilities. Allyn and Bacon, Inc., Boston.

Patten, B. 1972. Visually mediated thinking: A report on the case of Albert Einstein. J. Learn. Disabil. 6:415–420.

Ross, A. 1977. Learning disability: the unrealized potential. McGraw-Hill Book Co., New York.

Stanley, J.C., Keating, D.P., and Fox, L.H. 1974. Mathematical Talent: Discovery, Description and Development. The Johns Hopkins University Press, Baltimore.

Terman, L.M. et al. 1925. The mental and physical traits of a thousand gifted children. Genetic Studies of Genius. Stanford University Press, Stanford, CA.

Thompson, L. 1971. Language disabilities in men of eminence. J. Learn. Disabil. 4:34–45.

Torrance, E.P. 1969. Creativity. Dimensions Publishing Co., Belmont, CA.

Whitmore, J. 1980. Giftedness, Conflict, and Underachievement. Allyn and Bacon, Inc., Boston.

PART I

THE LEARNING-DISABLED/ GIFTED CHILD
Concepts and Characteristics

Chapter **1**

Giftedness and Learning Disability
A Paradoxical Combination

Abraham J. Tannenbaum and Lois J. Baldwin

Giftedness in children means different things to different people. No matter what definition is accepted, the identification of giftedness is an inexact science. This, in part, is attributable to imprecise methods and instruments. Besides, talent in childhood is not usually full-blown; instead, talent-in-the-making is coupled with an uncertainty about the future. Identification is, therefore, a matter of locating children who possess high potential when compared to other children. There is no guarantee that those with high potential eventually will excel by universal standards as adults, even when they receive the proper nurturance. Therefore, in creating a pool of "hopefuls," it is best to admit any child who stands any chance of achieving a great deal in the future. Of course, many "hopefuls" are really "doubtfuls." Because this is impossible to know in advance, it is best to uphold liberal admission criteria for all "hopefuls" in order to increase the chance that some hidden talent will be uncovered. In other words, imperfections in the identification measures force a choice between overincluding the nongifted and overexcluding the gifted, and it is safer to err on the side of overinclusion.

Yet, no matter how permissive are the criteria for bringing children into the pool, there is almost never anyplace for a child with learning disabilities. The symptoms of this handicap are so distracting that they divert attention from any signs of giftedness. This is regrettable, considering that such historic figures as Thomas Edison, Hans Christian Andersen, and Nelson Rockefeller managed to achieve renown despite their learning disabilities. It seems therefore, that as Gerken (1979) suggested, the identification of handicapped children as gifted is determined ex post facto.

Although the gifted and the learning-disabled children are seen very much in the public eye as *separate* subgroups of exceptional chil-

12   *Tannenbaum and Baldwin*

dren, there is little interest in those who fall into *both* categories. It is as if the two exceptionalities were contradictions, entirely incompatible and irreconcilable in any single child. Educators are often so preoccupied with a child's failures, they simply do not look for sparks of extraordinary potential. Often, they find it hard to believe that such sparks exist, even when they happen to notice signs of it. This chapter demonstrates that concepts of giftedness and handicap *are* compatible, and thus a viable method for identifying the gifted *can* include handicapped in its pool.

TOWARD A DEFINITION OF GIFTEDNESS

The human mind is capable of an almost endless variety of competencies, but many are never developed during a person's lifetime. Of the relatively few competencies that are nurtured to any extent, fewer still are honed to perfection. And even these highly developed skills are not always regarded as signs of excellence; a few succeed in attracting public acclaim while others remain unheralded and sometimes unnoticed.

One of the tantalizing mysteries about giftedness is how it is decided whether a particular kind of ability should be honored or ignored. For example, why is ballet considered high-level talent while acrobatics is not, even though both require rare psychomotor skills and imagination? If the reason is based on aesthetic appeal, why is the work of a theoretical mathematician considered a sign of excellence? Isn't its beauty obscure, except to a select few? If the criterion for great accomplishment is practical service to society, what practicality is there in a beautiful sculpture or violin concerto? If the intellectual complexity of the task makes a difference, why isn't championship chess considered a sign of greatness by everybody? There are no wholly satisfying answers to such questions, but this does not mean that public tastes are simply fickle. Every talent performs a different function in society, and the kinds of attention and credibility attached to a talent depend partly on the functional category in which it falls. There are four functional categories—*scarcity, surplus, quota,* and *anomalous* talents:

1. *Scarcity* talents are always in short supply because the needs that they address can never be satisfied fully. These are the talents that make everyday life safer, healthier, and more liveable. They are exemplified by such immortals as Jonas Salk, Sigmund Freud, Abraham Lincoln, and Martin Luther King, Jr. The rare abilities of such people are in constant demand. Although each makes a major con-

tribution to mankind, there is a need for new and greater leaps forward to solve lingering problems. For example, Jonas Salk played a key role in conquering polio, but other "Jonas Salks" are still needed to find cures for cancer and heart disease. Schools can justify doing something special for the gifted if for no other reason than to be prepared when the child with potential scarcity talent materializes. One such individual can "shake the world" by affecting the lives of all future generations.

2. Whereas scarcity talents take into account society's deepest needs, *surplus* talents satisfy some of society's profoundest cravings. These special abilities are mankind's "divine luxuries," and people possessing them are capable of beautifying the world without guaranteeing its continued existence. Surplus talents include Bach, Picasso, and Pavlova, all of whom became famous for enriching cultural life rather than for conquering cancer, bigotry, or mental illness. Surplus talents are not superfluous, but they derive their label from the fact that life could go on if they were no longer cultivated, although their absence would mean cultural tragedy.

3. *Quota* talents probably draw the greatest attention from school and society since they fill high-level, albeit finite, needs in the work force. People who possess these specialized abilities include physicians, teachers, engineers, lawyers, psychologists, and all others who have advanced training are subject to the laws of supply and demand. Earning a professional credential and being a member of a profession are not necessarily signs of high-level talent. Some skills that are needed to qualify for professional service can be acquired easily by most people; however, relatively few people take advantage of the opportunity. Many service professions require their members to have advanced academic study and successful performance in the field in order to be licensed. Those who do not qualify academically are not considered viable even though they may have the necessary skills to provide excellent services. Therefore, quota talents should not be equated with professionalism. Instead, the term should be reserved for reference to those who are at the peak of their professions or those who are capable of reaching the peak, regardless of what credentials are needed in order to qualify. As might be expected, quota talents seem to be among the highest priorities in educating the gifted, probably because they serve practical, everyday needs that are stable and status-related in society.

4. The last category is a catchall collection of *anomalous* talents, which require extraordinary mental functioning but are not widely appreciated as signs of excellence. They include a variety of prodigious

feats. Some of these feats may have practical value; others may be pure amusement. Examples include the ability to do complex mathematical calculations faster than a computer, the mastery of mountains of trivia, and some of the accomplishments listed in the *Guinness Book of Records*. This is the only category that also includes socially disapproved talents, which are generally regarded as detriments rather than benefits to society. Evidence of this can be seen when great leadership ability becomes demagogic, for example Adolph Hitler or when the gifted turn into technocrats willing to sell their talents to the highest bidder, as Albert Speer did in Nazi Germany. Schools sometimes invest heavily in anomalous talents, such as those who excel in sports. These students may attract considerable attention, but their popularity does not necessarily mean that they are qualified.

Psychological Perspectives

Giftedness is usually considered a psychological phenomenon in that it reflects the powers of the mind to actualize itself in rare and precious human performance or productivity. A great deal more is known about the extent of the mind's strength than the essence of its functioning. Scientific inquiry into giftedness began when Francis Galton (1874) divided human beings into 16 categories, ranging from idiocy to genius. Without the benefits of modern measures of ability, he recognized genius among those adults who had a reputation for accomplishing what few others could in their generation. His insights into persons who had earned renown in science led him to the conclusion that they were endowed with superior intellectual ability, tremendous energy, good physical health, a sense of independence and purposefulness, and exceptional dedication to their fields of productivity. These traits are remarkably similar to the traits that were discovered through psychometric methods in subsequent research on the gifted. When Terman initiated his Genetic Studies of Genius, there was a serious, large-scale attempt to investigate high potential in children and to determine whether that potential eventuated in fulfillment in their adulthood. This longitudinal study of intelligence test scores focused on more than 1,500 children with a minimum score of 140 (Terman, 1925). Terman proposed no theory of intelligence, but the Stanford-Binet test he developed and used to measure potential reflects an assumption that intelligence is a unitary factor associated with success at school and in careers after graduation.

The idea of equating giftedness with high scores on an intelligence test has been disputed by many behavioral scientists, among them the late Halbert Robinson (1977) who stated:

In the post-Terman era, it has indeed become possible to be a "gifted" individual without having any noticeable gift at all. We routinely categorize children as "gifted" by whatever cutoff score we happen to choose, in spite of the fact that they do not do better than average work in school or demonstrate in any other fashion an exceptional degree of talent, (p. 2).

Robinson's viewpoint is consistent with an existing belief that individuals can qualify as gifted only if they show extraordinary proficiency in ways other than scoring in the highest decile or percentile on a test of general intelligence. The ability to deal with abstractions is impressive only if the abstract ideas are in the context of a discipline or field of inquiry. In the years immediately preceding his untimely death, Robinson worked extensively on methods for diagnosing special aptitudes among precocious preschoolers. One of the more important items of unfinished business was a follow-up study of these children to determine whether the aptitudes they possessed in the first 5 years of life somehow related to the fields in which they excelled at school and even after graduation. This would have been an important companion piece to Terman's follow-up studies of children who scored high on an intelligence test. Most of these children grew up to be successful achievers, although it was impossible to forecast their eventual areas of specialization and excellence from their childhood test scores.

A movement away from reliance on intelligence test scores as the principal sign of giftedness received a major boost in 1971 from the United States Commissioner of Education whose report to the Congress (Marland, 1971) broadened the definition of giftedness to include special aptitudes. (The federal definition appears in the introduction to this book.) The popularity of the federal definition in schools throughout the country has not shielded it from some vigorous criticism. Renzulli (1978) charged that the definition omits the nonintellective factors that are vital in characterizing giftedness. He also pointed to the nonparallel nature of the six categories in which two (i.e., specific academic aptitude and visual and performing arts) denote fields of accomplished performance; the other four refer to cognitive processes that may be necessary to bring about superior achievement.

Finally, there is a tendency for practitioners to treat the six categories as if they were independent of each other, resulting in the development of separate identification systems for each category. Gallagher (1979) agreed with Renzulli that the six types of giftedness probably overlap in some ways. He also argued that the listing of leadership and psychomotor abilities is not yet justified because their meaning is not known, nor can high potential be identified for either one. Prob-

16 *Tannenbaum and Baldwin*

ably in recognition of these criticisms, the federal government dropped psychomotor ability from its listing, but the emphasis on varieties of talent generally remains acceptable in schools throughout the country.

In his own definition of giftedness, Renzulli (1978) added a non-intellective dimension to reinforce the more conventional performance indicators, as follows:

> Giftedness consists of an interaction among three basic clusters of human traits—these clusters being above average general abilities, high levels of task commitment, and high levels of creativity. Gifted and talented children are those possessing or capable of developing this composite set of traits and applying them to any potentially valuable area of human performance. Children who manifest or are capable of developing an interaction among the three clusters require a wide variety of educational opportunities and services that are not ordinarily provided through regular instructional programs (p. 261).

Renzulli's definition probably ranks with the one issued by the federal government for its widespread acceptance. Yet, there is room for quibbling about this approach. If the so-called "general abilities" include all kinds of mental strengths, specific as well as global, why separate creativity into a category of its own? Factor analytic studies have shown that creativity does not stand entirely apart from other intellective traits (Wallach, 1970); instead, it seems to overlap with general intelligence and is only partly independent of it. There is also reason to suspect that creativity is to some extent a nonintellective phenomenon (MacKinnon, 1962; Bloom, 1963). As for the nonintellective factor in Renzulli's definition, it is hard to imagine that task commitment is the only one related to giftedness. For example, Piechowski (1979) noted the importance of what he calls "overexcitability," or an exaggerated emotional reaction to various stimuli that propels the person with superior mental strength to higher levels of achievement. Self-concept, anxiety levels, work habits, and cognitive styles are some examples of personality variables that figure into human excellence. Finally, neither the Renzulli nor the federal definition takes into account the person's environment as the critical context for the fruition of human potential.

A Social-Psychological Perspective

The definitions of giftedness suggested by Terman, the federal government, and Renzulli are only a few of the many that have been advanced but they are by far the most popular. They differ basically in the sense that each adds its own ingredient without subtracting any from a previously stated definition. Thus, Terman's focus on general abilities is expanded in the federal definition to include specific apti-

Paradoxical Combination   17

tudes, and this in turn is expanded by Renzulli to include task commitment. To these, however, some more ingredients could be added. Before suggesting still another approach to characterizing giftedness, however, three basic premises need to be considered.

Premise 1   A distinction has to be made between giftedness in children and in adults. Children may be precocious, rapid learners, and superb grade-getters at school, but except in the rare case of a Mozart or a Mendelssohn, theirs are only promising but not yet proven talents. Giftedness in adults, on the other hand, is denoted by what they have done, not by what they may someday be capable of doing. Furthermore, giftedness is not synonymous with mastery or consumption of existing ideas; rather, it is the ability to produce new ideas. Children often prove their precocity by absorbing subject matter rapidly and abundantly, and they sometimes grow up to be superannuated precocious children with lots of acquired knowledge in their memory banks but without an innovative thought of any consequence. This type of person would probably be counted among the promising as a child but not among the fulfilled as an adult. Thus, because developed talent exists almost exclusively in adults, giftedness in children should be defined as their *potential* for becoming critically acclaimed *performers* or exemplary *producers* of ideas in spheres of activity that enhance the physical, moral, social, intellectual, emotional, and aesthetic life of humanity rather than by the quantities of knowledge absorbed.

Premise 2   Great performance or productivity results from varying blends of five factors—general ability, special aptitudes, nonintellective factors, environmental factors, and chance factors.

General Ability   General intelligence test figures are determined on a sliding scale in all high-level talent areas. Different levels of intelligence are required for various kinds of accomplishment—higher in academic subjects than, say, in the performing arts. There is no basis for making extreme assertions about the intelligence test score, such as entirely discounting its relevance to giftedness or claiming that all those destined to become great producers or performers in any area of human activity need to score at the 99th percentile or better. Instead, positions along this continuum should be adjusted according to the talent area, which means taking a stance closer to one extreme for some kinds of giftedness and nearer to the opposite extreme for others.

Special Aptitudes   It makes no sense to regard children as gifted only in terms of general intelligence. Giftedness means being exceptionally bright at doing something that is highly respected, and most people do not do many things equally well. Instead, they have special capacities and affinities for particular kinds of work. Some of these aptitudes are becoming more and more recognizable in young children; others are difficult to discern until early adolescence. For example, some kinds of musical talent appear as early as the preschool years, while insight into social and political structures develop much later in childhood. Whatever the aptitudes may be, it is necessary to assess them as soon as they become measurable in order to determine more precisely the child's special talents.

Nonintellective Factors Great accomplishment is not just an outgrowth of extraordinary ability. It depends also on a large number of nonintellective characteristics, such as ego strength, dedication to a chosen field of productivity or performance, willingness to sacrifice short-term satisfactions for the sake of long-term accomplishment, and many others. These traits are all part of the achieving personality regardless of the areas in which talent manifests itself.

Environmental Factors Stimulating home, school, and community settings are indispensible not only for maximizing potentialities but also for helping to determine the directions that they will take. Parents who serve as role models through their own achievement-orientation while creating an enriched educational environment outside of school can urge their children to advance as far as possible. The quality of classroom instruction as well as the attitudes of peers in and out of the classroom make a difference toward the child's mental outlook. As for the resources in the neighborhood, there are formal cultural institutions such as museums, concert halls, and libraries, as well as human resources, that can inspire and instruct. Without proper stimulation in the human environment, there is always the possibility, and often the likelihood, that children with outstanding mental endowment will "hide their lights under a bushel."

Chance Factors Studies of gifted persons generally overlook entirely unpredictable events that are critical to realizing promise and demonstrating developed talents. It is not only a matter of being in the right place at the right time, although that, too, is important. Many unforeseen circumstances in the opportunity structure and prevalent lifestyles of the person's peer group can make a big difference in the outlets for gifted performance. A brilliant medical researcher who was ready to achieve a breakthrough in disease control may suddenly and unpredictably be distracted by a personal crisis or by the lure of a social issue considered to be more relevant than human concerns. The "market" for lawyers may be so glutted that even those with freshly minted doctorates of jurisprudence who have leadership potential in the legal profession find little room for starting their practice. Chance factors can also serve as facilitators of achievement, as in the case of the gifted young singer or actor who happens to meet and study with the right coach and makes the most of that opportunity.

Premise 3 Each of these five intellectual, personalogical and so-cial-situational factors has a fixed threshold that represents the minimum essential for giftedness in *any* publicly valued activity. Research has not yet revealed what these thresholds are, but it seems that whoever achieves some measure of eminence has to qualify by *all* of these standards; the person who is unable to measure up to just *one* of them cannot become truly outstanding. In other words, success depends on a combination of qualifiers, whereas failure can result from even a single deficit. This is basic to understanding the relationship between promise and fulfillment. Children who seem to have superior intellectual power and the desire to perform well in various academic disciplines may never rise above mediocrity because their environment lacks richness and encouragement. Others may grow up in an appropriate environment and possess the intellectual power to perform with distinction but are handicapped by insufficient motivation or sloppy work habits. Therefore, it is futile to look for a single explanation as to why some children do or do not live up to high expectations. So-called "underachievers" cannot fit into only one typology.

Intelligence, spatial, and scientific aptitude thresholds are undoubtedly different for artists than they are for scientists. Thus, for example, Getzels' (1979) talented art students were able to demonstrate high potential in their field, even though their general academic abilities were no better than those of most college students. However, it is doubtful that any college student could become as distinguished as Roe's (1952) creative scientists without demonstrating superior academic potential at school. Those who fail to measure up to any of these minimum essentials for their respective fields of endeavor could never compare to the Getzels and Roe populations.

Thus, the proposed definition of giftedness as a potential for outstanding performance or productivity has meaning only if the complex combination of personal and situational facilitators are taken into account. These factors defy precise measurement because of necessary reliance on test instruments that lack perfect validity and reliability. Besides, the tests of intellective and nonintellective factors seem far more appropriate for consumers of knowledge than for potential producers or performers. The element of chance is by definition fortuitous and therefore unrelated to measurable antecedent conditions. By virtue of its "veto" power, then, every one of the five qualifiers is a *nec-*

20   *Tannenbaum and Baldwin*

essary prerequisite of high achievement, but none of them has *suffi-cient* strength to overcome inadequacies in the others.

WHO ARE THE LEARNING-DISABLED/GIFTED?

Perhaps because of rapid growth in the field of learning disabilities, there is considerable controversy and lack of clarity in defining this population. This chapter does not deal with the confusion in the literature, which is addressed elsewhere in this volume. The problem of recognizing giftedness in a learning-disabled population is confounded no matter how the nature of the handicap is characterized. Problems occur, even if what is perhaps the most operational of all definitions is accepted. This definition, found in PL 94-142, appears in the introduction to this volume.

Implicit in this definition are some of the obstacles that prevent learning-disabled/gifted children from being recognized for their extraordinary potentialities. Typical expectations of gifted children are that they will excel in school by completing their schoolwork accurately and quickly, that they will score high on achievement tests, and that they will earn good grades. The kinds of students that teachers often refer for testing and possible placement in gifted programs have exemplary study habits, do more than is expected on assignments, and demonstrate superior memory and reasoning skills. The learning-disabled child, on the other hand, rarely exhibits any of the learning and behavioral characteristics that schools look for in gifted students. To the contrary, in order to "qualify" as learning disabled, there must be a considerable discrepancy between the child's potential and actual work performance, a factor which is rarely perceived as compatible with giftedness. Furthermore, the learning disabled may be deficient in selectively attending to relevant and irrelevant stimuli, have inefficient learning strategies, have impaired short- and long-term memory processes, and suffer auditory and visual perceptual disturbances. Also, they may be handicapped by such counterproductive behaviors as withdrawal, clowning, hyperactivity, task avoidance, and slow impulse control. Or, they may have aggressive, disruptive habits that make it difficult for them to focus on their work and to succeed in establishing and maintaining friendships with other children.

Many learning-disabled/gifted children suffer in silence as they struggle to keep up with classroom assignments. Sloppy handwriting, difficulty in following directions, bizarre or phonetic spelling of words on writing assignments, or numbers placed in the wrong columns are some of the subtle indications that the problem is deeper than just an

Paradoxical Combination 21

unwillingness or inability to work hard enough to excel. Children who confuse "was" and "saw" while their gifted peers are reading books at or above grade level can hardly regard themselves as gifted. The stress and failure they experience at school are sensed by classmates, teachers, and parents alike, and the general feeling that these children are inept tends to diminish their self-esteem. This seems to be borne out in a study by Walsh (1956), who engaged gifted boys with reading problems in projective doll play and found that the boys portrayed their dolls as restricted, helpless, isolated, and rejected.

Children who develop negative self-concepts tend to view the world as hostile and disorderly and often develop deviant behaviors in order to cope with it. Discouraged or frustrated by their unrewarding attempts at learning, they may withdraw into their own fantasy worlds, protecting their fragile egos through apathy and educational inactivity. Or, as learning demands increase and undergo change, defensive maneuvers may take the form of clowning or fighting in order to divert attention from work demands and threat of failure. The social relationships of learning-disabled/gifted children are adversely affected by such behaviors. Teachers view these children as less desirable to have in class because they are regarded as uncooperative, inattentive, disorganized, tactless, and anti-social (Bryan and McGrady, 1972). Peers are antagonized by the behavior patterns of these children and therefore find it difficult to make and sustain friendships with them. It is not unusual for learning-disabled children to become isolates or class scapegoats. Their problems with gross motor skills or physical coordination often make them the last to be chosen for group games and sports. Academic failures place them in the "buzzard" reading group and eliminate them early during spelling bees, thus incurring the hostility of more competitive, skillful teammates who further isolate them from social activities at school.

The various school adjustment problems not only tend to obscure any signs of giftedness but also distract the teacher from suspecting that giftedness exists. The need to remediate deficits becomes a greater concern than the need to nurture special talents in children. These feelings are reflected in the huge discrepancy between the amounts invested in compensatory and honors programs. Even when teachers are aware of the coexistence of handicap and giftedness in one child, they find themselves in the unfamiliar role of planning both remediation and enrichment. Ironically, it may be an advantage for the child with hidden talents to show signs of handicap because then the teacher is alerted to seek diagnostic help which, in turn, can lead to the identification of the child's extraordinary abilities. Once the referral is

22   *Tannenbaum and Baldwin*

made, the multidisciplinary team can begin the process of gathering and sharing important information. They can help familiarize teachers with the learning characteristics of gifted children and how learning problems are not inconsistent with the possibility that extraordinary cognitive strengths might also exist.

PROBLEMS IN IDENTIFYING GIFTEDNESS

Unlike height and weight, which can be measured directly, human abilities can only be assessed by inference. Although there are some attempts at probing brain activity, such as reaction time, to different stimuli (Beck, 1975) as a way of estimating the potential for achievement, it is much too early to tell whether there is any payoff through such an approach. In the 1980s, conventional methods of sampling performance on a test and inferring from it the capacity to perform on a variety of problems at school and elsewhere are all that is available. But obviously, performance can only approximate capacity because it is subject to all kinds of "extraneous" influences (apart from intellective power) such as readiness, motivation, test conditions, and many other factors, all of which affect test results. Even if the precise problem-solving behaviors to sample were known, it could never be certain what special mix of ingredients goes into such behaviors and how that mix would vary from one child to the next. The mystery is even deeper for learning-disabled children whose handicaps have to be penetrated somehow in order to get a reading of their real capacities. Whitmore (1980) described Robert, a learning-disabled boy who scored 89 on a group intelligence test but raised his score to 163 when he was retested on the Stanford-Binet. It is mind-boggling to speculate on all the possible factors that might have accounted for the difference in performance. The results would have been far more consistent if Robert's abilities could somehow be measured directly rather than through inference from his responses to test items.

Under the best of circumstances, the measures of potential that are used in programs for the gifted are most effective in predicting success at school, but not in the world of work after graduation (Wallach, 1976). In other words, no existing battery of measures can predict with much confidence 1) who will qualify separately for each of the various high-level occupations, or 2) how those who manage to qualify for *any* of them will perform at their jobs. The supporting evidence is more dramatic for some kinds of careers than for others. For example, in a study of people listed in *Who's Who* (Chauncey and Hilton, 1965), results showed that performance on the Scholastic Aptitude Test

Paradoxical Combination   23

(SAT) was skewed toward the upper extreme, with 3.8 times as many people as expected scoring 696 and above. However, the figures also revealed that of those who made it into *Who's Who* and were tested on SAT, fully 25% were in the *lower* half of the college-bound distribution, scoring 499 or below. Indeed, there were as many coming from the lower 50% as from the upper 10% of the SAT distribution for college students. This suggests that success in some careers does not require outstanding scholastic potential in order for people to qualify for listing in *Who's Who*. Other careers, however, seem to depend on superiority as reflected on measures such as the SAT. For example, Roe (1952) investigated the backgrounds of distinguished scientists and discovered that in their early school days, they performed extremely well on tests that correlated highly with academic achievement. Indeed, their scores were impressive enough to label them "gifted" in many schools and qualify them for special enrichment programs.

Obviously, then, it is easier to use conventional measures of potential to identify the kinds of gifted people studied by Roe than to identify many of the kinds of gifted people listed in *Who's Who*. Besides, gifted performance in science and mathematics at school is a good forerunner of excellence in these disciplines after graduation because there is a similarity between the problem-solving experiences in the classroom and these same kinds of experience in the professions and industry. This is not true for people who qualify for *Who's Who* on the basis of their contributions to the world of business, politics or entertainment. The careers in which they make their reputations are hardly given much attention in the elementary and secondary curricula, thus making it difficult for educators to recognize such talent-in-the-making.

One serious mistake in identifying the gifted is to assume that it is a simple two-step process—diagnosis followed by treatment. This may work well in medicine or in prescriptive teaching for the handicapped, but it is out of place in programs for the gifted. As emphasized earlier, the available measurement tools are not nearly sophisticated enough to give an accurate reading of human potential. Nor are the domains of talent amenable to easy identification because many schoolchildren have little or no experience in practicing these talents. For example, there is no standardized test to measure potential for writing drama, and few children have the opportunity to practice such skills anyway. How, then, can schools identify the next Eugene O'Neill or Tennessee Williams unless teachers introduce drama-writing into the curriculum and sensitize themselves to children who show a special affinity for it? The principle is simple: if society wants to know who

24   *Tannenbaum and Baldwin*

stands a chance of someday writing an elegant couplet or a profound sonnet, someone has to teach these skills to children with more advanced aptitudes for language; if society is eager to find gifted dart-throwers, someone has to give able-bodied children with superior motor and muscle control a reasonable amount of instruction and practice in dart-throwing.

The more talents that are sought, the more expanded educational activities have to be relied upon to help in the identification process. Thus, enrichment is a vehicle for identification as much as identification is a facilitator of enrichment. This relationship has an oscillating nature in the sense that it is reciprocal and mutually reinforcing. The need for such oscillation (and less vacillation) is especially obvious for learning-disabled/gifted children whose handicaps usually limit their exposure to enrichment in favor of remediation. What these children need is a rare, hybrid-type educator who is sensitive to contrasting exceptionalities. As Karnes (1979) pointed out, special educators tend to focus on weaknesses and deficits because they are not trained in identifying the gifted; on the other hand, teachers of the gifted rarely have an opportunity to work with the handicapped and do not understand how handicapping conditions affect a child's development.

A WAY OF IDENTIFYING LEARNING-DISABLED/GIFTED CHILDREN

Guidelines for recognizing giftedness in children with learning disabilities are basically the same as those applicable to all children except that the methods of implementation are different. The process should begin as early in the child's life as possible, and it should go on for as long as possible because there are always opportunities for discovering new insights and correcting old errors of judgment. There are three stages in identification that can be depicted in the shape of a funnel—wide at the receptive end; becoming sharply narrower toward the middle, which has a built-in filter; and tapering off until the drainage end, where a sieve-like attachment does the final sifting and sorting. The stages are first, *screening*; second, *selection*; and third, *differentiation*. This sequence should be repeated continuously for children not yet screened and also for those who had not "made it" into the first stage previously.

Screening

The criteria for inclusion should be liberal at the wide mouth of the funnel. Many of the instruments used at this stage should assess remote and sometimes farfetched indicators of potential, not just actual performance at school. The purpose is to include even those children who show only vague hints of giftedness in order to determine later whether these exceptionalities do indeed exist. Eventually, the procedure should limit itself only to those content areas that the school elects to emphasize in its enrichment program. It would be wasteful, for example, to seek out children who have a flair for creative writing unless plans were completed or at least underway to cultivate these talents. Therefore, the selection of instruments and procedures has to be determined by the scope and objectives of the curriculum. In order to obtain the proper kinds of information, it is necessary to use multiple sources, including but not limited to the following:

Teacher Observations Teachers are often less prepared than parents to recognize giftedness in their children (Ciha et al., 1974; Jacobs, 1971). With the help of trait lists, however, teachers have improved considerably in forecasting future achievement. Feshbach et al. (1977) have developed an instrument that enables teachers to predict with impressive confidence the reading levels that kindergarten children will eventually reach in grade 3. Renzulli and Hartman (1975) designed an instrument that lists the characteristics of gifted children as reported in the research literature. The purpose of this instrument is to sensitize teachers to signs of giftedness in their classroom. Each child is assessed on traits grouped under such categories as proficiency in learning, creativity, motivation, and leadership. Although this instrument is widely used in identifying gifted children, considerable evidence is needed to determine the regression weights of the different traits and trait clusters. Also, this instrument may be useful to teachers searching for signs of giftedness in the classroom, but there is no evidence to show that it can be of assistance in recognizing gifted children with learning disabilities. The motivational and behavioral characteristics of these children are often obstacles in the identification process. Therefore, it may be helpful to consider how traits familiarly associated with the gifted become modified and sometimes distorted, yet retained, in the handicapped. Table 1.1 shows how attitudes and behaviors demonstrated by students with high tested intelligence and strong motivation often appear in the learning-disabled child with high tested intelligence.

Parental Reports Although parents often can be sharper than teachers in discerning high potential among young children, many "stage mother" types tend to push their children into every possible program for the gifted, regardless of qualifications. In the case of the learning-disabled child, however, the preoccupation may be with the

26   *Tannenbaum and Baldwin*

Table 1.1.   Characteristics of high-IQ, highly motivated vs. high-IQ, learning-disabled children

The child with high tested intelligence and strong motivation	The learning-disabled child with high tested intelligence
Perfectionist—high expectations of self and others	Frustrated with inability to master high priority, scholastic skills. The need to avoid failure leads to a refusal to perform required task. Unhappiness over failure to live up to own expectations often leads to frustration and anger. Denies learning problem by stating that school activity is "dumb" or too easy. Deceives by doing work so sloppily that it is impossible to evaluate.
Voracious consumer of knowledge—retains extraordinary quantities of information; desires to explore, to know, to discover	Bored with regular curriculum, particularly if it is textbook- and workbook-oriented. Has large knowledge base, which may have been acquired through intact sensory processes, but often suffers from "verbal diarrhea" to compensate for perceived failures in various school subjects. Bores classmates with long-winded or pompous disquisitions that reveal more information than anybody wants to know. May feel comfortable in revealing solid knowledge only in the safety of a one-to-one relationship with an adult. May divert conversation to more complex and challenging subjects. Reacts obstinately to criticism or doubt.
Possesses a variety of interests and special abilities	May also have a wide variety of interests, but is handicapped in pursuing them because of process and learning difficulties. Parents often report many interests at home, but child seems dull, uninterested in activities at school. Is capable of self-entertainment for long periods of time when there is no required work to do

Table 1.1. (*Continued*)

The child with high tested intelligence and strong motivation	The learning-disabled child with high tested intelligence
Language skills are highly developed	May use verbal skills to avoid or mask specific language and behavior disorders May not use a large vocabulary when speaking, but can explain meaning of words far beyond age expectancy Enjoys playing with words and their diverse meanings, even at inappropriate times and in inappropriate ways
Shows alertness, high energy level and accelerated pace of thinking	May be viewed as hyperactive because of need to be actively involved Frustrated by inactivity or too much emphasis on deficient skills in the classroom Impatient during social studies and science lessons that are textbook-oriented. Asks thought-provoking questions that may be misinterpreted; may also try to divert class discussions to current events Easily distracted by activities and conversations going on in other part of the classroom Has difficulty focusing attention on written tasks or workbook pages
Able to generate creative ideas about new problems and innovative solutions to old ones	May be performing a task in a new or creative way, but seems not to be following directions Dislikes rote and drill exercises, such as reciting arithmetic facts
Is unusually sensitive to the feelings of self and others	Sensitive to criticism by others, and highly critical of self and others, including teachers Can understand and express concern about the feelings of others even while engaging in anti-social behavior Able to size up situations and utilize them to own advantage; may become skillful at manipulating

continued

Table 1.1. (Continued)

The child with high tested intelligence and strong motivation	The learning-disabled child with high tested intelligence
	others, including parents and teachers
	Is sensitive to inconsistencies in teacher's disciplinary procedures and will complain about such unfairness
Possesses a keen sense of humor	May use a sense of humor to clown and divert attention from failure in school activities
	May use humor to demean or make fun of other students
Possesses extraordinary critical thinking skills and sees unusual relationships in objects, events, and ideas	May combine ideas or express solutions that peers and teachers find bizarre
	May be regarded as disrespectful because of tendency to question teacher's facts or conclusions

handicap and the means of compensating for it. In order to obtain hints of the child's giftedness from the parents' perspective, the school psychologist has to elicit considerable information about out-of-school activities and interests as well as early signs of skill development that seem unusual. Whatever insights and recollections that parents can provide in the course of an interview or in response to a questionnaire deserve close scrutiny. Some parents initiate an evaluation to determine why their child, who seemed so bright and alert prior to attending school, is suddenly angry and threatens not to go to class. In some cases, this may be a reaction to the school's failure to recognize special talents that the child possesses.

Evidence of General Ability If the enrichment program is geared exclusively to the academically gifted, then the major pool will probably consist of children scoring beyond 1 standard deviation above the mean on intelligence, scholastic aptitude, and standardized tests. For disadvantaged groups, the cutoff point may have to be even lower, and Feuerstein's (1979) mediated approach to testing will undoubtedly be helpful in measuring the child's potential rather than status. Much will depend also on other sources of information about the child's special abilities, work habits, and motivation. In addition, a lowering of the cutoff point on scholastic aptitude measures and more confi-

Paradoxical Combination   29

dence in other indicators of talent will help prevent overlooking the artistically and socially gifted.

Although learning-disabled children may earn high scores on an individually administered test of intelligence, the handicap will often depress the score to some extent, hopefully not below the 84th percentile or thereabouts at the Screening stage. One of the most widely used tests for determining general intelligence in learning-disabled children is the Wechsler Intelligence Scale for Children-Revised (WISC-R). This measure is divided into five Verbal and five Performance Subscales with two optional assessments in each area, all of which yield Full-Scale, Verbal, and Performance scores. A trained psychologist should be aware of the different scoring patterns that occur when a learning-disabled/gifted child takes the WISC. The following three patterns for learning-disabled children were identified by Clements and Peters (1967):

Pattern 1: Scattered scores in either or both the Verbal or Performance Scales occur in which there is usually a wide range between the child's high and low scores. Relatively low scores occur most frequently in Arithmetic and Digit Span in the Verbal Scale and Block Design, Object Assembly Coding, and Mazes in the Performance Scale.

Pattern 2: A Verbal score which is 15 to 40 points higher than the Performance score is the second pattern. Children displaying this pattern usually have difficulties with perceptual motor activities and/or particularly strong verbal language-oriented abilities.

Pattern 3: The reverse of the second pattern in which the performance score is 10 to 30 points higher than the verbal score, is the least frequently observed. Children displaying this pattern have more difficulty expressing themselves verbally and are frequently dyslexic.

In interpreting WISC-R test scores, the psychologist should look for patterns showing that the child has exceptional strengths in some areas. Scaled scores for such a child may range from 18 or 19 on some subscales and to 5 or 6 on others. Schiff et al. (1981) cited evidence to show that the Verbal-Performance discrepancies on the WISC-R are significantly greater for learning-disabled children with superior-tested intelligence than for learning-disabled and nonhandicapped children who have average scores. The reported mean difference in this study is 18.5 points, regardless of direction. An example of how scattered these scores can be is evident in the performance of Billy, a student presently attending a class for learning-disabled/gifted children. Table 1.2 shows his scores on each of the WISC-R subscales.

30   Tannenbaum and Baldwin

Table 1.2.   Billy's WISC-R test scores

Verbal		Performance	
Information	16	Picture Completion	12
Similarities	18	Picture Arrangement	14
Arithmetic	6	Block Design	12
Vocabulary	19	Object Assembly	9
Comprehension	12	Coding	1
Digit Span	10		

Although the scoring patterns help to identify children with high potential, another caution has to be exercised in interpreting the scores. The examiner should be concerned with the quality of the child's responses and how the child approached the tasks. Test scores are only remote indicators of abilities and disabilities, and in no way should they become the final assessment concerning individual learning potential. As Glasser and Zimmerman (1967) suggested:

> The kinds of success and failures or mistakes, rather than statistical treatment of scores, offer us a qualitative, phenomenological profile of personality attributes of vital significance. This point, the "how" of test responses, rather than the scores per se, cannot be overemphasized (p. 6).

Evidence From "Creativity" Measures   The most popularly used "creativity" instruments measure divergent thinking, and their reliability and validity are yet to be fully confirmed. Regardless of how doubtful, cautious, or enthusiastic people may be when assessing creativity this way, all would probably agree that such instruments are most (and perhaps only) appropriate if the enrichment program is designed to emphasize divergent thinking. If such thought processes are ignored in the curriculum, then searching for them amounts to auditioning people for their singing talent in order to qualify for the corps de ballet. Divergent thinking skills deserve more emphasis in the school curriculum than they are generally given, and assessing them as part of the identification process should depend on how prominent is the role of such skills in the program.

Evidence of Noncognitive Traits   Limitations in the predictive validity of Performance measures should encourage educators to correct the underemphasis on personality variables and behaviors, including self-directedness, pride in accomplishment, persistence, dedication, work habits, and other characteristics associated with achievement. A questionnaire was developed by the Bureau of Educational Research and Service at the University of Kansas for aspiring

Merit Scholarship winners. Consistently, the following items distinguished the eventual winners from the also-rans:

How would you rate yourself in terms of intellectual curiosity?
How would you rate yourself in terms of willingness to stand discomfort (a cold, illness, etc.) in completion of a school task?
How would you rate yourself in terms of willingness to spend time beyond the ordinary schedule in completing a given school task?
How would you rate yourself in terms of questioning the absolute truth of statements from textbooks, newspapers, and magazines, or of statements made by persons in position of authority such as teachers, lecturers, and professors?

These are examples of the kinds of information that can be obtained not only from the children about themselves, but also from their peers, parents, and teachers. A large number of questionnaires of this kind now exist, and although they are not all fully validated for a wide range of talents, even the "soft signs" that are revealed at the Screening stage can be highly enlightening.

Evidence of Productivity or Performance It is important for teachers to keep constant records of children's accomplishments in or out of school. A cumulative file that shows samples and other records of such projects may reveal unusual potential in an area of work valued by society, but this potential will not necessarily be emphasized in the classroom. The child prodigy is an obvious example of someone who builds up an early record of achievements; but for other children, the evidence of talent may be more obscure and harder to elicit. One of the best sources of information is often outside the school, usually in the home and the peer group. Parents and peers can certainly help to keep a child's record up-to-date, and teachers ought to be eager to obtain whatever information can help build a case for high potential in a child.

Selection

After the Screening stage, it is necessary to move toward the narrow end of the funnel and reduce the proportion of nongifted children in the pool. This requires changing the emphasis from remote indicators to those more clearly in the context of the curriculum. All children in the pool are then given a chance to "prove themselves" in real and simulated enrichment activity to show how well they respond to the challenge. For example, if the creation of psychodrama is part of the program, it is obvious that no existing test of verbal skills or social intelligence can possibly reveal who will excel in such activity. The

32   *Tannenbaum and Baldwin*

only way to make the proper identification is to allow only those children who show any signs of unusual language facility and social insight to try out for the psychodrama unit. Thus, the procedure oscillates between identification and enrichment. The special curriculum is not a privilege for a predetermined group of children labeled "gifted"; it is a testing ground on which the gifted sort themselves out from the nongifted. The quality of identification, therefore, depends greatly on the quality of the program.

Learning-disabled children who seem to possess special talents at the Screening stage should have opportunities to demonstrate their potential for excellence through enriched classroom experiences. However, many of them are placed in resource rooms, where the emphasis is usually on remedial work. Although these needs must be addressed, such children can easily be "turned off" by an educational program that is geared to developing basic skills instead of challenging and motivating inquiry into complex topics. A steady diet of "see Jane run" may be necessary but it cannot be the only nourishment for children who are also able to discuss some intricacies of the space shuttle. Spending at least 1 hour each day in the resource room may, in effect, deny the children an opportunity to participate in regular classroom activity during that time. There is also the tendency for the learning specialist to concentrate on providing assistance, correcting mistakes, and pressuring students to measure up to requirements. In these circumstances, learning-disabled children become more dependent on adults and less self-directing and self-correcting, which are so important for gifted behavior. As Meisgeier et al. (1978) noted in their own investigations:

> Gifted children with some kind of learning problem or other handicap have disengaged in school to such a degree that they are discovered in special education classes limping along with very little or no evidence of giftedness being manifested (p. 85).

On the other hand, learning-disabled/gifted children who are placed in an enrichment class for the gifted for part of the day can experience as much failure and frustration as those placed in remedially oriented classes. In order for these children to succeed, the teacher of the gifted has to understand how learning disabilities affect their behavior and how necessary it is to adapt teaching strategies to accommodate deficits and talents in the same children. Even with the help of an understanding, well-trained teacher, learning-disabled children may have difficulty in an environment of "all star" students because of the need to measure up to their classmates' levels of performance. Gifted children often tend to be extremely self-critical, and the learning-disabled children among them are no different. In fact, as they compare themselves with their nonhandicapped peers, they may become frustrated by the gap between their expectations and performance. Thus, instead of taking the academic risks necessary to cultivate intellectual growth, they often play it safe through avoidance or negative behavior. Beery (1975) and Covington and Beery (1976) reported studies showing that students with positive self-images often protect these feelings about themselves by taking the attitude of "nothing ventured, nothing lost"; that is, they refuse to take on highly demanding tasks in order to avoid the possibility of failure and the consequence of revising their self-images downward. Learning-disabled/gifted children, who alternate between flashes of brilliance and frustrations of failure, are particularly vulnerable to retreating from challenges because failure is always a threat in their lives.

An alternative to placing the learning-disabled/gifted child in a resource room for the handicapped or in a special enrichment group for the gifted is to organize a class of children with dual exceptionalities, even if it means crossing age lines. Hopefully, this would reduce the likelihood of children feeling isolated or "freakish" because of their unusual learning problems and intellectual interests. It would also obviate the need to juggle schedules of regular classrooms, resource rooms, and remedial services while giving a single teacher full control over schedules, curriculum, instructional materials, and teaching strategies. In such a setting, children who might otherwise have hidden their talents, except for occasional flashes of brilliance, would be given an opportunity to explore exciting new domains of knowledge and encouraged to take intellectual risks without fear of ridicule from classmates if they fail. By bringing out the best in these children the teacher is in a position to fulfill the requirement of Selection, which determines who would perform best in the most appropriate enrichment program.

Differentiation

At the lower end of the funnel there is a sievelike attachment that separates the gifted from the gifted as well as the gifted from the nongifted. This process, helped by several sifting and sorting attachments, should continue indefinitely. The main objective is to begin distinguishing potential mathematicians from musicians, engineers from philosophers, historians from politicians, and so on until the student's performance at school becomes more aligned with intelligent career choices. Much depends on the breadth and inspirational quality of the enrichment program; the gifted need exposure to a variety of al-

34   *Tannenbaum and Baldwin*

ternatives in order to avoid becoming locked into an area of specialization too early in life.

Thus, the final transition is made from 1) the Screening stage, which relies heavily on measures indirectly related to life in the classroom; to 2) the Selection stage, where tryouts are conducted in a real or simulated enrichment program; to 3) the Differentiation stage, where identification occurs mainly through the separate components of the curriculum. If enrichment is continuous throughout the children's schooling, Differentiation should not end as long as they remain in the program. In the last analysis, identifying learning-disabled/gifted children involves not only systematic observation and intelligent interpretation of test data, but also the development of the right kinds of educational opportunities that will facilitate self-identification. As Hagen (1980) pointed out:

> When combining data on various indicators of potential giftedness to arrive at a decision, you should always give major weight in your decision making to demonstrated achievement because it is the best single predictor of future achievement (pp. 39–40).

This is true for all gifted children, except that the learning-disabled children who are included among the gifted do not demonstrate achievement easily and obviously. A teacher must be ingenious and sensitive to lure to the surface what is otherwise well hidden, but the effort would be worthwhile because the payoff is sometimes incalculable.

REFERENCES

Beck, E.C. 1975. Electrophysiology and behavior. In: M.R. Rosenzweig and L.W. Porter (eds.), Annual Review of Psychology Vol. 26.

Beery, R. 1975. Fear of failure in the student experience. Pers. Guid. J. 54:190–203.

Bloom, B.S. 1963. Report on creativity research by the examiner's office of the University of Chicago. In: C.W. Taylor and F. Barron (eds.) Scientific Creativity: Its Recognition and Development, pp. 251–264. John Wiley and Sons, Inc., New York.

Bryan, T., and McGrady, H.J. 1972. Use of a teacher rating scale. J. Learn. Disabil. 5:199–206.

Chauncey, H., and Hilton, T.L. 1965. Are aptitude tests valid for the highly able? Science. 148:1297–1304.

Ciha, T.E., Harris, R., Hoffman, C., and Potter, M. 1974. Parents as identifiers of giftedness, ignored but accurate. Gifted Child Q. 18:191–195.

Clements, S., and Peters J. 1967. Minimal brain dysfunction in the school-age child. In: Frierson and Barbe (eds.), Educating Children with Learning Disabilities: Selected Readings. Appleton-Century-Crofts, New York.

Covington, M.V., and Beery, R. 1976. Self-Worth and School Learning. Holt, Rinehart, and Winston, Inc., New York.

Feshbach, S., Adelman, H., and Fuller, W. 1977. Prediction of reading and related academic problems. J. Educ. Psychol. 69:299–308.

Feuerstein, R. 1979. The Dynamic Assessment of Retarded Performers. University Park Press, Baltimore.

Gallagher, J.J. 1979. Issues in education for the gifted. In: A.H. Passow (ed.), The Gifted and the Talented: Their Education and Development, The Seventy-Eighth Yearbook of the National Society for the Study of Education, pp. 28–44, University of Chicago Press, Chicago.

Galton, F. 1874. English Men of Science. Macmillan Publishing Co., London.

Gerken, K. 1979. An Unseen Minority: Handicapped Individuals Who Are Gifted and Talented. In: N. Colangelo and R.T. Zaffron (eds.), New Voices in Counseling the Gifted, Kendall/Hunt Publishing Co., Dubuque, IA.

Getzels, J.W. 1979. From Art Student to Fine Artist: Potential, Problem Finding, and Performance. In: A.H. Passow (ed.), The Gifted and the Talented: Their Education and Development, The Seventy-Eighth Yearbook of the National Society for the Study of Education, pp. 372–387. University of Chicago Press, Chicago.

Glasser, A., and Zimmerman, I. 1967. Clinical Interpretation of the Wechsler Intelligence Scale for Children. Grune and Stratton, New York.

Hagen, E. 1980. Identification of the Gifted. Teachers College Press, New York.

Jacobs, J.C. 1971. Effectiveness of teacher and parent identification of gifted children as a function of school level. Psychol. Sch. 8:140–142.

Karnes, M.B. 1979. Young handicapped children can be gifted and talented. J. for the Educ. of Gifted. 2:157–172.

MacKinnon, D.W. 1962. The personality correlates of creativity: A study of american architects. In: Proceedings of the Fourteenth Congress on Applied Psychology. 2:11–39.

Marland, Jr., S.P. 1971. Education of the Gifted and Talented, Report to the Congress of the United States by the U.S. Commissioner of Education, Vol. 1. U.S. Government Printing Office, DC.

Meisgeier, C., Meisgeier, C., and Werblo, D. 1978. Factors compounding the handicapping of some gifted children. Gifted Child Q. 22:83–87.

Piechowski, M.M. 1979. Developmental potential. In: N. Colangelo and R.T. Zaffrann (eds.), New Voices in Counseling the Gifted, Kendall/Hunt Publishing Co., Dubuque, IA.

Renzulli, J.S. 1978. What makes giftedness? Phi Delta Kappan, 60:180–184, 261.

Renzulli, J., Hartman, R., and Callahan, C. 1975. Scale for rating the behavioral characteristics of superior students. In Psychology and Education of the Gifted, W. Barbe and J. Renzulli (eds.), Irvington Publishers, New York.

Robinson, H.B. 1977. Current myths concerning gifted children. N/SLTI Gifted and Talented Brief. October, No. 5:1–11.

Roe, A. 1952. The Making of a Scientist. Dodd, Meade and Co., New York.

Schiff, M.M., Kaufman, A.S., and Kaufman, N.L. 1981. Scatter Analysis of WISC-R Profiles for Learning Disabled Children with Superior Intelligence. J. Learn. Disabil. 14:400–404.

36   Tannenbaum and Baldwin

Terman, L.M. 1925. Mental and Physical Traits of a Thousand Gifted Children. Stanford, Stanford University Press, CA.

Wallach, M.A. 1970. Creativity. In: P.H. Mussen (ed.). Charmichael's Manual of Child Psychology, 3rd Ed. John Wiley and Sons, Inc., New York. p. 1211–1272.

Wallach, M.A. 1976. Tests tell us little about talent. Am. Sci. 64:57–63.

Walsh, A. 1956. Self concepts in bright boys with learning difficulties. Unpublished doctoral dissertation, Teachers College, Columbia University.

Whitmore, J.R. 1980. Giftedness, Conflict, and Underachievement. Allyn and Bacon, Inc., Boston.

Chapter 2

The Nature and Identification of Learning Disabilities and Their Relationship to the Gifted Child

Gerald M. Senf

In the context of the early 1980s, the concept of learning disabilities must be called into closer examination because of the tremendous dependence it has on federal (and subsequently state) regulations. In this context, it is more difficult to relate the concept of learning disability to any other category of exceptionality let alone the gifted, which also has distinct ties to federal funding. The very notion of the handicapped and what is involved in their service revolves around governmental sanction. Without federal and state monies, the burden of cost would be shifted, and the definition of the constituent groups might change drastically. Herein lies the two-edged sword of government influence: if not for the intercession of federal funds and influence, current conceptualizations of handicapped persons might be different, but fiscal support might also be lacking.

The present system is a crossbreed between categories of handicapped certified by the federal government (and subsequently by state governments) as "real" and those conditions and specific syndromes to which practitioners have become attuned in clinical and research work throughout the decades. Ironically, the learning-disabled children who are now denied their inheritance by present psychometrically based government regulations may be the true heirs of that intellectual heritage.

THE NATURE OF LEARNING DISABILITIES

Consideration of the concept of learning disabilities, particularly in relation to a concept as complex as that of the gifted, requires some appreciation of its variation over time and in different locations. Al-

37

though the field of learning disabilities can be etched within the last two decades, the historical roots extend over a century (Cruickshank, 1977; Senf, 1973; Wiederholt, 1974). A detailed history does not have to be considered in the present context, but some of the recent historical trends are important in order to understand the potential relationship between learning disabilities and the gifted.

In some circles, learning disabilities are thought to be the near exclusive province of the public education system. Others rightfully contest this simplification. Although the federalization of learning disabilities has resulted in the initial *concept* being transformed into a *category* of handicapped to expedite administrative, fiscal, and statutory concerns, many who exist outside of the public education framework perceive learning disability in quite another context. In fact, as Adamson and Adamson (1979) pointed out, there is continued pressure to define learning disability in the context of biological disorders so that services are paid for by third party insurance payers. Thus, the educational label of "learning disabilities" (or some variant) within the public school system may permit remedial assistance but is mirrored by other labels; for example, "minimal brain dysfunction," which brings fiscal assistance from insurance carriers in the private sector. This sociological phenomenon needs to be acknowledged because it reflects underlying conceptual differences that greatly affect the term learning disabilities and, hence, its relationship to that of the gifted.

Cruickshank (1977) correctly noted that, although a recent development, the field of learning disabilities possesses a lengthy intellectual history. Modern learning disabilities cannot be disassociated from the work of Orton (1937), Strauss and Lehtinen (1947) nor the pioneering work of many others in the late 1940s, 1950s and early 1960s (see Myklebust, 1968). Yet, learning disabilities is a sociocultural as well as a psychoeducational phenomenon. It is much more than a disorder that afflicts many school children; learning disabilities is a subspecialty within the education profession.

The sociological context of a developing profession is basic to its domain of service. In fashioning their field, learning disabilities specialists have worked to define their domain as distinct from other fields of education, such as remedial reading and mental retardation, and from other professional disciplines concerned with developmental disabilities, such as pediatrics, neurology, psychology, and neuropsychology. Defining the characteristics of the learning-disabled child, and by inference designating the "appropriate" service agent, has been tantamount to defining the domain of the professional subspecialty of the same name.

THE CONTEXT OF DIAGNOSIS AND
TREATMENT: HISTORICAL PERSPECTIVE

Before the concept of learning disabilities became fashionable, or at least prior to when federal monies were expended to remediate these disorders in public schools, the private facilities, university-affiliated clinics, and occasionally "left-over" space within the public school were typical service sites. Without public funding, the locus of service was dramatically different from what is seen in the 1980s. *More important, the range of the practitioner's concern used to be considerably broader than that which has since been addressed by public schools.*

The effort in what was to become the field of learning disabilities can be characterized by the involvement of the "whole person" in the instruction or remedial concern. This is in contrast to the prevailing view, which is somewhat mitigated by research on the social context of the learning-disabled person (e.g., Hallahan and Bryan, 1981). This view focuses squarely on the academic performance of the individual, specifically with an expectation by relevant others that the individual could (and should) perform much better. In the public school context, "education specialists," many retrained from the areas of reading, speech and language, and general education, attempt to bring the child's academic achievement in line with his or her potential.

The focus on eliminating "underachievement" culminated in regulations for identifying learning-disabled children. After considerable debate, PL 94-142 identified a learning disability as the discrepancy between intelligence and one or more of the areas of reading, writing, spelling, mathematical computation, written expression, oral expression, and comprehension. Intellectual history was sacrificed to administrative expedience (Senf, 1978). The strictly product-related skill deficiency approach to learning disabilities was widely accepted because of the lengthy legislative history which preceded the regulations. From the initial lobbying efforts of the mid 1960s until the acceptance into law, the need to establish reasonably concrete procedures for determining who was and who was not "learning disabled" became increasingly important. *Definition* in laws was superceded by identification *procedures* outlined in the regulations. Specifically, the discrepancy between intelligence (as measured by traditional intelligence tests, such as the Wechsler Intelligence Scales for Children (WISC), the Stanford-Binet, or often the Peabody Picture Vocabulary Test) and achievement in one of the seven basic skill areas noted above became the essence of learning disabilities—not just in law but in the thinking of the vast majority of practitioners (Kirk et al., 1981). The

40 *Senf*

willingness to accept such a conceptualization rested in part on the fact that many newcomers failed to know the history of their field. Furthermore, the practical reality was that only with such psychometric evidence were fiscal resources for remediation available within the public school setting. In essence, the measurement criteria became definition.

The history has been lost to the present practitioner and officially disregarded by virtue of the federal regulations. These factors have resulted in a pronounced discontinuity with history of the field. Coupled with the educational community's desire to establish its own territory (Lieberman, 1980) and adopt the learning-disabled child as an object of their particular concern, the domain of issues during the 1970s became dramatically restricted; the range of ideas and multidisciplinary knowledge concerning learning problems was also narrowed.

Although it is recognized that PL 94-142 called for the most extensive auxiliary services for the handicapped schoolchild ever mandated by law, the money to purchase those services was never to be forthcoming. Nor was there any organizational structure developed to effect the necessary liaisons with nonschool personnel, such as psychiatrists, clinical and developmental psychologists, optometrists, occupational and rehabilitation personnel, and health personnel. Lacking money, time, and organizational structure for delivery of such services, the law promised services that only the most rich, dogged, or socially adept could obtain for their child.

As related disciplines "fell away" from the public school effort for the learning-disabled children, the work did not cease. Private- and university-affiliated clinics maintained interdisciplinary perspectives through their numbers and impact, not only in the broader social context but also in the published literature, quickly became dwarfed by the strictly educational approaches espoused by the public education system. For example, a striking decrease in the number of interdisciplinary articles published by the *Journal of Learning Disabilities* over its 15-year history can be observed. By the mid 1970s, the impact of the public law predominated, and many of the pages focused on law-related concerns, such as articles regarding aspects of the law itself, legal compliance, formulation of individualized educational plans (IEPs), measurement issues regarding the identification of the learning-disabled children, and mainstreaming.

There seems to be greater continuity with early historical trends, both in thinking and in practice, outside of the public school setting. Such settings have been less directly reoriented by the infusion of federal and state monies, laws, and attendant regulations. At the ex-

Nature and Identification 41

treme, many researchers seem to be unaware of the passage of PL 94-142 and its attendant impact on the public school setting. Because this did not affect them directly, researchers continued as they had been. Perhaps many of them did not realize the impact of the PL 94-142 on the constitution of their research samples inasmuch as the law was dictating who might be labeled within the school context. Because there are many specific lines of inquiry and modes of service outside the public school, it is impossible to accurately determine or succinctly relate the specific course of the various intellectual trends or the impact PL 94-142 had on each of them. Because the concern is to relate the definition and assessment procedures in learning disabilities to the area of the gifted, it is reasonable to group together those nonpublic school efforts and draw from them distinctions which weigh heavily as a counterpoint to the public school *conception*.

In contrast to the public school conception of learning disabilities, the essence of which is the discrepancy between potential and actual school-skill performance, the clinic conception has different elements: 1) a concern for the "total child"; 2) a concern for the child in the context of environment, including family and peers; 3) particular concern, often specific to the orientation of the observer, for aspects of the child not ordinarily considered by the public school, such as the child's neurological integrity, biological history, psychological development, and emotional status; and 4) correlated aspects of performance, such as visual skill and auditory capabilities and language skills.

It is important to draw distinctions between 1) the conceptionalization and practices of those not intimately involved with public school programs for the learning disabled children; and 2) the statutory requirements and derivative practices related to the law governing public school action. Their relationship to the gifted will vary accordingly. Most succinctly, the learning-disabled/gifted child has greater recognition in the clinic than in the public education setting. This fact stems from the public school's use of the simplistic intelligence achievement discrepancy mode of thought, whether or not specific psychometric formulas are utilized. The clinic setting, however, has attended to the broad diversity of symptomatology, which inevitably characterizes the disabled learner. Despite the provisions of PL 94-142 (1975) for related services, very few services within or through the public school are geared to the whole child. This fact is important in that the identification of a child who is gifted and who might also be learning disabled becomes extremely unlikely. Fewer here are identified than in the theoretical joint set comprising the overlap between the learning-disabled and gifted populations. This is because many public schools are

42   Senf

insensitive to the symptomatology characteristic of the learning-dis-
abled/gifted child.

This insensitivity extends beyond the social, emotional, and personality disturbances which can accompany the failure of gifted children in the context of an otherwise superior performance. A system
such as the one that exists in the public education domain should be
capable of measuring the discrepancy between seven school skills and
intelligence test scores by noting one or more of those skills that are
significantly below "expectancy." However, given the variation in academic skill among the highly talented, it is not unlikely that the skill
level in one or more of these seven areas would significantly trail behind what is predicted from the child's intelligence. For example, are
children with intelligence test scores in the 99th percentile to be termed
learning disabled if they perform at grade level in mathematics? According to the federal learning disability regulations, if mathematics
significantly lags behind the predicted level based on the intelligence
quotient, these children could be classified learning disabled. Yet,
there is an extremely low likelihood that a child's performance appropriate to his or her grade level would ever signal a teacher or parent
to investigate potential learning disabilities. This would require the
observer to interpret the governmental equation literally.

Utilizing most any formula which compares expected performance (based on intelligence test scores) with achievement, it could
readily be demonstrated that *most* gifted children perform significantly
below their expected level in one or more of the seven school skill
areas. This is the nature of individual differences. No such analysis is
conducted in practice. Rather, the gifted child thought to have a learning disability must show some signs of social, emotional, or personality
disorder in order to be considered for follow-up testing and supportive
services.

In this context, the notion of learning disability as it has existed
in the clinic setting throughout the last 50 years comes into play. No
definition of learning disabilities ever hinged on a simple discrepancy
formula between intelligence test scores and performance in one or
more of seven basic school skill areas. Rather, the functioning of the
total child was ascertained and decisions were made in the context of
the total welfare of the client. In that context, it would be determined
that despite giftedness, certain disabilities affect intellectual endeavors
so as to prohibit the maximization of potential. It is less important,
that the child is above average in all skill areas commensurate with
intelligence than that the child copes successfully and gains pleasure
from life. *When* the learning-disabled/gifted child is noticed within the
public school context, it is because he or she is observed as a dis-

turbed person. *The learning-disabled/gifted child is seldom referred for psychological assessment because of a skill deficiency but rather for the psychological manifestations of distress.*

Paradoxically, numerous so-called learning-disabled/gifted children could be identified through routine calculation of intelligence test scores and school skill discrepancies. However, this point overlooks a more important principle—that it is not the depression of one or more of the school skills that characterizes the learning-disabled/gifted child, but rather personality and behavioral disturbances which characterize those with "true" disabilities. Exactly whether or not the same underlying processes are responsible for the personality and behavioral disorders or whether the personality and the behavioral disorders are secondary to the specific areas of diminished skill is basically an issue for individual case study. It seems reasonable, however, to assert the likelihood that underlying learning disabilities are not simply the cause of school-skill problems, which in turn negatively impact the child's personality and behavioral outcomes; rather, the learning disability itself has a pervasive impact on the total child. The same disability which affects a school skill also affects information processing in the social and emotional realm. This general disruption is not the *result* of the school-skill problem but an integral part of the total symptomatology.

In this context, it is important to recognize that the traditional chicken-and-egg questions of whether personality and behavioral problems result from school skill deficiencies or whether they all emanate from a single underlying disability may not be as important as thought previously. Causation must be understood in the context in which the behavior occurs. The potential for feedback to the organism from its experience is so immediate that a linear concept relating such global terms as "inadequate skill performance" and "personality/behavioral problems" makes little sense. Rather, the ongoing dynamic interaction makes the linear conception misleading. Failure effects personality/behavior problems and personality/behavioral problems prohibit skill acquisition. A more reasonable and productive conceptionalization recognizes this interactive nature of personality and performance (Senf, 1972).

LEARNING DISABILITIES SYMPTOMS AMONG THE GIFTED

In its 15–year history, the *Journal of Learning Disabilities* has published only a few articles concerned with the learning-disabled/gifted child. One involves biographical notes about a number of well-known individuals who were alleged to have a specific learning disability

44   *Senf*

(Thompson, 1971). This particular article provides interesting hints as to the relationship between learning disabilities and giftedness, and corroborates the thesis that the psychopathological aspects of learning disabilities characterize the learning-disabled/gifted person.

The other relevant article is interesting from a couple of perspectives (Schiff et al., 1981). First, it examines the psychometric characteristics of learning-disabled/gifted children on the WISC-R. Second, it provides insight into the functioning of the learning-disabled/gifted person which, bolstered by clinical information that is also provided, yields a picture consistent with what was described previously. Specifically, persons in this sample were not initially isolated because of inadequate performance in one of the "skill areas" so much as they were referred because of their psychological difficulties. In psychometric interviews, Schiff observed:

> The children tended to be emotionally upset and disorganized. All expressed a sense of unhappiness, and many felt they did not fit in anywhere. They often complained of being isolated or scapegoated; images of being corroded, out of control, monster-like, or dumb prevailed. Virtually all had some idea that they could not make their brain, body, or both, do what they wanted it to do. They often reported organizing difficulties in simple mathematical calculations, spelling, and handwriting. They reported extremely upsetting feelings with physical education and gross motor activities, and often perceived themselves powerless in a fearsome and attacking world. Many sought angry revenge against teachers and children who made fun of them or picked them last in games. The emotional implications of the group as a whole include inadequate impulse control, defective self-concept, narcissistic hypersensitivity, and poorly developed integrative functions; these emotional problems are similar to those reported by Adamson and Adamson (1979).

The area of learning disability has become so heavily cognitive that the peculiar problems of learning-disabled/gifted children have not yet been squarely met. It is as if the learning-disabled/gifted child represents a deviant group within the learning-disabled population— a group whose deviance absolutely requires examination of emotional and social functioning. This is significantly less often addressed within the broader learning-disabled population. The learning-disabled/gifted children may nevertheless reveal much about aberrant processes involved in academic skills because their deficits stand in bolder relief against their strengths than do those of their more average learning-disabled peers. Because the understanding of the social, emotional, and ego functioning of learning-disabled children in general is so poor, it is not surprising that little is known about particular problems encountered by the highly intelligent and creative learning-disabled person.

Nature and Identification   45

The research in learning disabilities regarding social functioning centers around peer status. Here, it is routinely found that learning-disabled students are found more typically among the class isolates and less frequently among the class stars (Siperstein et al., 1978). Although these data are hardly surprising, such findings provide necessary substantiation. A number of studies report that the self-esteem of some learning-disabled children is lower than that of their normal counterparts, although broad terms like "self-esteem" mask the specific aspects of the child's internal uncertainty.

The particular syndromes vary, but there seem to be few learning-disabled children who consider themselves to be unscathed in activities other than academic. Their failure in school is either symptomatic of a broader information-processing disability or failure has generalized to other aspects of functioning, despite the fact that the skill theoretically might enable them to function quite adequately in these other situations. Such differential issues have not been subject to study. Whether it is the fact that the children are primarily deficient in the social context or whether their failure in the academic context generates a predisposition for self-defeating behaviors in the social context, where they would otherwise perform normally, is not known. Studies of learning-disabled children indicate that they are both viewed as different (Hallahan and Bryan, 1981) and that they do seem to act sufficiently differently—such that even naive observers can notice the learning-disabled child distinct from the norm (Bryan and Bryan, 1978). A very basic information-processing deficiency is suggested. This deficiency prohibits the extraction of relevant cues from the social environment so that the learning-disabled child both acts and is perceived by others as idiosyncratic with respect to the normal social context. Little theoretical work has been done in this area. It has only been pointed out that these discrepancies exist; no effort yet has tried to integrate them into a framework of individual psychology. Certainly, this area is open to creative explanation.

**IMPLICATION OF PSYCHOMETRIC DEFINITIONS
FOR SERVICES TO THE LEARNING-DISABLED/GIFTED CHILD**

Assessment of the learning-disabled child follows a number of basic steps. First, what is often called screening or early identification is accomplished by a variety of methods (e.g., Senf and Comrey, 1975). The parent or medical practitioner frequently notes irregularities in the child's behavior and brings them to the attention of appropriate school personnel. More typically, the schoolteacher notices some difficulty, as often in the child's *behavioral characteristics* (such as degree of activity or lack of success in interpersonal relationships) as in academic performance. The teacher or another adult suggests that the child should be diagnostically evaluated.

Here, the course of activity within and without the public school context can be distinguished. Within the public school context, the child is seen typically by a diagnostician, whose primary focus involves the academic capabilities of the child and prerequisite skills or associated global measures thought to be related to academic skills. Intelligence test subscales, subscales on the Illinois Test of Psycholinguistic Abilities, direct assessment of academic skills, and indices of perceptual-motor skills (such as obtained through the Bender Gestalt Test or some similar procedure) are often obtained. *Unless the gifted child is particularly lacking in social skills, is extremely overactive, or substantially interpersonally deviant, referral to the clinical psychologist is not likely to be made! Furthermore, unless the child is severely disturbed, no emotional disorder will be noticed.* No learning disorder will be uncovered because the school psychologist usually will not administer the requisite achievement indices in the "seven basic school skill areas" necessary to identify a child as learning disabled.

Although such a broad statement must be false a reasonable percentage of the time, the assertion is that the school psychologist is primarily a psychometrician schooled in the measurement of intelligence and attendant assessment devices geared for information which is to be utilized for placement into predetermined programs (Senf, 1981). Furthermore, the school psychologist will not examine intraindividual discrepancies within a child who indicates above average intellectual capability.

The implication is that the school psychologist will not uncover any disorder except the grossest emotional disturbance in the gifted child. Because the learning disability profession is primarily practiced in the public school domain, at least as far as the educational side is concerned, it is important to examine why many psychologists would be insensitive to the plight of the learning-disabled/gifted child.

Even discounting the pathological bias of the referral agent, there are extraordinary psychometric difficulties which prohibit the examiner from finding a child to be both gifted and learning disabled. First, the referral question presented to the psychologist must be examined. Typically, with a gifted child, it can be presumed that the question does not involve lack of achievement because most persons are rather quick to perceive the obvious overall competence of the child. Hence, the question provided to the psychologist is not why the child is performing "only at grade level" in a content area, but rather what other

Nature and Identification   47

circumstances could be the cause of behavior that is withdrawn, hyperactive, inattentive, argumentative, disruptive to the group, or otherwise self-defeating. Personal problems often create or contribute to learning problems.

Given this broader referral problem, the psychologist may fail to administer a sufficiently detailed educational examination so that the actual discrepancies between basic academic areas and intelligence test scores are never determined. Instead, a general assessment battery (sometimes augmented by a parent interview and perhaps some projective techniques) is administered. The psychologist may overlook the possibility that deficiencies in underlying psychological processes, the hallmark of learning disabilities, are responsible for the gifted child's wide-ranging problems.

Another impediment to useful diagnosis should be acknowledged. Many practitioners within public education agencies do not look for problems. Recognizing the lack of programs to deal with such problems, the absence of problems or their diminishment can be viewed as implicit in their job description (Senf, 1981). They may feel that it is better to resolve the problem through quick consultation with the referral agent rather than establish, by virtue of their diagnostic edict, the necessity of a placement in special education for each child tested, even if such placement would be beneficial.

No witness to the contemporary educational scene could reasonably have believed that the public system could ever have delivered the "related services" written into PL 94-142. The alleged multidisciplinary character of school personnel is reduced in scope by self-selection. Not everyone is capable of working within the strictures of the public education system. The strictures call for an adherence to the goal structure of the public school setting. Within that setting, there are diffuse goals; but few would claim that these goals champion the individuality of children and the necessity for the professionals in the system to foster such individuality (Senf, 1981).

Furthermore, given the orientation of the school system that all of its employees serve it and its goals, not only do persons select themselves as they deem themselves capable of submitting to the overall goals of an educational system, but the educational system itself further homogenizes practices and opinion in order that it might exhibit a coherent organizational effort. This folie à deux between the practitioner and the broader school system strips the multidisciplinary team of its intellectual diversity. Although an administrator, psychologist, learning disability specialist, social worker, etc. may meet to determine the child's educational program, all are intimately aware of the system's

48   *Senf*

goals and limitations, as well as the resultant position it must take vis-à-vis the parent and the child in recommending (and delivering) services. "Related services," as called for in PL 94-142, can become little more than a skeleton in the public school closet.

CONCLUSION

Services for learning-disabled/gifted individuals relate ultimately to the sociology of the public school. The plight of these children is that the related services they directly need are essentially absent from their school's special education service system. A number of historical factors have created this situation, including a territorial dispute over the control of public education by the educational establishment and the rejection of those outside of the full-time education payroll. The broader issues however, lie outside that scope of discussion. Until education can integrate into its employ the other "related disciplines" on a regular contractual or salaried basis, there will be no true interdisciplinary effort in public education. The learning-disabled/gifted child will remain underidentified and underserved.

REFERENCES

Adamson, W.C., and Adamson, K.K. 1979. A Handbook for Specific Learning Disabilities. Gardner Press, New York.

Bryan, T., and Bryan, J. 1978. Understanding Learning Disabilities. 2nd Ed. Alfred Publishing Co., Inc., Sherman Oaks, CA.

Cruickshank, W.M. 1977. Myths and realities in learning disabilities. J. Learn. Disabil. 10:51–58.

Hallahan, D.P., and Bryan, T.H. 1981. Learning disabilities. In: J.M. Kauffman, and D.P. Hallahan (eds.), Handbook of Special Education. Prentice-Hall, Inc., Englewood Cliffs, NJ.

Kirk, S.A., Senf, G.M., and Larsen, R. 1981. Current issues in learning disabilities. In: W. Cruickshank and A. Silver (eds.), Bridges to Tomorrow Volume II, The Best of ACLD. Syracuse University Press, Syracuse, NY.

Lieberman, L.M. 1980. Territoriality—who does what to whom? J. Learn. Disabil. 13:124–128.

Myklebust, H.R. 1968. Progress in Learning Disabilities, Vol. 1. Grune and Stratton, New York.

Orton, S. 1937. Reading, Writing and Speech Problems in Children. W. W. Norton and Co., Inc., New York.

Schiff, M.M., Kaufman, A.S., and Kaufman, N.L. 1981. Scatter analyses of WISC-R profiles for learning disabled children with superior intelligence. J. Learn. Disabil. 14:400–404.

Senf, G.M. 1972. An information integration theory and its application to normal reading acquisition and reading disability. In: N.D. Bryant and C.E. Kass (eds.), Leadership Training Institute in Learning Disabilities, Vol. II. 303–391.

Nature and Identification 49

Senf, G.M. 1973. Learning disabilities. In: H.J. Grossman (ed.), Pediatric Clinics of North America. 20:607–640.

Senf, G.M. 1978. Implications of the final procedures for evaluating specific learning disabilities. J. Learn. Disabil. 11:124–126.

Senf, G.M. 1981. Issues surrounding the diagnosis of learning disabilities: Child handicap versus failure of the child-school interaction. In T.R. Kratochwill (ed.), Advances in School Psychology, Vol. 1. Lawrence Erlbaum Associates, Inc., Hillsdale, NJ.

Senf, G.M., and Comrey, A.L. 1975. State initiative in learning disabilities: Illinois' Project SCREEN, report I: The screen early identification procedure. J. Learn. Disabil. 8:451–457.

Siperstein, G.N., Bopp, M.J., and Bak, J.J. 1978. Social status of learning disabled children. J. Learn. Disabil. 11:98–102.

Strauss, A., and Lehtinen, L. 1947. Psychopathology and Education of the Brain-Injured Child. Grune and Stratton, New York.

Thomson, L.J. 1971. Language disabilities in men of eminence. J. Learn. Disabil. 4:34–45.

Wiederholt, J.L. 1974. Historical perspectives on the education of the learning disabled. In: L. Mann and D. Sabatino (eds.), The Second Review of Special Education. JSE Press, Philadelphia.

Chapter 3

Learning Disabilities as a Category of Underachievement

Ronald A. Berk

Probably the most difficult task that every practitioner and researcher must tackle before identifying a learning-disabled child is to define the construct *learning disabilities*, preferably in operational terms. The considerable amount of confusion and fragmentation in the field of learning disabilities which has occurred over the past 20 years can be traced to this initial step. If the definition is imprecise or ambiguous, then all succeeding tasks contingent upon that definition, such as screening, diagnosis, and remediation, will be afflicted by the imprecision or ambiguity. Therefore, clarification must begin with the definition.

This chapter surveys and analyzes definitions proposed by field experts as well as legislative mandate in order to provide some insight into the existing problems with screening and diagnosis. The presentation is organized according to the following topics: 1) historical developments, 2) common elements in the definitions, 3) criticisms of federal definitions, 4) theoretical versus operational definitions, and 5) definitions used in research and practice. Several conclusions regarding the current state of definitions will then be given. One of these is that learning disabilities has become a category of underachievement.

HISTORICAL DEVELOPMENTS

Prior to the 1960s, a variety of terms referred to the disorders that were later to fall under the rubric of learning disabilities. These included

---

This chapter is based on an article by the author, titled "Toward a definition of learning disabilities: Progress or regress?," in *Education and Treatment of Children*, 1983. In press.

52   Berk

minimal brain dysfunction, psychoneurological learning disorder, central processing dysfunction, exogeneous, and perceptually handicapped. More specific disorders were given labels such as dyslexia for severe reading disabilities and aphasia for delays in learning to talk. The number of these terms increased ad infinitum as specialists attempted to describe the conditions they observed.

In 1962, Kirk coined the term *learning disabilities* in the first edition of his popular textbook, *Educating Exceptional Children* (Kirk, 1962). Shortly afterwards, he introduced the term in a presentation at the 1963 Conference on Exploration into the Problems of the Perceptually Handicapped Child. At this conference, Kirk also tried to sort out the multiplicity of terms and labels which had been applied to the children of interest:

> There are two kinds of terms that have been applied to those children, either alone or in combination.
> The first group of terms refers to causation or etiology. We try to label the child with a term that has biological significance. These terms are *brain injury, minimal brain damage, cerebral palsy, cerebral dysfunction, organic driven-ness, organic behavior disorders, psychoneurological disorders*, and a host of other terms. All of these terms refer to a disability of the brain in one form or another as an explanation of the deviant behavior of the child.
> The second group of terms refers to the behavior manifestations of the child, and include a wide variety of deviant behavior. Terms such as *hyperkinetic behavior, perceptual disorders, conceptual disorders, Strauss syndrome, social dyspraxia, catastrophic behavior, disinhibition, learning disorders*, and the various forms of aphasia, apraxia, agnosia, dyslexia and a host of other terms which describe the specific behavior deficit of the child (pp. 1–2).

These two groups of terms were the precursors of the medical and behavioral categories of definitions, respectively. Kirk then presented the term *learning disabilities*:

> Recently, I have used the term "learning disabilities" to describe a group of children who have disorders in development in language, speech, reading, and associated communication skills needed for social inter-action. In this group I do not include children who have sensory handicaps such as blindness or deafness, because we have methods of managing and training the deaf and the blind. I also exclude from this group children who have generalized mental retardation (p. 3).

The definitions of learning disabilities which were to be included in the literature during the next 2 decades are listed in Table 3.1. Some of them were formulated by individuals; others were developed by committees associated with various parental, professional, educational, or governmental organizations.

Category of Underachievement 53

Table 3.1 Chronology of selected definitions of learning disabilities over the past 2 decades

Date	Source	Definition
1962	Samuel A. Kirk	A learning disability refers to a retardation, disorder, or delayed development in one or more of the processes of speech, language, reading, spelling, writing, or arithmetic resulting from a possible cerebral dysfunction and/or emotional or behavioral disturbance and not from mental retardation, sensory deprivation, or cultural or instructional factors (p. 263).
1963	Helmer R. Myklebust	The term "psychoneurological learning disorders" is used to include deficits in learning, at any age, which are caused by deviations in the central nervous system and which are not due to mental deficiency, sensory impairment, or psychogenicity. The etiology might be disease and accident, or it might be development (p. 27).
1964	Barbara Bateman	Manifest an educationally significant discrepancy between their estimated intellectual potential and actual level of performance related to basic disorders in the learning processes, which may or may not be accompanied by demonstrable central nervous system dysfunction, and which are not secondary to generalized mental retardation, educational or cultural deprivation, severe emotional disturbance, or sensory loss (p. 220).
1966	Task Force I—sponsored by National Society for Crippled Children and Adults and National Institutes of Neurological Diseases and Blindness, National Institutes of Health (Clements, 1966)	The term "minimal brain dysfunction syndrome" refers to children of near average, average, or above average general intelligence with certain learning or behavioral disabilities ranging from mild to severe, which are associated with deviations of function of the central nervous system. These deviations may manifest themselves by various combinations of impairments in perception, conceptualization, language, memory, and control of attention, impulse, or motor function (pp. 9–10).

continued

Table 3.1 (Continued)

Date	Source	Definition
1966	James J. Gallagher	Children with developmental imbalances are those who reveal a developmental disparity in psychological processes related to education of such a degree (often four years or more) as to require the instructional programming of developmental tasks appropriate to the nature and level of the deviant developmental process (p. 28).
1968–69	National Advisory Committee on Handicapped Children; Children with Specific Learning Disabilities Act of 1969 (PL 91-230)	Children with special learning disabilities exhibit a disorder in one or more of the basic psychological processes involved in understanding or using spoken or written languages. These may be manifested in disorders of listening, thinking, talking, reading, writing, spelling or arithmetic. They include conditions which have been referred to as perceptual handicaps, brain injury, minimal brain dysfunction, dyslexia, development aphasia, etc. They do not include learning problems which are due primarily to visual, hearing, or motor handicaps, to mental retardation, emotional disturbance, or to environmental disadvantage (p. 4).
1969	James C. Chalfant and Margaret A. Scheffelin	Characteristics which are often mentioned include disorders in one or more of the processes of thinking, conceptualization, learning, memory, speech, language, attention, perception, emotional behavior, neuromuscular or motor coordination, reading, writing, arithmetic, discrepancies between intellectual achievement potential and achievement level, and developmental disparity in the psychological processes related to education (p. 1).
1975	Part A of the Education of the Handicapped Act (PL 91-230), as amended by the Education for All Handicapped Children Act of 1975 (PL 94-142), which is Part B	Children with specific learning disabilities are defined as those children who have a disorder in one or more of the basic psychological processes involved in understanding or in using language, spoken or written, which disorder may

Year	Source	Definition
		...imperfect ability to listen, think, speak, read, write, spell, or do mathematical calculations. Such disorders include such conditions as perceptual handicaps, brain injury, minimal brain dysfunction, dyslexia, and developmental aphasia. Such term does not include children who have learning problems which are primarily the result of visual, hearing, or motor handicaps, of mental retardation, of emotional disturbance, or of environmental, cultural, or economic disadvantage (Sec. 602).
1979	Samuel A. Kirk and James J. Gallagher	A specific learning disability is a psychological or neurological impediment to spoken or written language or perceptual, cognitive, or motor behavior. The impediment (1) is manifested by discrepancies among specific behaviors and achievements or between evidenced ability and academic achievement, (2) is of such nature and extent that the child does not learn by the instructional methods and materials appropriate for the majority of children and requires specialized procedures for development, and (3) is not primarily due to severe mental retardation, sensory handicaps, emotional problems, or lack of opportunity to learn (p. 285).
1981	National Joint Committee for Learning Disabilities—composed of representatives from American Speech-Language-Hearing Association, Association for Children and Adults with Learning Disabilities, Council for Learning Disabilities, Division for Children with Communication Disorders, International Reading Association, and The Orton Dyslexia Society (see Hammill et al., 1981)	Learning disabilities is a generic term that refers to a heterogeneous group of disorders manifested by significant difficulties in the acquisition and use of listening, speaking, reading, writing, reasoning or mathematical abilities. These disorders are intrinsic to the individual and presumed to be due to central nervous system dysfunction. Even though a learning disability may occur concomitantly with other handicapping conditions (e.g., sensory impairment, mental retardation, social and emotional disturbance) or environmental influences (e.g., cultural differences, insufficient/inappropriate instruction, psychogenic factors), it is not the direct result of those conditions or influences (p. 5).

56   *Berk*

Medical Definitions

The substance and orientation of these definitions reflect the different perspectives and changes in the field which occurred within that period of time. The influences of medicine, psychology, and education were the most profound. For example, several of the earlier definitions stressed *medical-neurological* or biologically based factors by expressing learning disabilities as etiologies. These usually related to a particular type of brain dysfunction or disorder of the central nervous system. This focus is illustrated in the definitions of Myklebust and Clements (see also Cruickshank, 1967; Johnson and Myklebust, 1967; Ross, 1976; and Wender, 1971). These definitions fostered the notion that the locus of damage or dysfunction was internal to the child.

Confronted with this charge of detecting brain dysfunction, the educational diagnostician conveyed dissatisfaction and frustration. First, the medical vocabulary was foreign. Second and more important, however, the required assessment procedures, instruments, and competencies were not within the purview of educators, especially learning disability specialists, and medical evidence was essential in order to link learning disabilities to minimal brain damage. Bryan and Bryan (1978) explained the problem:

> The stronger the evidence for brain damage, such as seizures and paralysis, the less likely the diagnostic conclusion is to be "minimal" damage. The less direct the medical evidence, the more reliance upon social and academic performance, and the more likely the diagnosis of "minimal brain dysfunction." By definition, the linkage of brain damage with learning disabilities through direct evidence becomes an impossibility. (p. 35)

Finally, even if the difficulties of locating dysfunctions in the brain were overcome and specific damage was identified, instructional programming to ameliorate or eliminate the damage would be pointless. There is little meaningful activity via prescriptions in which the educator could engage in order to make any corrective difference.

Behavioral Definitions

As a result of the discontent over etiological definitions, a major shift in emphasis could be anticipated. The definitions that followed relied heavily upon educational and psychological (or psychoeducational) factors. These *behavioral* definitions concentrated on behavioral characteristics such as the inability to read, listen, think, speak, write, spell, or perform arithmetic calculations, irrespective of etiology. These elements are evident to varying degrees in all of the other definitions in Table 3.1. The attempt to blend diverse psychoeducational variables into a single framework was most clearly documented in the 1968 National Advisory Committee on Handicapped Children definition, which was included in PL 91-230, Children with Specific Learning Disabilities Act of 1969, the Elementary and Secondary Amendments of 1969. This legislation was extended in 1974 as part of PL 93-380, the Education of the Handicapped Amendments, and again in 1975 when the definition was changed only slightly for inclusion in PL 94-142, the Education for All Handicapped Children Act of 1975. These federal definitions underscored the domain of *language-related problems* as the distinguishable category of disorders which constitutes special (or specific) learning disabilities.

The other definitions proposed by the authorities listed in Table 3.1 represented particular educational, psychological, or psychoeducational positions. For example, Kirk (1962) emphasized specific learning problems, Bateman (1965) stressed the discrepancy between achievement and potential, Gallagher (1966) focused on the irregular development of mental abilities, and Chalfant and Scheffelin (1969) related psychological processes to academic disorders.

COMMON ELEMENTS IN THE DEFINITIONS

An analysis of all of these definitions and others which have accumulated reveal several common elements or components that circumscribe the limits of what are called learning disabilities (see Chalfant and King, 1976; Gearheart, 1981; Myers and Hammill 1976; Wallace and McLoughlin 1979). Johnson and Morasky (1980) extracted five functional characteristics that are explicitly or implicitly contained in most definitions:

1. Some principle of discrepancy or disparity between a child's actual performance and predicted potential or capacity
2. General role of the central nervous system, although few contemporary definitions focus on the necessity for demonstrating neurological pathology or dysfunction for inclusion in a learning disability category
3. Primary physiological problems are excluded
4. Some special problem areas are excluded, such as cultural disadvantage, mental retardation, and emotional disturbance
5. The relevance of the problem to the learning process in terms of educational growth, development, and performance (pp. 5–6)

Perhaps the simplest observation that can be made about these definitions is that they delineate what learning disabilities are as well as what they are not; that is, there are elements of inclusion and elements of exclusion in each definition.

58   Berk

Elements of Inclusion

There are four elements of inclusion in most definitions: 1) normal intelligence; 2) ability-achievement discrepancy; 3) academic disorder; and 4) psychological process disorder.

1. *Normal intelligence*   This distinguishing characteristic pertains to the level of intelligence. The child with a learning disability should possess normal intelligence and can possess gifted intelligence based on verbal or nonverbal measures of language concepts. Although the notion that a learning disability is not attributable to a child's lack of intelligence or mental subnormality is generally accepted in the profession, there is no explicit statement about intelligence level in any of the definitions in Table 3.1. The intelligence element is inferred from that part of the "exclusion clause," indicating that a learning disorder is not primarily attributable to mental retardation. Given the criteria that traditionally identify the mentally retarded, definitions of learning disability automatically exclude children who are below a certain level of intelligence. This approach to designating the intelligence element leads to the conclusion that the specification of intelligence level in all of the definitions is vague, indirect, and indefinite.

2. *Ability-achievement discrepancy* (underachievement)   Children who have learning disabilities should also have normal mental ability; in addition, they should exhibit an achievement deficit relative to their ability in at least one academic subject area. In other words, in spite of average or above average potential, severe learning problems must be clearly evidenced. This difference between measured ability and measured achievement has been expressed as a "discrepancy," "disparity," "imbalance," "deficit," "gap," or "intraindividual difference" in the various definitions. It is noteworthy that a statement of discrepancy or underachievement does not appear in either the National Advisory Committee on Handicapped Children (1968) definition or the PL 94-142 (1975) definition. In 1977, however, the *Procedures for Evaluating Specific Learning Disabilities*, published in the *Federal Register* of the United States Office of Education (U.S.O.E.) in 1977, did stipulate:

> [A]   child has a specific learning disability if:
> (1)   The child does not achieve commensurate with his or her age and ability levels in one or more of the areas listed [below] . . . when provided with learning experiences appropriate to the child's age and ability levels; and

Category of Underachievement   59

(2) The [multidisciplinary] team finds that a child has a severe
discrepancy between achievement and intellectual ability in
one or more of the following areas:
  (i)   Oral expression;
  (ii) Listening comprehension;
  (iii) Written expression;
  (iv) Basic reading skill;
  (v)   Reading comprehension;
  (vi) Mathematics calculation; or
  (vii) Mathematics reasoning (p. 65083).

The omission of a "severe discrepancy between achievement and intellectual ability" in the original definition is a major oversight inasmuch as the discrepancy element has emerged as the primary focus of the criteria for identifying learning-disabled children.

Despite the emphasis given to the ability-achievement discrepancy and the proliferation of methods to operationally define "discrepancy," none of the definitions provides any guidelines or standards for determining what is a significant or severe discrepancy. Although this ambiguity in the federal specifications is not surprising in view of the earlier congressional definitions, it is nevertheless troublesome from the standpoint that the responsibility is then thrust on local and state agencies. As Ysseldyke and Algozzine (1982) so metaphorically and accurately observed, "local or state education agencies must flesh out the skeletal structure offered by the federal agency" (p. 44).

3. *Academic disorder* The areas of academic disorder or ability-achievement discrepancy usually stated in the definitions are reading, writing, spelling, and arithmetic. Listening, speaking, and thinking are also listed in the federal definitions. These areas were partitioned further in the *Procedures* (U.S.O.E., 1977) quoted previously. It is interesting to note that the words "may be" are used in these definitions. This suggests the possibility that an individual's process disorder need not be manifested in an academic deficit in order to satisfy the legal requirements for a specific learning disability.

4. *Psychological process disorder* Underlying the ability-achievement discrepancy is a disorder in basic psychological or learning processes such as memory, perception, closure, modality, and sequencing. Impairment in one or more of these processes may take the following forms: a) loss of the process, b) inhibition of the development of the process, or c) interference with the function of the process (Myers and Hammill, 1976). Children frequently exhibit problems with varying degrees of severity in several processes. The

60   *Berk*

processes related to understanding and using spoken and written language are usually stated in the definitions of learning disabilities. The authors of most of the definitions in Table 3.1 view these processing abilities as the precipitating or causative factors involved in the discrepancy. Interestingly, although process disorders appear in the 1968 and 1975 federal definitions, they are not mentioned as part of the identification criteria in the *Procedures for Evaluating Specific Learning Disabilities* (U.S.O.E., 1977).

Associated with the definitions are certain models of psychological processes. Two models that have received a considerable amount of attention in the field are Chalfant and Scheffelin's (1969) information-processing model and Kirk and Kirk's (1971) psycholinguistic model. Wallace and McLoughlin (1979) summarized the salient features of these models:

1. The learner must be able to receive, integrate, and do something with information which he [or she] takes in.
2. All modalities (vision, hearing, touch, etc.) must be considered important factors in learning, either on an individual basis or combined.
3. Psychological processes overlap, are ongoing, and are not unitary functions.
4. The effort is made to distinguish between processing information in a meaningful or nonmeaningful way, in a symbolic or nonsymbolic way, and in a verbal or nonverbal way.
5. These descriptions generally include an explanation of their effects on academic learning (pp. 30–31).

The last feature is particularly significant in that the linkage between the processes and academic disorders has been extremely difficult to establish. The processes are typically "test-identified" (Mann, 1971). In fact, the perceptually oriented tests, such as the Illinois Test of Psycholinguistic Abilities and Developmental Test of Visual Perception, that accompanied the learning disability movement tend to interpret the intent of the process component in the various definitions. The implication is that a process disorder is manifested in a language disorder. Unfortunately, the tests designed to measure auditory, visual, sensory integration, and haptic process disorders have less than desirable technical characteristics (Salvia and Ysseldyke, 1981).

Elements of Exclusion

Elements of exclusion delineate the characteristics of children that exclude them from being identified as learning disabled. These elements relate to problems of mental subnormality, visual or hearing

Category of Underachievement   61

impairment (sensory deficit), motor deficit, severe cultural neglect, and/or severe emotional disturbance. All of the behavioral definitions in Table 3.1, except those by Gallagher (1966) and Chalfant and Scheffelin (1969), can be considered "definitions by exclusion." They designate what a learning disabled child is not. The exclusion clause specifies, in essence, that if a child is not deaf, blind, emotionally disturbed, mentally retarded, or disadvantaged, yet exhibits learning problems, he or she must have a learning disability. These elements were reinforced in relation to an ability-achievement discrepancy in the 1977 criteria outlined in the *Federal Register* (U.S.O.E., 1977):

> (b)   The [multidisciplinary] team may not identify a child as having a specific learning disability if the severe discrepancy between ability and achievement is primarily the result of:
> (1) A visual, hearing, or motor handicap;
> (2) Mental retardation;
> (3) Emotional disturbance; or
> (4) Environmental, cultural or economic disadvantage (p. 65083).

It is often stated or implied in the definitions that these other handicapping conditions must be *primary* problems or causal agents. For example, suppose a mentally retarded child satisfied all but one of the inclusion criteria in the definition of a specific learning disability (i.e., normal intelligence). That child would be classified and placed according to the primary condition, and would be ineligible for learning disability programs and services because the learning disability might be considered as a secondary condition caused by retardation. Although this primacy qualification was not intended to preclude or otherwise discourage the teacher of the mentally retarded from treating the child for the learning disorder as well as the other problems, the net effect of the exclusionary statement has been to deny many mentally retarded children the benefits of learning disability-type programming. This dilemma is also generalizable to children with the other "primary" handicaps.

Certainly the authors of the definitions did not anticipate that the exclusion clause would automatically exclude special types of handicapped children with learning disabilities from receiving appropriate remedial services. Nonetheless, this inadvertent denial of services to children who are entitled to them has been one ramification of the clause. Perhaps some of the ensuing problems and controversy over the exclusion clause would not have arisen had the elements of inclusion in the definitions been clearly described (Hammill, 1974).

If each definition was stripped of its exclusion clause, what remains is essentially a statement that *a learning disability is an inability*

62   Berk

to learn. This suggests a strong sense of circularity within the definition, leaving the core of the problem undefined and unspecified. More will be said about this obvious ambiguity in the next section.

CRITICISMS OF FEDERAL DEFINITIONS

The foregoing analysis of the major elements of the definitions in Table 3.1 has exposed a few of the weaknesses, problems, disadvantages, and points of controversy which demand attention. This negative appraisal is consistent with the conclusions reached by many of the experts in the field (Bryan, 1974; Bryan and Bryan, 1978; Bryant 1972; Gearheart, 1981; Hallahan and Cruickshank, 1973; Lerner 1981; Mercer, 1979; Myers and Hammill, 1976; Wallace and McLoughlin, 1979). Although most of the comments addressed the general definitional issue of how to devise unambiguous and noncontradictory criteria that would be consensually accepted by the professionals, there have been specific attacks on the two key federal definitions—the 1968 PL 91-230 definition and the 1975 PL 94-142 definition. The 1975 version was just a slight rewording of the earlier definition with no substantive changes. Each sentence in these definitions has been scrutinized, and criticisms have been directed from different perspectives (Cruickshank, 1977; Hammill, 1974; Hammill et al., 1981; Kirk, 1974; Myers and Hammill, 1976; National Joint Committee for Learning Disabilities, 1981; Wiederholt, 1974).

Functions

Before examining these criticisms, however, it is essential to consider the purposes and functions of the definitions. Certainly if a definition is criticized for not being operational and it was never conceived with that intent in mind, such a criticism would be invalid. Initially, the federal definitions provide *theoretical* statements for understanding and delimiting the conditions called specific learning disabilities. They are not intended to be *operational* definitions, which guide the selection of children for particular research studies or the diagnosis and treatment of children in a school or clinical setting. In addition, these definitions were designed to serve primarily administrative and financial functions. They furnish a foundation for developing screening and identification procedures from which classifications can be made, incidence (or prevalence) rates estimated, and funds distributed. The decision on the amount of funding that each state agency will receive for educational programs for learning-disabled children and for professional training depends almost entirely on how the federal definition is interpreted (see Bersoff and Veltman, 1979, pp. 16–19).

Criticisms

Given these functions, the federal definitions are *ambiguous*. But this ambiguity is also attributable to the nature of the construct and the target population. The domain encompassing learning disabilities is broad in scope and complex in substance. Historically, it evolved from numerous and diverse categories of handicapping conditions. Consequently, the children falling within the limits of this domain represent different learning handicaps; they fail to learn for a variety of reasons. This builds in a heterogeneity of characteristics in the population. Furthermore, the widespread practice of categorizing almost any child with learning problems as learning disabled, irrespective of etiology or symptomatology, compounds the heterogeneity. Many programs serving these children have tended to become "dumping grounds."

Another persistent criticism related to these definitions is the difficulty of *obtaining professional consensus*. Although the 1968 definition was perhaps more acceptable to researchers and practitioners than most others, there is still considerable disagreement and dissatisfaction with the 1975 version. To a large extent, this trouble can be explicated in terms of the historical developments in the field, specifically the nature of the professional population. As discussed earlier, the roots of the learning-disability movement were planted in medicine, education, and psychology. Although much of the progress that has occurred represents to varying degrees the confluence of theoretical and philosophical approaches in these disciplines, the original diversity in the professional population has been retained and even increased via the specializations which have emanated from the movement itself, e.g., learning-disability specialists, reading specialists, diagnostic-prescriptive teachers, educational diagnosticians, and speech/language/audiology specialists. Consequently, the variability and quantity of professional viewpoints on "what is a specific learning disability" would be more conducive to disagreement than agreement.

Disagreements with the definitions have often focused on particular words, phrases, and clauses. In fact, much of the controversy that has erupted over some of the terminology stems from this inherent diversity of professional viewpoints. There are six specific criticisms:

1. *The term "children" is unnecessarily restrictive.* The use of the term *children* in the definitions implies that learning disabilities do not afflict adults and that the law applies only to children. This is misleading and incorrect. There has been a recent trend toward programming for adults with learning disabilities. Other developments in the field include the name changing of professional

64   Berk

associations (e.g., Association for Children and Adults with Learning Disabilities—previously, adults were omitted from the title) and the founding of new organizations for this segment of the population (e.g., LAUNCH, an acronym for Leadership, Action, Unity, Nurturing, Citizenship, and Harmony). These developments furnish sufficient evidence to warrant inclusion of adults in the definitions. Obviously they are part of the population of learning-disabled persons.

2. *"Basic psychological processes" cannot be identified or clearly defined.* It is doubtful whether authorities on learning disabilities can identify what these processes are and precisely how they should be defined. As noted previously, these processes have assumed meaning via the tests developed to measure them. These test-identified processes, especially in the perceptual/language area, have proven to be a baneful result of the learning-disability movement; not only do the tests provide the illusion of defining the basic processes, but their popularity belie their poor psychometric foundation.

The original intent of the phrase was lost and replaced with a few theories of psychological processes and accompanying tests. The phrase was supposed to focus on the intrinsic causes of learning disabilities as opposed to extrinsic or environmental causes, and to direct attention away from the medical-neurological orientation so predominant in the early years. Since the 1968 definition, however, the phrase has engendered confusion and debate instead of clarifying this important causal distinction.

3. *"In understanding or in using language, spoken or written" is redundant.* Understanding and using spoken language are synonymous with "listen" and "speak," and understanding and using written language are synonymous with "read," "write," and "spell."

4. *"Spell" is redundant.* Spelling is subsumed under written language. It also does not appear in the seven areas designated in the *Procedures for Evaluating Specific Learning Disabilities* (U.S.O.E., 1977). Sentence one of the definition needs to be rewritten in order to eliminate these redundancies.

5. *"Conditions" cannot be clearly defined.* Although the list of conditions, including perceptual handicaps, brain injury, minimal brain dysfunction, dyslexia, and developmental aphasia, were specified for the purpose of clarifying "disorders," it has just added confusion and misinterpretation. The professional polemics over the definitions of these conditions have not yet abated. Therefore, they only invite further controversy.

6. *"Does not include . . . which are primarily the result of"* makes *assumptions that are not supported in practice.* This clause assumes that diagnosticians can competently distinguish between primary and secondary handicapping conditions. It is often very difficult to discern whether an emotionally disturbed child developed an achievement deficit as a result of the emotional problem, or whether a learning-disabled child acquired emotional problems attributable to poor achievement performance. In fact, it is almost impossible to differentiate between handicaps such as learning disability, emotional disturbance, and mental retardation where the conditions exist in a mild to moderate degree. For nonachievers with borderline intelligence and disruptive classroom behavior, the differences between these discrete categories can be negligible (Hallahan and Kauffman, 1977). In other words, for the vast majority of learning-disability referrals, not only is it difficult to determine which condition is primary, but in many instances, the conditions themselves are not readily identifiable.

Another problem with this exclusion clause is "the widespread misconception that learning disabilities can occur neither in conjunction with other handicapping conditions nor in the presence of environmental, cultural, or economic disadvantage" (Hammill et al., 1981, p. 338). This interpretation is incorrect. The definition states only that learning disabilities are not *"primarily* the result of visual, hearing, or motor handicaps, of mental retardation, of emotional disturbance, or environmental, cultural, or economic disadvantage" (italics added). The primacy qualification implies that these other conditions or situations can be secondary or tertiary problems, as manifested in multiply handicapped learning-disabled children.

Response to the Criticisms

As these criticisms of the federal definitions have mounted since the 1970s, so have the suggestions for changes. However, the bulk of these suggestions have been isolated and expert-specific (e.g., Myers and Hammill, 1976). Not until February, 1980 was there any initiative to recommend changes on a systematic basis. The National Joint Committee for Learning Disabilities was formed with this charge in mind. It was composed of representatives from six professional organizations concerned with the definition of learning disabilities (see Table 3.1). The work of the Committee culminated in a critique of the PL 94-142 definition and a proposal of a new definition. This was presented in a position paper at the final meeting in January of 1981 (see Table 3.1).

66   Berk

The Committee was convinced that its definition was a substantial improvement over extant definitions, particularly the PL 94-142 definition. Although the definition does address most of the aforementioned criticisms, it also uses expressions that are either not clearly defined or difficult to verify in practice. These are:

1. *"Significant difficulties,"* which is analogous to "severe discrepancy" in the *Procedures for Evaluating Specific Learning Disabilities* (U.S.O.E., 1977)
2. *"Due to central nervous system dysfunction,"* which is imbued with the same problems of establishing causality as basic psychological processes
3. *"It is not the direct result of those conditions or influences,"* which is analogous to the exclusion clause and primacy qualification in the PL 94-142 definition

The definition has certain advantages over its predecessors because it omits some of the ambiguous, redundant, and misleading terminology; however, the three expressions noted above tend to offset these advantages. This is unfortunate because the improvements do seem to advance the field toward a "better definition." In all likelihood, the gains resulting from the Committee's efforts will eventually be masked by the criticisms and controversy which have plagued previous efforts. As a theoretical definition of learning disabilities, it can always be criticized as ambiguous. The contribution of this new definition beyond federal definitions and its acceptance by the profession, however, will only be demonstrated in time.

THEORETICAL VERSUS OPERATIONAL DEFINITIONS

In the foregoing discussion of federal definitions, a distinction was made between theoretical and operational definitions. This distinction is crucial inasmuch as professionals have typically expected more of definitions than they were ever intended to deliver. Often, theoretical definitions such as those in Table 3.1 have been criticized for not furnishing operational guidelines for research and practice. A *theoretical* or constitutive definition of learning disabilities defines the construct "learning disabilities" using other constructs indicated by the elements of inclusion and exclusion (see Margenau, 1950, p. 236). In order to be scientifically useful, the construct must possess constitutive meaning; that is, it must be capable of being used in theory. (For a further discussion of this issue, see Torgerson, 1958, pp. 4–5.)

By contrast, an *operational* or epistemic definition defines the construct at the level of observation by providing explicit instructions, guidelines, or criteria. From a research perspective, Kerlinger (1973) offered the following description:

> An *operational definition* assigns meaning to a construct or a variable by specifying the activities or "operations" necessary to measure it. Alternatively, an operational definition is a specification of the activities of the researcher in measuring a variable or in manipulating it. An operational definition is a sort of manual of instructions to the investigator. It says, in effect, "Do such-and-such in so-and-so a manner." In short, it defines or gives meaning to a variable by spelling out what the investigator must do to measure it (p. 31).

Typically, the theoretical definitions of learning disabilities have been *operationalized* with specific identification criteria, such as "2 or more years below grade level," rather than with a statement of operational definition per se. Thurlow and Ysseldyke (1979) commented that "[d]espite the fact that there has been no operational definition of learning disabilities, and the fact that criteria used in identifying children as learning disabled have been both highly variant and nebulous, educators *have* for some time been making decisions about children" (p. 16).

Considering the functions of these two types of definition, the theoretical definition must be developed first. Once the conceptualization of learning disabilities is understood and the admissible conditions delimited in that definition, then restrictive operational definitions for specific research and practical purposes can be generated. These definitions, however, should reflect the theoretical underpinnings of the construct. This usually has been manifested in terms of the elements of inclusion and exclusion (see Chalfant and King, 1976).

This notion of definition development suggests that one theoretical definition should be adopted, and there may be any number of attendant operational definitions designed to serve different purposes (Senf, 1977). Such diversity evidenced as learning disabilities has been operationalized in research studies and practical applications.

DEFINITIONS USED IN RESEARCH AND PRACTICE

Several surveys of the definitions and criteria used to identify learning-disabled children for research purposes and for special services eligibility have been reported. They revealed how the theoretical defini-

68   *Berk*

tions are interpreted (or misinterpreted) and what elements in those definitions are deemed most important and meaningful.

Research

In any study of learning-disabled children, the target population must be defined and the sample selected. In essence, the criteria for selecting the sample operationalize the definition of learning disabilities accepted by the researcher. They are more often derived from state definitions than from federal definitions—either the 1968 PL 91-230 definition or 1975 PL 94-142 definition (Kavale and Nye, 1981). As such, the selection or identification criteria can be categorized according to the four elements of inclusion (normal intelligence, ability-achievement discrepancy, academic disorder, and psychological process disorder) and also to the elements of exclusion described previously.

Three independent analyses of the criteria employed in research articles between 1968 and 1980 were published in 1981 (Harber, 1981; Kavale and Nye, 1981; Olson and Mealor, 1981). While the two major learning-disability journals were of primary interest in all three analyses, eight other educational and psychological journals, which publish studies using learning-disabled subjects, were also surveyed by Kavale and Nye (1981). The percentages of studies specifying each type of criteria expressed as elements of inclusion and exclusion are presented in Table 3.2. (*Note*: These percentages are based on only the number of studies reviewed that did specify identification criteria.)

There are obviously marked discrepancies in the findings of the three analyses. These may be attributable to one or more of the factors listed at the bottom of the table—number of studies, journals reviewed, and years reviewed. Although Harber's results should be embedded in the results of the other two analyses and Olson and Mealor's results should be reflected in Kavale and Nye's results, few consistencies emerge.

Several observations about these statistics can be made:

1. An ability-achievement discrepancy is the most prominent or a prominent element of inclusion in a majority of the studies reviewed. This is consonant with earlier results reported by Torgesen and Dice (1980). The consistency of this evidence throughout all of the analyses indicates the emphasis attached to a discrepancy score in identifying learning-disabled children.
2. A statement about normal or above normal intelligence as a criterion for being learning disabled seems to have received increased attention in recent years. In the studies published since 1978

Category of Underachievement 69

Table 3.2 Definitional criteria used in research studies of learning disabled subjects compiled in three independent surveys

Element	Harber (1981)	Olson and Mealor (1981)	Kavale and Nye (1981)
Normal intelligence	53%	42%	26%
Ability-achievement discrepancy	68%[a]	51%	69%[a]
Academic disorder	27%	87%[a]	24%
Psychological process disorder	5%	35%	57%
Exclusion clause	42%	72%	73%
Number of studies specifying criteria	62	71	304
Journals reviewed	J. Learn. Disabil. Learn. Disabil. Q.	J. Learn. Disabil. Learn. Disabil. Q. J. School Psychol. Psychol. Schools	J. Learn. Disabil. Learn. Disabil. Q. J. School Psychol. Psychol. Schools Except. Child. J Spec. Educ. J Educ. Psychol. Child Dev. J. Exp. Child Psychol. Educ. Res. Q.
Years reviewed	1978–80	1975–80 (except Learn. Disabil. Q.)	1968–80 (except Learn. Disabil. Q. and Educ. Res. Q.)

[a] Most prominent element of inclusion.

(which specified criteria), more than half reported an intelligence criterion. This is surprising in view of its omission as an element of inclusion in all of the definitions; it is either implied or a part of the exclusion clause.

3. The linkage of the ability-achievement discrepancy with a psychological process disorder has diminished with the recency of the studies reviewed. In Harber's analysis of studies between 1978 and 1980, 5%, or three studies, mentioned impairment in one or more of the basic learning processes; one study included the presence

70   Berk

of hard and soft neurological signs. The analyses of studies for 1975–1980 and 1968–1980 reported 35% and 57%, respectively. This trend may be indicative of the impact of the 1977 *Procedures*, which do not acknowledge "process disorders" as part of the identification criteria and of the difficulties encountered in measuring these processes reliably and validly (Salvia and Ysseldyke, 1981; Thurlow and Ysseldyke, 1979).

4. Areas of academic disorder were identified in a large percentage of the studies analyzed by Olson and Mealor, but the percentage was extremely low in both the Harber and the Kavale and Nye analyses. There is no readily apparent explanation for this inconsistency. Interestingly, the listing of the seven areas of possible "severe discrepancy" in the 1977 *Procedures* has had little influence on the researchers' specification of those areas.

5. An exclusion clause was designated in a significant number of the studies in the three analyses. It was the most prominent feature in the Kavale and Nye review. The categories of exclusion frequently included emotional disturbance, sensory handicaps, mental retardation, and cultural disadvantage. These correspond to the major categories in the federal definitions and in the 1977 *Procedures*.

These observations suggest that in much of the research conducted with learning-disabled subjects, the term "learning disabled" tends to be operationalized with an ability-achievement discrepancy score rarely linked to a process disorder. This is considered in conjunction with not being emotionally disturbed, deaf, blind, mentally retarded, or culturally disadvantaged. It was evident in all of the analyses that these criteria vary markedly from study to study. In addition, 40% of the original pool of studies reviewed between 1975 and 1980 did not specify any criteria for identification. Clearly this state of operational definitions in research on learning disabilities is an "impediment to the orderly accumulation of knowledge" (Senf, 1977, p. 8).

Practice

In order to gain some insight into how practitioners define learning disabilities and whether the federal definitions are being adopted, several surveys were undertaken during the 1970s. Some were relatively limited in scope, examining the practices in individual states such as Colorado (Vaughan and Hodges, 1973), while others sought to determine what definitions were being used by the 50 state departments of

Category of Underachievement   71

Table 3.3   Definitions of learning disabilities adopted by state departments of education based on two independent surveys

Definition adopted	Gillespie et al. (1975) (N = 50)	Mercer et al. (1976)[a] (N = 50)
1968 PL 91-230 definition	16%	26%
Modified 1968 PL 91-230	38%	36%
Other definition	38%	32%
No definition	8%	6%

[a] Includes follow-up data on eight states compiled by Mercer (1979); not included in originally published results.

education. Two surveys conducted by Gillespie et al. (1975) and Mercer et al. (1976) were particularly informative. Their results are summarized in Table 3.3. Among the 50 states, few accepted the 1968 federal definition.

In a more recent study by Thurlow and Ysseldyke (1979), 44 Child Service Demonstration Centers in 26 states were surveyed regarding their use of the 1968 definition, the 1975 PL 94-142 definition, the 1977 *Procedures*, some other definition, or no definition at all. These centers were established to develop and refine exemplary instructional programs capable of serving as models of what services ought to be. Of the 38 centers responding to the definition question, the following results were recorded: 1) 1968 definition—24%; 2) 1975 definition—5%; 3) 1977 *Procedures*—68%; and 4) other—8%. Obviously these centers found the PL 94-142 definition less desirable than the PL 93-230 definition. But the 1977 criteria for identification specifying an ability-achievement discrepancy in one or more of seven academic areas were adopted by more than two-thirds of the centers. This corroborates the major operational criterion employed by the researchers, as shown in Table 3.2.

Other definitional information compiled by Mercer et al. (1976) can be related to the findings in Table 3.2. Based on 42 states responding in the survey, the elements of inclusion and exclusion were analyzed. The percentages of state definitions addressing these elements were reported as follows: 1) normal intelligence—26%; 2) ability-achievement discrepancy—29%; 3) academic disorder—74%; 4) psychological process disorder—86%; and 5) exclusion clause—62%. These statistics denote a strong emphasis on process and/or language disorders. In fact, this element emerges as the core of the state definitions of learning disabilities. Furthermore, the areas of academic disorder (i.e., reading, writing, spelling, and arithmetic) and the var-

72   *Berk*

ious exclusionary categories were also prominent. These elements are directly associated with either the 1968 PL 91-230 definition or variations of that definition. These types of definitions were adopted by over half of the states.

The different emphases in Tables 3.2 and 3.3 seem to be a function of the theoretical-versus-operational definition issue. The figures in Table 3.2 reflect the researchers' attempts to operationalize "learning disabilities"; the figures in Table 3.3 are derived from constitutive definitions. The researchers focused on the ability-achievement discrepancy and the exclusionary categories, whereas the state departments of education attached the greatest weight to the process disorders, academic disorders, and the exclusionary categories.

In all instances, for identification or placement decisions there was a heavy reliance on test scores. A multidisciplinary team composed of a variety of professionals often made the final decision. Indeed, recent studies of this team decision-making process indicated that available psychometric information such as ability-achievement discrepancy scores has little influence on the actual decisions (Ysseldyke et al., 1980; Ysseldyke et al., 1982a). Eligibility decisions tended to be made in spite of data, either supportive or not supportive of the decision.

This analysis of state definitions of learning disabilities revealed the generic nature of the term (Lloyd et al., 1980). There is substantial evidence that the definitions remain nonoperational and highly variant. Gillespie et al.'s (1975) summary remarks captured the flavor of these practices:

> A child displaying specific behavioral characteristics could be eligible for learning disabilities programs in some states, but not in others. Moreover, in all but two states, the child must fit the description of learning disabilities used by the state if he or she is to receive special services provided by state monies (p. 62).
> [S]tate legislation suffers from a professional failure to define and make explicit the behavioral characteristics of the learning disabled child. As a result, no complete operational definition exists. Even when agreement does occur in legislation, definitions tend not to be behavioral in nature and are, therefore, of little use for making relevant educational decisions (p. 67).

CONCLUSION AND RECOMMENDATIONS

This critical review of definitions of learning disabilities and the efforts to circumscribe the specific characteristics of those disabilities suggest that definite progress has occurred in four areas: 1) sorting out the key issues and points of controversy; 2) isolating the characteristics of learning-disabled children from other handicapping conditions; 3) eliminating some of the ambiguous, redundant, and misleading terminology; and 4) establishing rules and regulations for identifying these children. Despite all of these developments, however, the most recent PL 94-142 federal definition and the 1981 National Joint Committee for Learning Disabilities definition emphasize the role of psychological processes and the central nervous system, respectively. These constructs are extremely difficult to define and to measure; usually, they are test-named and test-identified.

Confronted with an array of global concepts in these definitions, researchers and practitioners have tended to expeditiously devise their own operational criteria for identification. The ability-achievement discrepancy has emerged as the primary element in this process, which is reflective of the 1977 *Procedures*. Consequently, learning disabilities has become a category of *underachievement* (Algozzine and Sutherland, 1977; Ysseldyke and Algozzine, 1979), and the research evidence that is accumulating substantiates this position (Kirk and Elkins, 1975; Ysseldyke et al., 1982b).

This progression of theoretical and operational definitions is especially troublesome because there is no empirical foundation at any level; clinical intuition and expediency form the underlying rationale. For example, although there has been a considerable amount of attention devoted to ability-achievement discrepancies with more than a dozen different procedures recommended, there is virtually no evidence to indicate whether any particular procedure is better than any other in identifying children with learning disabilities (Berk, 1982). In fact, if a local educational agency (LEA) employs the "2 or more years below grade level" criterion, an ability-achievement discrepancy (or expectancy) formula, and clinical judgment as part of a multidisciplinary team assessment, it is not known whether any one or a combination of those procedures can correctly differentiate learning-disabled children from all other children.

Ceteris paribus, it is imperative that classroom teachers, learning disability specialists, educational administrators, and school psychologists perform a scrupulous reexamination of the methods being used to screen and diagnose children with learning disabilities and the definitions from which they are derived. The use of tests which are purported to measure psychological processes is indefensible in view of the state of assessment devices. Furthermore, the most popular ability and achievement tests require scrutiny from a technical perspective. If the essential research to ascertain the effectiveness of a given method is not conducted, not only will extant practices remain psychometrically indefensible, but the damaging consequences of mislabeling or misclassifying children will be inexcusable.

REFERENCES

Algozzine, B., and Sutherland, J. 1977. Nonpsychoeducational foundations of learning disabilities. J. Spec. Educ. 11:91–98.

Bateman, B. 1964. Learning disabilities—yesterday, today, and tomorrow. Except. Child. 31:167–177.

Bateman, B. 1965. An educator's view of a diagnostic approach to learning disorders. In: J. Hellmuth (ed.), Learning Disorders. Special Child Publications, Seattle. 1:219–236.

Berk, R.A. 1982. Effectiveness of discrepancy score methods for screening children with learning disabilities. Learn. Disabil.: An Interdiscipl. J. 1:11–24.

Bersoff, D.N., and Veltman, E.S. 1979. Public Law 94-142: Legal implications for the education of handicapped children. J. Res. Dev. Educ. 12:10–22.

Bryan, T.H. 1974. Learning disabilities: A new stereotype. J. of Learn. Disabil. 7:304–309.

Bryan, T.H., and Bryan, J.H. 1978. Understanding Learning Disabilities (2nd Ed.). Alfred Publishing Co., Sherman Oaks, CA.

Bryant, N.D. 1972. Subject variables: Definition, incidence, characteristics, and correlates. In: N.D. Bryant and C.E. Kass (eds.), Final Report: LTI in Learning Disabilities, pp. 5–158. (Vol. I. U.S.O.E. Grant No. OEG-0-71-4425-604, Project No. 127145.) University of Arizona Press, Tucson.

Chalfant, J.C., and King, F.S. 1976. An approach to operationalizing the definition of learning disabilities. J. Learn. Disabil. 9:228–243.

Chalfant, J.C., and Scheffelin, M.A. 1969. Central Processing Dysfunctions in Children: A Review of Research. NINDS Monograph, No. 9. United States Department of Health, Education, and Welfare, Bethesda, MD.

Clements, S.D. 1966. Minimal Brain Dysfunction in Children: Terminology and identification. NINBB Monograph, No. 3, Public Health Service Bulletin, No. 1415. United States Department of Health, Education, and Welfare, DC.

Cruickshank, W.M. 1967. The Brain-Injured Child in Home, School and Community. Syracuse University Press, Syracuse, NY.

Cruickshank, W.M. 1977. Myths and realities in learning disabilities. J. Learn. Disabil. 10:51–58.

Gallagher, J.J. 1966. Children with developmental imbalances: A psychoeducational definition. In: W. Cruickshank (ed.), The Teacher of Brain-Injured Children: A Discussion of the Bases of Competency, pp. 21–34. Syracuse, University Press, Syracuse, NY.

Gearheart, B.R. 1981. Learning Disabilities: Educational Strategies. C.V. Mosby Co., St. Louis.

Gillespie, P.H., Miller, T.L., and Fielder, V.D. 1975. Legislative definitions of learning disabilities: Roadblocks to effective service. J. Learn. Disabil. 8:660–666.

Hallahan, D.P., and Cruickshank, W.M. 1973. Psychoeducational Foundations of Learning Disabilities. Prentice-Hall, Inc. Englewood Cliffs, NJ.

Category of Underachievement   75

Hallahan, D.P., and Kauffman, J.M. 1977. Labels, categories, behaviors: ED, LD, and EMR reconsidered. J. Spec. Educ. 11:139–149.

Hammill, D.D. 1974. Learning disabilities: A problem in definition. Div. Child. Learn. Disabil. Newsl. 4:28–31.

Hammill, D.D., Leigh, J.E., McNutt, G., and Larsen, S.C. 1981. A new definition of learning disabilities. Learn. Disabil. Q. 4:336–342.

Harber, J.R. 1981. Learning disability research: How far have we progressed? Learn. Disabil. Q. 4:372–381.

Johnson, D.J., and Myklebust, H.R. 1967. Learning disabilities: Educational principles and practices. Grune and Stratton, New York.

Johnson, S.W., and Morasky, R.L. 1980. Learning Disabilities. 2nd Ed. Allyn and Bacon, Inc., Boston.

Kavale, K., and Nye, C. 1981. Identification criteria for learning disabilities: A survey of the research literature. Learn. Disabil. Q. 4:383–388.

Kerlinger, F.N. 1973. Foundations of Behavioral Research. 2nd Ed. Holt, Rinehart and Winston, Inc., New York.

Kirk, S. A. 1962. Educating Exceptional Children. Houghton Mifflin Co., Boston.

Kirk, S. A. 1963. Behavioral diagnosis and remediation of learning disabilities. In: Proceedings of the Conference on Exploration into the Problems of the Perceptually Handicapped Child. Fund for Perceptually Handicapped Children, Evanston, IL. 1–4.

Kirk, S.A. 1974. Introduction to the State of the Art: Where are We in Learning Disabilities? Association for Children with Learning Disabilities and California Association for Neurologically Handicapped Children Publications, Los Angeles.

Kirk, S.A., and Elkins, J. 1975. Characteristics of children enrolled in the child service demonstration centers. J. Learn. Disabil. 8:630–637.

Kirk, S.A., and Gallagher, J.J. 1979. Educating exceptional children. 3rd Ed. Houghton Mifflin Co., Boston.

Kirk, S.A., and Kirk, W.D. .1971. Psycholinguistic Learning Disabilities: Diagnosis and Remediation. University of Illinois Press, Chicago.

Lerner, J.W. 1981. Learning Disabilities: Theories, Diagnosis, and Teaching Strategies. 3rd Ed. Houghton Mifflin Co., Boston.

Lloyd, J., Hallahan, D.P., and Kauffman, J.M. 1980. Learning disabilities: A review of selected topics. In: L. Mann and D.A. Sabatino (eds.), The Fourth Review of Special Education, pp. 35–60. Grune and Stratton, New York.

Mann, L. 1971. Psychometric phrenology and the new faculty psychology: The case against ability assessment and training. J. Spec. Educ. 5:3–14.

Margenau, H. 1950. The Nature of Physical Reality. McGraw-Hill Book Co., New York.

Mercer, C.D. 1979. Children and Adolescents with Learning Disabilities. Charles E. Merrill Publishing Co., Columbus, OH.

Mercer, C.D., Forgnone, D., and Wolking, W.D. 1976. Definitions of learning disabilities used in the United States. J. Learn. Disabil. 9:47–57.

Myers, P., and Hammill, D. 1976. Methods for Learning Disorders. John Wiley and Sons, Inc., New York.

Myklebust, H.R. 1963. Psychoneurological learning disorders in children. In: S.A. Kirk and W. Becker (eds.), Conference on Children with Minimal Brain Impairment. University of Illinois, Urbana.

National Advisory Committee on Handicapped Children. 1968. Special

Education for Handicapped Children. First Annual Report. United States Department of Health, Education, and Welfare, Washington, D.C. January 31.

National Joint Committee for Learning Disabilities. 1981. Learning disabilities: Issues on definition. Unpublished position paper, January 30. (Available from Drake Duane, NJCLD Chairperson, c/o The Orton Dyslexia Society, 8415 Bellona Lane, Towson, MD 21204).

Olson, J.L., and Mealor, D.J. 1981. Learning disabilities identification: Do researchers have the answer? Learn. Disabil. Q. 4:389–392.

Public Law 94-142. 1975. Education for All Handicapped Children Act, S.6, 94th Congress [Sec 613(a) (4)] 1st session, June. Report No. 94-168.

Ross, A.O. 1976. Psychological Aspects of Learning Disabilities and Reading Disorders. McGraw-Hill Book Co., New York.

Salvia, J., and Ysseldyke, J.E. 1981. Assessment in Special and Remedial Education. 2nd Ed. Houghton Mifflin Co., Boston.

Senf, G.M. 1977. A perspective on the definition of LD. J. Learn. Disabil. 10:537–539.

Thurlow, M.L., and Ysseldyke, J.E. 1979. Current assessment and decision-making practices in model LD programs. Learn. Disabil. Q. 2:15–24.

Torgerson, W.S. 1958. Theory and Methods of Scaling. John Wiley and Sons, Inc., New York.

Torgesen, J.K., and Dice, C. 1980. Characteristics of research on learning disabilities. J. Learn. Disabil. 13:531–535.

United States Office of Education. 1977. Assistance to states for education for handicapped children: Procedures for evaluating specific learning disabilities. Federal Register, 42:62082–62085.

Vaughn, R.W., and Hodges, L. 1973. A statistical survey into a definition of learning disabilities: A search for acceptance. J. Learn. Disabil. 6:658–664.

Wallace, G., and McLoughlin, J.A. 1979. Learning Disabilities: Concepts and Characteristics. 2nd Ed. Charles E. Merrill Publishing Co., Columbus, OH.

Wender, P. 1971. Minimal Brain Dysfunction in Children. Wiley Interscience, New York.

Wiederholt, J.L. 1974. Historical perspectives on the education of the learning disabled. In: L. Mann and D.A. Sabatino (eds.), The Second Review of Special Education, pp. 103–152. Journal of Special Education Press, Philadelphia.

Ysseldyke, J.E., and Algozzine, B. 1979. Perspectives on assessment of learning disabled students. Learn. Disabil. Q. 2:3–13.

Ysseldyke, J.E., and Algozzine, B. 1982. Critical Issues in Special and Remedial Education. Houghton Mifflin Co., Boston.

Ysseldyke, J.E., Algozzine, B., Richey, L., and Graden, J. 1982a. Declaring students eligible for learning disability services: Why bother with the data? Learn. Disabil. Q. 5:37–44.

Ysseldyke, J.E., Algozzine, B., Shinn, M.R., and McGue, M. 1982b. Similarities and differences between low achievers and students classified learning disabled. J. Spec. Educ. 16:73–85.

Ysseldyke, J.E., Algozzine, B., and Thurlow, M.L. 1980. Placement Team Decision-Making: A Naturalistic Investigation, Research Report No. 41. University of Minnesota Institute for Research on Learning Disabilities, Minneapolis.

Chapter **4**

The Gifted Child
with a Learning Disability
Clinical Evidence
Stanley L. Rosner and Jeannette Seymour

The gifted child with a learning disability has been invisible in many school settings because teachers have been unable to conceptualize the existence of such an individual. The presence of these two syndromes simultaneously often leads to a behavioral presentation in which neither giftedness nor learning disability is apparent. Youngsters often develop secondary problems when either need is not met. The assessment and programming for such youngsters is an area that demands a good deal of careful and sensitive "clinical feel."

DEFINITIONS AND CLINICAL DIRECTION

Clinical identification must start with definitions. In education, diagnosticians are faced with a series of definitions, generating different levels of measurement for different purposes. Classical starting points can be important in order to understand how current practice in the field has evolved. One of the earliest pictures of gifted children was presented by Lewis Terman (1925). His complete survey of 1,500 gifted subjects began in 1921 and continued for a period of 40 years (Terman and Oden, 1951). His gifted students included a population which scored in the top 1% on the Stanford-Binet Intelligence Test with a score of 140 or above. The purpose of the Terman studies was to differentiate children with normal intelligence from gifted children. Terman discovered that the children identified by his study maintained a lead throughout life if they had the proper guidance. According to Terman, children with an intelligence test score of 140 or above surpass the average child in physical development, social adjustment, character traits, and educational achievement. Like Terman, Hollingworth (1926) also found gifted students to be physically larger than average

77

78   *Rosner and Seymour*

for their age but smaller for their grade because many were accelerated in their education.

Some writers have criticized the research of Terman. Khatena (1978) attributed the superior emotional and physical ratings of the Terman subjects to socioeconomic factors rather than to inherent differences between gifted and average students. He based this information on his own research. He found his gifted subjects came from above average homes with parents he described as intellectually superior. Torrance (1977) found fault with the Terman research for failing to search for intellectually gifted among the disadvantaged or culturally different groups.

Two other definitions that are often cited are those by Hollingworth and Witty. Hollingworth (1926) believed that the attainment of literacy and the ability to deal with abstraction was definitive and measurable. Witty (1951) did not limit the definition of giftedness to a single score on an intelligence test. He characterized gifted children as accelerated in reading and language with a remarkable acceleration in vocabulary. According to Witty, a gifted youngster could be one who performed remarkably in a worthwhile area even if the area was not specifically academic in nature.

With minor exceptions, the picture of giftedness presented in the literature leaves little room for conceptualizing a gifted youngster who is also learning disabled. This is because a part of most definitions involves superior achievement in important subject areas. Only in passing do they strike at the possibility that giftedness exists outside of that construct generally accepted as intelligence. By practices in the 1980's, it would have to be concluded that educators have concentrated almost exclusively on the quantitative aspects.

Zorbaugh noted, "Superior children are the accident of birth. Superior adults are the result of training" (Brumbough, 1956, p. 10). To elaborate upon the influence of nurturing on a child's intellectual development, Grotberg (1974) made the following statements about the parent-child relationship.

> It is important to note how frequently emotional factors are identified as critical to promoting gifts and talents in children. Not only do parents help their children more when they themselves have a good sense of who they are, a feeling of stability and emotional security, and a sense of control and worth, but they also need to be supportive and encouraging of their children. Patterns of parental indifference, rejection, and oversolicitude impair the children's development and may crush their talents; one expression of this turmoil is underachievement (p. 38).

This stress on psychosocial influences is extremely important in the view of the authors.

Clinical Evidence 79

These are as succinct statements of the nature-nurture debate as one can find; however, the issue goes beyond nature-nurture to legislative mandate. Rules, regulations, and bureaucratic standards seem to have more to do with the identification of the gifted than what educators have long believed to be relevant.

"Giftedness" can vary from state to state, and this variation is primarily numerical. For example, an amusing thing happened in Pennsylvania in the spring of 1981. The state legislature convened, looked at the financial position of the Commonwealth, and decided that giftedness as measured by intelligence tests began with a score of 140 rather than the previously accepted score of 130. In its infinite wisdom the legislature eliminated approximately 6,000 youngsters, thereby destroying their parents' dreams of glory and, in essence, making a decision which many legislators have very little training to make. The point is that the legislature dictates controls for the practice of the profession. Legislation can eliminate the findings of researchers and clinicians in order to meet a particular budget need or the demands of a particular constituency.

The clinician with a sense of insecurity regarding the appropriate guidelines for giftedness is in approximately the same condition as the clinician who is attempting to understand how to define learning disability. PL 94–142 defined children with learning disabilities as those with a processing disorder. Although this definition (see the Introduction of this book) addresses the special needs of the learning-disabled child who is not gifted, it omits a definition of the gifted youngster who is also learning disabled.

The term has had a variety of ancestors. It is not inaccurate to suggest that dyslexia or strephosymbolia, as once defined, incorporated many of the characteristics which currently exist under the label "learning disability." Orton (1928), for example, stated:

> Errors in direction in reading and writing come from failure of one hemisphere of the brain to establish clear-cut dominance over the other. Without well-established dominance, the child receives conflicting signals from printed matter . . . would receive "engrams" from both halves of the brain—one the mirror image of the other (p. 97).

While Orton's definition is reading-based, it certainly incorporates many of the same characteristics found in terms used in the 1980s to define learning-disabled youngsters. In the *Journal of Educational Research*, Krippner (1968) noted that one of the few characteristics that appears universally when defining learning-disabled youngsters is their inability to read. In 1968, the World Federation of Neurology suggested that developmental dyslexia was:

80   *Rosner and Seymour*

. . . a disorder manifested by difficulty in learning to read despite conventional instruction, adequate intelligence, and sociocultural opportunity. It is dependent upon fundamental cognitive disabilities which are frequently of constitutional origin.

Perhaps the most broadly drawn definition of learning disability is that of Clements (1966), who suggested that:

Minimal brain dysfunction syndrome refers to children of near average, average, or above average general intelligence with certain learning or behavioral disabilities ranging from mild to severe, which are associated with deviations of function of the central nervous system. These deviations may manifest themselves by various combinations of impairment in perception, conceptualization, language, memory and control of attention, impulse or motor function (pp. 9–10).

Recently, a task force, called together by The Johns Hopkins University and the Maryland State Department of Education and composed of college educators and practitioners, took 2 days to arrive at the following definition of the learning-disabled child:

Learning disability is a generic term that refers to a heterogeneous group of learning disorders caused by varying forms of central nervous system (CNS) dysfunction.

Central nervous system dysfunction can be the result of such factors as anatomical difference, genetic factors, neuromaturational delay, biochemical imbalance, metabolic imbalance, severe nutritional deficiency, or trauma. Many children with manifest CNS dysfunction do not necessarily have learning disabilities (e.g. cerebral-palsied persons). At the present time, evidence of CNS dysfunction is not necessarily elicited during medical examination and/or specific research procedures. However, such evidence can be elicited through psychological, educational and/or language assessment.

These learning disorders are manifested by significant difficulties in the acquisition and use of such language skills as listening, speaking, reading, and writing as well as mathematics. These disabilities are intrinsic to the individual. Even though they may occur concomitantly with other handicapping conditions (e.g. sensory impairment, mental retardation, social and emotional disturbance) or environmental influences, (e.g. cultural differences, insufficient/inappropriate instruction, psychogenic factors), they are not the direct result of these conditions and influences.

While it is recognized that there may be learning-disabled children of less than average intelligence, a marked discrepancy in achievement areas should be documented by the evaluation teams before labeling such a youngster learning disabled.

It must also be recognized that a youngster who is near or at grade level with significantly above average ability may also have a learning disability.

The predisposing characteristics of learning disability are represented by various combinations of one or more of the following:
1. Disorders in information processing
   a. Taking in information

b. Putting information together, seeing the relationships
c. Memory of information
d. Expressing information
2. Disorders in the functions of attention, concentration and impulse control
3. Disorders in the functions of perception
a. Sensory
b. Sensorimotor
c. Social

This last definition appears to incorporate a wide variety of the characteristics upon which most practitioners in the field agree, particularly those who adopt a delimited concept of the etiology of learning disability.

It is obvious from the variety of definitions and guidelines cited that universal agreement is far from a reality. As a result, public and private practitioners alike have arrived at their own working definitions. These operational or working definitions are frequently unspoken, but are generally based on the concept that it is impossible to have rigid guidelines in defining the needs and skills of either gifted or learning-disabled youngsters. It would seem that an individual case approach is the only reasonable way to proceed because it requires that clinicians and teachers view each individual independently and not as a set of quantitative characteristics measured against a definition. It is probably at this point that six bureaucrats from state departments of education have just fainted. This type of individual attention and definition goes against the very grain of organized, neat, systematic, legislatively-bound guidelines. Certainly real danger exists in adopting this type of approach to assessment because it requires the practitioner to be competent, perceptive, and to possess an ability to derive meaning from the qualitative as well as the quantitative data generated by the tests. Many bureaucrats may assume that sufficient quantitative guidelines will reduce the need for competence on the part of the clinician. Clinicians, however, argue that individual case studies and not legislative guidelines are needed for educational judgment.

The case study approach is certainly not without its proponents even in the literature. Harris and Avery (1978), for example, used a case study approach to point out one of the practical difficulties in identifying the learning-disabled/gifted child. The definition of learning disability that they ultimately used is a youngster not functioning up to his or her intellectual potential. Harris and Avery noted a common problem in identification; that is, that youngsters with learning disabilities and excellent intellectual endowment are capable of performing at a level which does not cause real concern in most school

82   *Rosner and Seymour*

settings in light of the fact that they are "at grade level." Regardless of how much college professors talk about the importance of reaching potential, achievement at grade level continues to be a "real world" standard. In short, the youngster must stand out in some obvious fashion for somebody to notice that although his or her achievement is quite adequate by general school standards, it is not in keeping with a personal standard of potential. Clinicians, therefore, rely on the ability of teachers, school administrators, or parents to perceive the discrepancy. In the absence of such sensitivity, clinicians never have the chance to make the diagnosis of giftedness or learning disability. Many of these youngsters simply pass through the school system; it is often then assumed that they are doing quite well without the recognition that one of the least renewable resources is being wasted—intellectual ability.

REFERRAL

The dual diagnosis of gifted and learning-disabled tends to be grossly underreferred for evaluation. In spite of the point made repeatedly in the literature about learning acquisition not being solely tied just to intellectual adequacy, teachers seem to have considerable difficulty seeing a youngster as gifted without superior academic performance in addition to the high intelligence test scores. Although most informed educators would probably agree that there is nothing contradictory about a youngster who is in both a mathematics program for the gifted and a remedial reading program, experience in a fairly typical suburban school district showed that this combination of programs is seldom found. The apparent lack of youngsters being provided with appropriate programming for both their giftedness and their learning disability is based on the inability of many teachers to see these two conditions as existing simultaneously. As a result, the private practitioner is more likely than the school psychologist to see these youngsters for evaluation.

Parent-initiated referrals often have one of three complaints. The first complaint is often: "My child seems bright enough"; "Everybody says that my child is bright, but he or she doesn't seem to be doing as well as he or she should be doing in school"; or "When I talk to the teacher, the teacher says my child is doing as well as most of the other kids in class. I have a feeling he or she is really not doing as well as he or she can." The second complaint suggests a degree of anger at the school for not using the appropriate methods to teach the youngster. This complaint by parents is frequently worded to imply the fol-

Clinical Evidence 83

lowing: the reason for the lack of progress is that the child is smarter than the teacher; the teacher is unwilling to accept this and to provide appropriate methods to enable these children to actualize their ability. The third complaint of parent referrals can be phrased aggressively or in more defensive terms. It suggests that there is a gap between the parents' perception of the youngster's learning ability and the school's perception of the child's learning ability. It generally follows that the school is unwilling to see the youngster as having exceptional endowment in the absence of very superior achievement. Having read about programs for the gifted and becoming quite frustrated by their youngsters' lack of success in the school situation, parents frequently ask for an assessment of their youngsters' giftedness when in reality their secret concerns lie elsewhere. Thus, the bias seems to lie with under-referral by the classroom teacher and overreferral by the parents, who seek an explanation for the discrepancy that they see or a placement that will vicariously elevate the status of their youngster's ability.

THE FOCUS OF CLINICAL EVALUATION

Whether the clinician is a school psychologist or a learning disability specialist, if his or her conclusion is that current and historical definitions are not totally adequate, then he or she is left with the basic tools with which the clinician has always had to work: first, a structure for observation (for the most part, tests); second, a fund of experience gained in looking at real cases; and, third, that very unscientific but genuine commodity—qualitative evaluation and intuition. Observations that have been collected from 20 years of clinical experience emerge from this base. Only a small number of these observations has involved the evaluation of gifted youngsters with learning disabilities.

This type of evaluation necessitates the assessment of a youngster's intellectual functioning. It is generally agreed that a satisfactory measure of actual intelligence does not exist. In the hands of a skilled clinician, the Wechsler Intelligence Scale for Children-Revised (WISC-R) is a reasonable measure of where a youngster is currently able to function. It is the most frequently used structure for observing intelligent behavior. On the WISC-R there do not seem to be patterns that cut across the dual categories of gifted and learning disability. Rather, the insights to be gained are those which develop from listening with a sensitive ear to individual responses and assessing the quality and structure of a youngster's answer rather than simply whether it fits the category of a 2-, 1-, or 0-point response.

84   *Rosner and Seymour*

In considering individual responses, it seems that the response of a gifted youngster with a learning disability frequently indicates the use of psychological defenses to compensate for what has been termed the "narcissistic wound" of experiencing a learning disability. When asked a relatively simple low-level question, it is characteristic of this type of youngster to respond with the kind of intellectualization that in essence says to the clinician, "I refuse to accept the judgment that I am stupid even if I cannot master the basic processes of reading and writing to the degree that my teachers expect or to the degree that I expect of myself." For example, if asked, "Who discovered America?", the child might answer, "Most people think it was Christopher Columbus but there are some people who say that it was really Leif Erickson and Christopher Columbus shouldn't have gotten the credit. There are other people who have written, and a television program that I saw said that the first people to really get to America were people from Ireland in boats made out of leather." By such responses, these youngsters assure the examiner and themselves that they are capable and do have intelligence in spite of the embarrassment of not being able to demonstrate that intelligence by the mastery of a school subject.

Another characteristic type of response, particularly among adolescents, is one in which youngsters assert their ability to think outside of commonly accepted norms. They justify this with what they perceive as acceptable data or information. In answer to the question on the unrevised WISC: "Why should women and children be saved first in a shipwreck?" one such youngster might reply, "I don't believe that. That's a sexist position. Men and women should be treated equally. Some people might argue that children have longer to live, but I believe that they ought to really evaluate the contribution that each of the people can make to society before they decide who gets saved."

Another type of response to the discrepancy between excellent intellectual potential and flawed learning ability is for youngsters to take occasional refuge in only giving responses that they are certain will be perfect and to be unwilling to attempt to answer questions about which they are uncertain. Experience teaches that if a reasonable relationship is established with such youngsters, they might move if pushed from an initial response to an easy "don't know" to a quite acceptable response even when it is not totally adequate from their own point of view.

At times, there is the dramatic impact of a gifted youngster who has a learning disability and comes from a family in which there are other gifted individuals, most notably the parents. Parents of excellent intellectual endowment frequently have not only an expectation that

Clinical Evidence 85

their children will perform at a certain level, but also a kind of automatic assumption that the youngster will be as driven as the parent in the search for achievement. A dramatic example of this is a youngster named Vicki. Vicki was extremely bright, and while her learning disability was quite mild, it was a source of great concern to her mother and father. When the examiner was reviewing the intelligence test results to assure Vicki's parents that she was bright, he advertently set the Coding section of the WISC-R on the desk close to her father. The examiner reached for the Coding test to show the parents that Vicki had done somewhat less well on this perceptual-motor measure and noted that while he turned toward Mrs. H, Mr. H. had completed the Coding items that his daughter had left unfinished.

An even more characteristic descriptor of learning-disabled/gifted youngsters is perplexity. These youngsters seemed perplexed by their inability to perform certain tasks. They have a keener than average perception of falling short in tasks which they feel they should have the capacity to complete in an appropriate manner. The Block Design Subtest sometimes illustrates the most graphic and direct sample of problem-solving behavior on the intelligence test. Children with poor perceptual-motor skills frequently attempt to talk themselves through the solution on this test, as if their excellent verbal facility can provide the understanding and structure that is lacking in their sensory integration.

It is particularly important for very bright learning-disabled youngsters to utilize a battery of measures sufficiently broad in scope so that the total human being can be truly examined. Of critical importance is a thorough open-ended case history interview as well as a thorough feedback interview at which both parents and the youngster are present. Another necessity is to use measures in each area that will represent the truest sample of behavior. The result of such a test as an informal reading inventory is particularly meaningful. An informal reading inventory aids the clinician in identifying the learning-disabled/gifted child by measuring a broad sampling of reading ability against intellectual capacity. Very bright youngsters, however, have the ability to "fake out" even such clinical measures as an informal reading inventory. They seem able to perceive that the answer to questions at the lowest grade levels are frequently contained in the questions themselves. As a result, they are able to answer relatively basic questions at pre-primer, primer and up through grade levels 2 and 3 without having very good mastery of the mechanics of the reading process. Prior to grade levels 4 and 5, they also seem quite capable of using context heavily in filling in word perception skills. Probably they have not mastered the basics of word recognition, but they rely quite heavily on their ability to understand the patterns of language. Unfortunately, even for the brightest youngster this can break down as the curriculum moves into more complex subject-oriented content material.

Isaacs (1974) noted that:

> Literature on the gifted may be misleading because it may tend to stress achievement and fail to mention the gifted child's problems. Not uncommonly is he in need of remediation in reading. Many gifted children have been known to read several levels below their potential, a fact which would make average children candidates for remediation. When it is realized that the gifted should be able to read several levels above grade placement, their problems when regarded in proper perspective, loom even larger than do the problems of average children (p. 113).

Other typical clinical measures used in assessing learning disabilities have not led to patterned or characteristic styles of functioning for the learning-disabled/gifted youngster compared with other youngsters. The typical patterns of interference with attention and concentration, inconsistency in the ability to make associations, and gaps in those skills which are prerequisite to mastering formal learning may exist in much the same fashion in the learning-disabled/gifted youngster as in an average learning-disabled youngster.

An area frequently overlooked by the learning-disability field is the psychological adjustment and reaction of the child to his dual status—being at the upper limits of one critical intellectual area and at the lower limits of another. Krippner (1968) observed that a tendency exists among talented youngsters with learning disabilities to show greater adjustment difficulty. He categorized this difficulty in the areas of social immaturities, psychopathic tendencies, neurotic tendencies, psychotic tendencies, and unfavorable educational experiences.

It has been suggested that careful diagnosis will reveal that gifted youngsters suffer some of the same emotional-psychological problems as nongifted groups. In addition, they have unique problems induced by their giftedness and attendant problems which may be characterized as psychosocial (Isaacs, 1974).

Although interesting, this generalization does not provide a prescription for ways to meet the needs of such youngsters. A key variable in their difficulty is the tendency to use defenses to escape their sense of inadequacy when they fail to meet the demands placed on them by important others and themselves. As noted already, a typical defense is that of intellectualization, where these youngsters become super bright and extremely knowledgeable about particular subject areas

Clinical Evidence 87

such as dinosaurs, or the operation of the telephone, or the use of computers. Or, they may become a kind of trivia expert in a wide variety of areas in order to prove to themselves that they are capable of digesting material. In many ways, intellectualization is quite adaptive to the demands of the school situation. Youngsters who can talk credibly will frequently be seen as having some redeeming academic value even if their reading, writing, and mathematics skills are not up to par.

Several writers, such as Harris and Avery (1978) and Krippner (1968), stressed the neurological components of the learning disabilities experienced by gifted youngsters. Although this data seems clear and acceptable, it is important to note that what operates in an educational world is not the neurological impairment, but the products of that neurological impairment two steps removed. The neurological impairment expresses itself in developmental lags or developmental unevenness. The developmental difficulty can be expressed in a behavioral disorder, a learning disorder, or both. The functioning of that rather abstract process called "ego" determines the youngster's adjustment to the learning disability—not the direct impact of neurological factors alone. Many clinicians have been impressed with the fact that children with virtually identical developmental pictures can arrive at very different places in terms of academic achievement. It is a function of the interaction of the psychological and environmental factors which shapes the total structure called ego.

The narrowing of interest is another defense frequently used by gifted youngsters. This reflects both the areas where difficulty exists as well as the areas where giftedness produces excellent functioning. Youngsters may have difficulty mastering the reading process, and yet will zealously devote themselves to mathematics, where they operate on a different conceptual level. Here, they may feel free of the torment of mastering the illusive squiggles of printed language. Such youngsters frequently carry this specialization to the point of excluding all careers that might demand many reading skills. Instead, they look favorably on all careers involving primarily mathematics. By the time these youngsters reach adolescence, they are often molded into a behavior that involves a variety of defenses with a unifying theme—a strong oppositional quality that could be called negation.

Negation is a theme which characterizes adolescence in general. Bright but disillusioned with their inability to meet the demands of the system, these youngsters have perfected the use of negation as a defense against the rejection they perceive by the system. In turn, they reject the standard rules, invest a good deal of energy in being extremely perceptive of the shortcomings of their teachers and administrators, and often accurately perceive the weak links of the school. They demonstrate a keenly perceptive ability to play upon the areas of deficiency in the teachers. For example, if the youngsters are unable to meet the particular textual demands, they may attack areas where they know that the teacher feels uncertain about the conceptual demands. They become the rather unpleasant gadflies in an academic setting, where war already wages between the middle-aged and the adolescent.

> Very often a child who is disabled in one way or another may dwell on the harm done to him by heredity, physicians, his parents, schools, or by society in general. Sometimes these feelings are justified; sometimes they are imaginary. One thing, however, is certain. If a child lives in an environment in which he is opposed, thwarted or rejected, as happens often with the exceptional, he will often begin at an early age to develop the kind of behavior which we find in a person who perceives himself as one who is being abused. He will feel hostile and probably project his hostility onto others (Frampton, 1955, p. 120).

CLINICAL EXAMPLES

Direct clinical evidence provides the clearest route to understanding gifted individuals who are also learning disabled. The following case material illustrates the significant aspects of assessment of these youngsters.

As noted, the route of referral for gifted individuals with a learning disability is frequently circuitous. Occasionally, it takes a lengthy period of time before a referral is initiated. Labuda and James (1974) suggested that one reason for the delay is that these children are able to draw attention away from the area of deficit by compensating or covering over the problem.

Case Study 1

A man sought evaluation at the age of 36. This individual was a successful director of research for a large manufacturing corporation. He held a bachelor's degree from one of the campuses of the State University system in California and a master's degree from Ohio State University. He had completed most of the course work toward a doctorate when he decided not to continue pursuing this goal, but simply to get a job and put his education to work.

Mr. Norman reported that he had grown up in a comfortable, middle-class home and that his parents demanded high achievement. Although he felt that he always got reasonably good grades, he had

Clinical Evidence   89

had some difficulty developing reading skills. It was his impression that he had not really read until he was in about grade 3. His father's solution to this problem was to demand that he sit with him and read a chapter from a book each day. Mr. Norman suggested that this was quite unpleasant, and the only reason he did it was that his father was a very forceful individual. From his point of view, his school success was based on a much greater amount of work and effort than that put forth by the average youngster. Mr. Norman's current concerns were that it took him longer than most people to read material (a not uncommon complaint among nonlearning-disabled adults); that he had a tendency to transpose letters and words; that he frequently read the wrong word in a sentence or paragraph or even on a poster for a movie; and that at times he would group words together in an ungrammatical fashion. He noted further that he had difficulty with brief messages and newspaper headlines, and often he had to reread to fully comprehend what was written.

He reported being happily married for approximately 5 years. He felt quite realistically that he was doing very well in his current job, but in the first job he had out of college, he "totally froze," was unable to produce, and was ultimately dismissed. Mr. Norman has been in psychoanalysis for 6 years.

Of course it becomes possible to dismiss all of the difficulties that Mr. Norman noted as neurotic symptoms. This seems too facile an explanation. His test data reflects the struggle of a gifted individual living with a learning disability over an extended period of time. His inability to understand why he had the difficulty may indeed have driven him to neurotic anxiety rather than the converse situation of a neurosis underlying the symptoms.

A striking aspect of Mr. Norman's performance was his desire to demonstrate that he had excellent intelligence. He generally went well beyond the limits of what was required on verbal items from the Wechsler Adult Intelligence Scale (WAIS), achieving a Verbal score well within the superior range. His subtest scores consistently ranged from superior to very superior levels, with particular strength exhibited on measures of his word knowledge, social judgment, and background of information. Word knowledge represented a particular area of pride to him, and he commented that he had worked very hard to develop an excellent vocabulary. In spite of this, he continually asked if his responses were correct. He dramatically expressed this concern about his intellectual adequacy with respect to one particular item that he missed on the Similarities Subtest. Following the testing, Mr. Norman wrote a letter to the psychologist with instructions about billing his insurance plan. He began the letter with a brief paragraph in which he wrote out an answer to the Similarities Subtest item that he had missed on the test. (He had realized that he had missed the item and so had researched the answer in the interim.)

Mr. Norman's functioning on the less verbal tasks was in striking contrast to his Verbal score, both in terms of involvement and in terms of adequacy of performance. He never really seemed to operate on a perceptual-motor level. For example, even on the Block Design Subscale, there was a considerable amount of "talking himself through" the solution rather than operating on the level of perceptual cues. He also exhibited impatience with these tasks.

Mr. Norman's figure drawings and Bender Gestalt were primitive, poorly conceptualized and attached with an uncharacteristic impulsiveness. He seemed to want to get this part of the testing "over with." The educational derivative of this perceptual-motor difficulty was Mr. Norman's clear-cut problem with handwriting. It was an unplanned combination of printing and script, sometimes within the same word.

Although he scored in the 99th percentile in defining words on a standardized test, he scored only at the second percentile in reading rate. It was apparent reading aloud was a struggle. When given an informal Word Recognition inventory, in which he had to read words presented rather rapidly, he became quite uncomfortable and suggested that "it takes a minute for the word to get into my brain." He did reasonably well understanding several short paragraphs. He explained the compensations he had devised to handle reading tasks— that reading is so burdensome to him he tends to check around in the paragraph for some words or concepts which are familiar and then to rely upon his background knowledge to fill in the rest of the detail.

Mr. Norman then, seems to represent what clinicians seldom see: the "living laboratory", so to speak—a person whose learning difficulties were not identified and dealt with in childhood. His early functioning can only be inferred, but the substantial amount of evidence increases the probability of accurate inference. As a youngster, demands were made on him to fulfill his intellectual potential; he did this to the best of his ability. Although he developed a number of defenses and coping mechanisms that allowed him to perform at a reasonably adequate level, he did not realize his overall potential. He achieved a reasonably degree of success in a variety of areas, but persistently doubted that things were as they should be, particularly in reading. He had devoted time and energy to wondering and worrying about why he functioned in this manner.

Case Study 2

A youngster of superior intellectual ability, at the time of examination, was 7½ years old and in a grade 2 classroom. The examination of this youngster led to the clinical observation that he was fidgety, unable to sit still, and would frequently lie down on the table in front of the examiner rather than sit in a normal posture. He was, in short, quite "hyperactive." The complete examination suggested first, that his hyperactivity was rooted as much in his psychological adjustment to the world as in a neurological base. Furthermore, it indicated that his academic performance was indeed well above what could be expected based on his intelligence. His academic skills ranged from grades 5–7. Although the measure used was a rather superficial test of achievement, he had clearly mastered the basic processes of reading, spelling and mathematics. There seem to be two common problems clearly demonstrated by this youngster. First, there is a tendency to view hyperactivity as always neurologically based rather than as an interaction of neurological and psychological factors and in some cases, primarily a psychological problem; second, there is a need to see certain youngsters as learning disabled, even when their academic achievement lives up to their intellectual ability.

Case Study 3

An example of a gifted youngster with a rather clear-cut specific learning disability is suggested from data provided by a youngster named Wendy. Wendy's mother, Mrs. W., came for evaluation, not because she was concerned about any difficulty that the youngster had, but because she felt that the school was making too much of Wendy's failure to respond adequately to the reading program. Mrs. W. believed that the phonics approach used in the reading program was too heavy, and that Wendy was apparently oriented toward learning words in a visual manner.

The history suggested real difficulty when Mrs. W. was pregnant with Wendy. Medication and bedrest were required in order to maintain the pregnancy. Mrs. W. noted that delivery was easy and Wendy developed normally. She seemed particularly proud of the fact that Wendy was "a fast talker" and could put words together by the time she was 7 months. On the other hand, she noted that the youngster was slower in motor development (although this was dismissed as a product of her being overweight) and also that her placid personality as a baby continued into childhood. At times, the parent received

92   *Rosner and Seymour*

positive reinforcement in some areas of the youngster's behavior which led the parent to overlook or to rationalize away other areas of apparent deficit.

Wendy has two other sisters, both of whom are considered gifted. Her father is a cardiologist. Currently a housewife, her mother graduated from college and is very active as a volunteer in the school.

There are several critical points about Wendy which make her an interesting example of a younger learning-disabled/gifted child. First, she functioned quite well in most of the areas of the intelligence test, with the exception of the measures of attention and concentration. Second, she was not identified as either gifted or learning disabled through the middle of grade 2. It was only at her parents' insistence that she was examined at all. The school suggested that she had an auditory perception problem. This was indeed confirmed in the evaluation. Also confirmed was her tendency to function less well on measures of auditory attention and concentration. In spite of this, she was kept in a program heavily oriented toward phonics; the school showed little flexibility for providing an alternative to the current reading program. Wendy reacted to this type of management by becoming increasingly dependent upon the teacher to provide words she did not recognize. This was clearly observable in the testing situation. On an informal reading inventory, she requested help from the examiner rather than attempt difficult words herself. There seemed, indeed, to be a withdrawal from this unpleasant and poorly planned program.

Elkind (1973) noted that:

> The educational program for a gifted child with learning disabilities must be so constructed that we capitalize on his strong modalities of learning while at the same time strengthening those modalities that are weak and need shoring up. . . . At the same time these adaptations and adjustments are being made, the child should be receiving supportive reinforcement and training to ameliorate his deficiencies. . . . Classroom management techniques can also be developed to accommodate the gifted child with learning disabilities. With appropriate modification and adaptations of programs and classroom management techniques, the gifted child with learning disabilities can function and flourish in a setting whether it be in the regular classroom, in enrichment groups, in special classes for the gifted children, or in special schools for the gifted children. The gifted child with learning disabilities can fulfill the potential that is within him and achieve the open-endedness of human ability (p. 97).

The data provided by Elkind and youngsters such as Wendy stress the fact that programming for such youngsters is not very different from programming appropriate strategies or approaches for any youngster. For example, evidence of consistent, clear-cut difficulty in

Clinical Evidence 93

auditory discrimination would indicate two needs: 1) to facilitate the development of auditory discrimination; and 2) to provide a reading program which does not rely heavily on areas of obvious weakness for the child. Mrs. W's observation that Wendy was in an inappropriate reading program clearly seems to be the most accurate one. By insisting that Wendy operate within the school's program, the school was serving the curriculum and not the child. The most striking data regarding this youngster was an Associative Learning Test administered to her. This test assesses the aspects of sensory input which would enhance a child's ability to master symbols. On this measure, Wendy evidenced an ability to make associations except with word-like symbols; she seemed to reflect clearly an emotional resistance to word-like forms. In a sense, Wendy represents the kind of youngster who has a "learned disability" rather than a learning disability. In the absence of more appropriate programming, it is likely that the discrepancy between her potential and her ability to read will continue to increase resulting in increased difficulty in other areas.

Dr. and Mrs. W's attitude toward their daughter's problem is not uncommon. On the other hand, parents feel concern about the school not doing right by the child; at the same time, they may feel that the problem is best left alone, and the youngster will "outgrow it" because other areas of functioning seem to be quite adequate. For youngsters like Wendy, the presence of excellent resources in a variety of areas seems to mask the learning problem from the parents. These children may become so resistant to and negative about the school experience that the problem can no longer be ignored.

Sometimes, the gifted learner who has a learning disability becomes most noticeable in adolescence. This is the time that the youngster traditionally moves from a classroom situation with one teacher to having to develop relationships with teachers of a variety of subject areas in several classes. The opportunity for establishing close relationships with the individual teacher decreases. Fewer exceptions are made for the hardworking, well-motivated youngster who seems bright but performs poorly. The loosening of the teacher-pupil relationships are coupled with the ordinary stresses of adolescence, frequently leading to youngsters becoming quite negative and using their energy to circumvent or act out against the system. Case Study 4 is a classic example of this kind of behavior.

Case Study 4

George's intelligence test score was well within the very superior range, and there was very little unevenness manifested in his functioning.

School records suggested George had produced low average work, and he presented a picture of chronic underachievement. Several teachers observed that he was a "bright youngster who simply was not using his full potential"; however, his ability to use language well and to form good relationships with his teachers at the elementary level was quite helpful in getting passing grades. As expectations for greater independence increased at the intermediate level, he began to experience more difficulty; yet, he continued to pass. Every year, handwringing comments were made about his not quite realizing his potential for reasons no one knew. In an almost classic manner characteristic of adolescents, George began to act out against the system by not using his brightness to keep out of trouble. Rather, he seemed to wave his negative, acting out behavior in front of those individuals most likely to reprimand him for such behavior. For example, George's experimentation with marijuana generally took place on school grounds or in the boys' lavatory. Also, he would cut classes or school and then would generally make himself quite visible in the community. George also involved himself in what might be considered as provocative behavior, which his teachers evidenced in part by his ostentatious neglect of all demands and assignments. His teachers noted the flair with which George was able to let them know about his unwillingness to meet their demands. The message that came across was seldom one of inability. Because inability is associated with weakness, admission of inability only added further insult to the youngster's already shaky self-concept.

The testing data on George is unremarkable in many ways. His learning status was one of a mild, chronic inability to learn. However, he had remarkable perceptiveness and an ability to identify the correct combinations of stimuli that could get any teacher angry and marching to the principal's office to complain about "unmanageable George." After meeting with the assistant principal, George could tell a highly accurate story about acting perfectly calm; he could point out all the flaws in the procedure used to punish him. He might suggest that by enforcing such rules, the assistant principal was merely being a lackey for the principal. Furthermore, he would point out that the use of such punishment in the past had had virtually no impact on him and in all likelihood would have no impact on him this time. And as if George had had nothing to do with what happened, he would suggest to the psychologist that the assistant principal had totally "lost his cool," screaming uncontrollably.

The psychoanalytic literature speaks of regression in the service of ego. In this case, the youngster sought to serve his own need to

Clinical Evidence 95

gain a sense of ego adequacy by proving his ability to control other people. Such behavior is clearly not totally the outcome of the youngster's learning disability. It seems, however, that George's defensive and maladaptive behavior might never have become present or reinforceable without his learning disability as a stimulus. Once these behaviors begin, they are likely to continue because others in George's environment continue to react to them.

CONCLUSION

Perhaps the most obvious conclusion to be drawn about the clinical assessment of learning-disabled/gifted youngsters is that the clinician can only hypothesize and is not in the position to draw any real conclusions. An inconsistent bias exists toward underreferral of such youngsters. They are seen frequently for rather narrow purposes (for example, do they qualify for the gifted program?). Legislative and political considerations often dictate definitions of giftedness and learning disability, such as giftedness equaling an intelligence score of 130. The definitions with which the clinician has to work are clinically unsatisfying. They rely primarily on quantitative standards that limit any real understanding of the youngster's patterns of strengths and weaknesses. It is absolutely necessary to consider that giftedness and learning disability exist concurrently. It is also necessary to fund projects in which clinicians and legislators can work cooperatively to define standards that are both psychoeducationally sound and legally manageable.

The "rules" which grow out of sound educational theory and practice for the assessment of learning-disabled/gifted youngsters are not completely different from the rules of assessment of any youngster whose skills and abilities need evaluation. First, an appropriate battery of tests must be utilized. This battery of tests must be broad enough to encompass critical human skills as the target behaviors. The best possible sample in each area must be chosen. The clinician must realize that a sample of behavior is influenced by a variety of factors, including the impression that a youngster makes on the examiner. Clearly, further education of professionals is necessary to enable these youngsters to be evaluated and given appropriate programs.

This discussion has attempted to suggest that the identification of learning-disabled/gifted youngsters represents a significant educational problem. Neither learning disability nor giftedness has been defined in an adequate operational fashion. Often, decisions are made on legislative definitions. In light of the unique nature of their problems, any evaluation must emphasize broadly based, qualitative assessment. Strictly quantitative results often lack the flavor of the youngster's style of response and behavior and, therefore, are not reliable. The behavior of learning-disabled/gifted children is often heavily influenced by the fact that they are continually faced with gaps between their limited self-expectations, overestimated parental demands, and the reality of what they are able to produce.

Clinical experience as well as research suggests that the youngsters' attempts to deal psychologically with being gifted and learning disabled leads to a number of energy-draining defenses and behaviors. A careful review of actual case material often provides more insight than an average profile of the group.

There is a critical need to take a closer look at the psychological impact of this simultaneous condition. Wasted human potential is not the only cost at stake; more important, the actualization of these individuals as human beings can be limited and distorted.

REFERENCES

Brumbaugh, F.N. 1956. Intellectually gifted children. In: M.E. Frampton, and E.D. Gall, (eds.), Special Education for the Exceptional, Vol. 3. Porter Sargent Publishers, Inc., Boston.

Clements, S.D. 1966. Minimal Brain Dysfunction in Children: Terminology and Identification, Na-1415. United States Public Health Service Publication, Washington, D.C.

Elkind, J. 1973. The gifted child with learning disabilities. Gifted Child Q. 17:98–102.

Frampton, M., and Gall, E.D. (eds.) 1955. Special Education for the Exceptional. Porter Sargent Publishers, Inc., Boston.

Grotberg, E. 1974. Parent roles in fostering reading. In: M. Labuda (ed.), Creative Reading for Gifted Learners: A Design for Excellence. International Reading Association, Newark, DE.

Harris, D., and Avery, S. 1978. Gift behind the difficulties. Pointer. 23:65–68.

Hollingworth, L. 1926. Gifted Children: Their Nature and Nurture. MacMillan Publishing Co., New York.

Isaacs, A. 1974. Creative reading can be a balance and an anchor in guiding the gifted. In: M. Labuda (ed.), Creative Reading for Gifted Learners: A Design for Excellence. International Reading Association, Newark, DE.

Khatena, J. 1978. Some advances in thought on the gifted. Gifted Child Q. 22:55–61

Krippner, S. 1968. Etiological factors in reading disabilities of the academically talented, in comparison to pupils of average and slow learning ability. J. Educ. Res. 61:275–279.

Labuda, M., and James, H. 1974. Fostering creativity in children who differ. In: M. Labuda (ed.), Creative Reading for Gifted Learners: A Design for Excellence. International Reading Association, Newark, DE.

Orton, S.T. 1928. An impediment to learning to read: a neurological explanation of the learning disability. Sch. and Soc. 28:286–290.

Terman, L.M. 1925, 1930, 1947, 1959. Genetic Studies of Genius, Vols. 1, 3–5. Stanford University Press, Stanford, CA.

Terman, L.M., and Oden, M. 1951. The Stanford studies of the gifted. In: P. Witty (ed.), The Gifted Child. D.C. Heath and Co., Boston.

Torrance, E.P. 1977. Discovery and Nurturence of Giftedness in the Culturally Different. Counc. Except. Child., Reston, VA.

Witty, P. (ed.). 1951. The Gifted Child. D.C. Heath and Co., Boston.

PART II

ISSUES IN IDENTIFICATION
Problems and Practices

PART II

ISSUES IN IDENTIFICATION
Problems and Practices

Chapter 5

Models for Identifying Giftedness
Issues Related to the Learning-Disabled Child
Lynn H. Fox and Linda Brody

Intellectual and academic giftedness is typically assessed by standard-ized aptitude and/or achievement tests, sometimes in conjunction with teacher evaluations. For the learning-disabled/gifted child, the gift-edness may be masked by the disability. The purpose of this chapter is twofold: first, to survey conceptual and operational definitions of giftedness in relation to the concept of a learning-disabled/gifted child; and second, to discuss specific measures that are used to screen chil-dren for giftedness in order to determine their appropriateness or po-tential for identifying learning-disabled children.

DEFINING GIFTEDNESS

Attempts to identify the learning-disabled/gifted child are complicated by a lack of agreement among educators as to the definition of gift-edness for children. Throughout the history of the gifted child move-ment, social-philosophical, psychological, and pragmatic considera-tions have contributed to the development of a wide variety of defi-nitions of giftedness. Some of the more common definitions and re-lated issues are summarized in the following section.

Conceptual Definitions

Conceptual definitions of giftedness typically include a reference to intelligence, without specifically defining the term. This is not sur-prising in light of the general lack of agreement about the meaning of

---

Portions of this chapter were adapted from Fox, L.H. 1981. Identification of the academically gifted. Am. Psychol. 36:1103–1111. Copyright © 1981 by the American Psychological Association. Adapted by permission of the publisher.

102   *Fox and Brody*

the term beyond "that which an intelligence test measures" (Thorndike, 1921). According to Wechsler (1975), intelligence tests measure "the capacity of an individual to understand the world about him and his resourcefulness to cope with its challenges" (p. 139).

Terman (1925) initiated the first major research study in which giftedness or intellectual talent in children was operationalized in terms of performance on intelligence tests. Terman sought students who scored in the top 1% on the Stanford-Binet Intelligence Scale. Although this study had great impact on current thinking about giftedness, some people consider the operational definition used by Terman, which was based on intelligence test scores only, too restrictive.

Some broader definitions have been proposed, such as that the talented and gifted child is "one who shows consistently remarkable performance in any worthwhile line of endeavor" (Witty, 1958, p. 62). Renzulli (1978), however, noted that definitions of giftedness generally differ only in terms of the number of performance areas that are specified and/or in the degree of excellence that must be exhibited, such as the 90th versus the 98th percentile on an achievement measure.

Definitions may also differ as to whether or not potential alone is a sufficient condition for giftedness. A child who exhibits potential but performs poorly in school or on achievement tests could be considered gifted by some definitions; other definitions specify that the child must also exhibit high achievement. For example, Fliegler and Bish (1959) defined gifted students as those who possess both potential and functional skills necessary for academic achievement in the top 15% to 20% of the school population. Newland (1976) noted that according to such a definition, the concept of underachieving gifted individuals is paradoxical. Whitmore (1980) maintained, however, that "one must include as gifted those individuals who excel in only one or a few categories of ability and those who reveal on aptitude tests high potential for learning that has not been evidenced in their academic performance" (p. 67).

The Study of Mathematically Precocious Youth (SMPY), initiated by Stanley in 1971 at The Johns Hopkins University, introduced a new perspective on the definition of giftedness. He searched for youths who, at an early age, reasoned extremely well in mathematics. This was evidenced by high scores on difficult tests (those intended for much older students). Stanley equated precocity, as measured by test performance, with specific academic talent (Stanley, Keating, and Fox, 1974). According to Stanley (1976), a high score on a test intended for older students is predictive of long-range, lasting differences in ultimate ability and not just a temporary advantage. Thus, a student might be identified as academically gifted in one or more specific areas without necessarily exhibiting general intellectual superiority in all areas.

Although the terms *academically talented* and *gifted* are often used interchangeably, Renzulli (1978) defined giftedness in terms of the interaction of three clusters of traits: above average general ability, high levels of task commitment, and high levels of creativity. Accordingly, "gifted and talented children are those possessing or capable of developing this composite set of traits and applying them to any potentially valuable area of human performance" (Renzulli, 1978, p. 261). The rationale for this concept is based on the cumulative research on creative and productive adults (Albert, 1975; Cox, 1926; MacKinnon, 1965; McCurdy, 1957; Roe, 1952).

Feldman (1979) differed from Renzulli by arguing that all children are gifted (although not all in the academic and intellectual areas). He said: "farfetched though it may sound, I think it not at all implausible that a broadened view of giftedness would reveal that every child is gifted in some socially valued way" (p. 663). Newland (1976), however, suggested the "sociopsychological approach," in which the percentage of gifted students identified would be based on society's projected needs for leadership in specific areas.

Sternberg (1981) proposed an information-processing theory of intelligence rather than a psychometric one. In this model, there are three broad components of giftedness: metacomponents—such as the higher order processes used in problem solving (e.g., selection of strategies for problem solving); performance components—the processes used in problem solving, such as inference; and acquisition, retention, and transfer components—the skills used in learning, storing, and applying information. According to Sternberg, gifted individuals are those who are capable of "high quality and quantity of interaction among the various kinds of components in the system . . . they are more sensitive to the feedback that the various components can provide" (p. 91).

Legal and Operational Definitions of Giftedness

Prior to 1971, only four states (California, Illinois, Nebraska, and Pennsylvania) had legally or formally defined giftedness. A 1971 report to Congress by the Commissioner of Education sparked more interest in the identification of talented students (Marland, 1972). This document deplored the condition of education for gifted children, questioned the reliance on intelligence test scores as the sole criteria for selecting children for programs, and for the first time, proposed a definition of

104   *Fox and Brody*

gifted and talented children at the national level. This definition (see the Introduction to this book) defined giftedness as outstanding ability or achievement in one or more of five areas.

By 1978, 42 states either had developed definitions for giftedness in law or regulation or had at least formulated working guidelines modeled along the lines of the federal definition (Karnes and Collins, 1978). General intellectual ability was specified in all of the 42 states. Separate categories for specific academic aptitude and creative thinking were included in the definitions in 36 states. In three states, intellectual giftedness is operationally defined as a score that is 2 standard deviations above the mean on an individual test of intelligence. In most states, however, the definitions are less specific and refer to students who score in some upper range (2%–10%, or 1⅓–2 standard deviations above the mean) on measures of ability (Karnes and Collins, 1978). The federal definition requires only that students be identified by experts.

Although experts typically recommend the use of individual tests of intelligence, such as the Wechsler Intelligence Scale for Children-Revised (WISC-R) or the Stanford-Binet, in practice most local school systems rely on a combination of teacher recommendations and scores on group tests of intelligence and achievement. This is not surprising given the high cost in time and money of administering individual tests and the general lack of federal, state, or local monies for education of the gifted and talented.

The operational definition for specific academic aptitude proposed by Stanley (1979) begins with an initial screening on an in-grade achievement test. Students who score in the upper 3% qualify for further testing on a more difficult measure of specific aptitude. The criterion score on the more difficult tests used for selection for the SMPY programs has varied depending on the test used, the nature of the program, and the age of the student.

The Learning-Disabled/Gifted Child

Clearly, the concept of learning-disabled/gifted children is viable according to some definitions but not others. Such children would not be considered gifted if high levels of achievement or aptitude are required in all intellectual/academic areas because the learning-disabled child would have deficits in one or more areas. If precocity in only one area is necessary to be considered gifted, the learning-disabled child may exhibit precocity in an area untouched by the disability. A definition that emphasizes a child's potential rather than achievement would be more likely to include the learning-disabled/gifted child who

Models for Identifying 105

has high potential but whose disability was limiting school performance. The use of multiple screening measures should detect giftedness in a learning-disabled/gifted child, who may score poorly when tested on only one measure.

SCREENING FOR GIFTEDNESS

One or more of the following measures are typically used for screening gifted children: individual or group intelligence tests, group aptitude and achievement tests, teacher recommendations or checklists, and measures of creativity. The appropriateness of each of these for use with a learning-disabled/gifted child will be considered.

Intelligence Tests

Evidence of the long-term predictive validity of individual intelligence test scores for identifying the academically gifted comes largely from Terman's longitudinal study of children with intelligence test scores of 140 or higher on the Stanford-Binet. As adults, the subjects outperformed other comparison groups on the Concept Mastery Test, a difficult test of verbal reasoning; the proportion of the Terman group members who graduated from college, earned advanced graduate degrees, and pursued professional careers was considerably larger than that of the general population (Oden, 1968). The numbers who published articles and books, held patents, or earned awards and honors were also impressive.

For learning-disabled/gifted students, intelligence tests may be used to measure potential in a child who is not achieving well in school but whose ability can be measured by an intelligence test. The problem arises, however, if the disability depresses scores on the intelligence test. Thus, the child will fail to meet the overall criteria for inclusion, such as a score of 130, in spite of high ability in some areas. In this case, an individual intelligence test such as the WISC-R allows the clinician to examine performance on subtests and to look for areas of relative strength and weakness. High scores on parts of the test may suggest giftedness while poor performance in other areas suggests disability.

Wechsler designed the WISC and WISC-R to distinguish between what he labeled verbal and performance areas of intelligence. Statistically, a 15-point discrepancy between these two scores is significant at the .01 level. This has led clinicians to seriously consider a 15-point or greater Verbal-Performance discrepancy as an indication of a possible problem, and studies have attempted to link Verbal-Performance discrepancies with learning disabilities or brain damage (Rourke et al., 1971; Clements, 1963). Kaufman (1979), however, found that 25% of the subjects in a normative population had a Verbal-Performance discrepancy of at least 15 points. He questioned how a 15-point discrepancy could be diagnostic of a learning disability when it occurs in one out of four normal children. Other studies have supported Kaufman's position that although some learning-disabled children may exhibit this discrepancy, its presence is not sufficient for diagnosis because many normal children have this discrepancy and many learning-disabled children do not (Anderson et al., 1976; Tabachnick, 1979; Bloom and Raskin, 1980; Vance et al., 1976; Richman and Lindgren, 1980). However, if a child's Verbal or Performance score greatly exceeds the other so that one falls into the superior range and the other does not, the possibility that the child is both gifted and learning disabled should be considered.

Dissatisfaction with the limitations of the Verbal-Performance discrepancy for diagnosis has led to attempts in the field to recategorize the WISC-R subscales into other categories. Kaufman (1975, 1979) did a factor analysis of the WISC-R using the standardization sample. He found three factors: 1) Verbal Comprehension including Information, Similarities, Vocabulary and Comprehension, 2) Perceptual Organization including Picture Completion, Picture Arrangement, Block Design, Object Assembly and Mazes, and 3) Freedom from Distractibility including Arithmetic, Digit Span, and Coding. He noted the resemblance of the Verbal Comprehension and Perceptual Organization factors to Wechsler's Verbal and Performance Scales. Bannatyne (1974) proposed four scales: 1) Spatial—equal to Picture Completion, Block Design, and Object Assembly; 2) Conceptualizing—equal to Comprehension, Similarities, and Vocabulary; 3) Sequencing—equal to Digit Span, Arithmetic, and Coding; and 4) Acquired Knowledge— equal to Information, Arithmetic, and Vocabulary. In Chapter 6 of this book, Fox reports on an attempt to relate Bannatyne's scales to a group of learning-disabled/gifted children in which no consistent pattern was found. More research is needed to determine what, if any, unique patterns characterize the learning-disabled/gifted child.

Another approach for diagnosing learning disabilities using the WISC-R has been to examine the variance between individual subtests. The subtest scores can be compared directly to each other or they can each be compared to a common number (usually the mean of the subtest scores for either the Verbal or Performance portion of the test). Wechsler provided a table in the test manual (Wechsler, 1974) that shows the differences between scaled scores required for statistical significance at the 15% level of confidence. How much difference is required depends on the particular subtests being compared. As a general rule, Wechsler suggested that a difference of three or more points between any pair of subscales may be considered significant at the 15% level of confidence. The significance would be greater with greater differences. Using this approach, for example, a child whose Similarities score was 17 and whose Coding score was 10 might be suspected as being a learning-disabled/gifted child. Kaufman (1979) advocated computing the mean scaled scores for the Verbal and Performance subscales and comparing each subscale to the child's mean scores. He suggested that values of 3 or more points above the mean should be considered strengths, and values 3 or more points below the mean should be considered weaknesses.

The Stanford-Binet Intelligence Test was used by Terman in his study of gifted children and is often used by psychologists to measure intelligence. Its norms encompass a wider age group than the WISC-R so that it can be used with children as young as 2 years of age as well as with older adolescents. This facilitates comparisons across age groups. The Stanford-Binet, however, does not include subtest scores. Although a trained examiner can look at item-response patterns to determine strengths and weaknesses, it is a much more difficult and less reliable process than with the WISC-R, where subtest scales have already been determined. In addition, the Stanford-Binet has fewer nonverbal components than the WISC-R. The WISC-R, therefore, seems to be a better choice than the Stanford-Binet for identifying strengths and weaknesses in a learning-disabled/gifted child.

Attempts have been made to adapt both the Stanford-Binet and the WISC-R for use with culturally disadvantaged children. Meeker (1969) developed the Structure of Intellect-Learning Abilities Test (SOI-LA), adapting items from the Wechsler Tests and the Stanford-Binet to Guilford's Structure of Intellect (SOI) model (Guilford, 1967). The test obtains scores for each SOI factor measured by the intelligence tests, identifying strengths and weaknesses so that the weaknesses can be remediated. The SOI-LA has been used to specify patterns of strengths and weaknesses for black and Chicano students (Meeker and Meeker, 1973) and to assess gifted potential among the Navajos (Meeker, 1977). More research is needed on the use of this measure with learning-disabled/gifted students, whose disabilities may inhibit performance on an intelligence test in much the same way as cultural deprivation.

Another attempt to improve the assessment of culturally diverse children is the System of Multicultural Pluralistic Assessment

(SOMPA), developed by Mercer and Lewis (1978). It is composed of three models: the medical system, social system, and pluralistic model. SOMPA includes a parent interview as well as student assessment and incorporates the WISC-R as one part of an in-depth clinical case study approach. The WISC-R results are interpreted relative to the socio-cultural group to which the child belongs. SOMPA attempts to assess potential that may be masked by sociocultural and health factors. An Abbreviated Binet for the Disadvantaged (ABDA) was devised by Bruch (1971) for disadvantaged black children. Although these tests might not be appropriate for learning-disabled/gifted students from a variety of backgrounds, the approach might be useful if specific items could be identified that would measure high ability in a learning-disabled child.

Group tests of intelligence are used more often with children in school systems than individual tests because of the time and cost involved in administering a test individually. Even though scores on group tests often correlate highly with scores on individual tests of intelligence, group tests often fail to identify many students who would qualify on individual measures. Pegnato and Birch (1959), for example, reported that for junior high school students, a cutoff score of 130 on a group test (Otis Quick-Scoring Mental Ability Test) identified only 23% of those who scored 136 or higher on the Stanford-Binet whereas a cutoff of 115 correctly identified 92%. In another study of 332 gifted students who scored 130 or higher on the Revised Stanford-Binet scale, only half scored 130 or higher on a group test of intelligence (Martinson and Lessinger, 1960). Thus, it may be wise to use scores of 120 or even 115 on group tests for purposes of screening, but not for decisions about program placement. For children who are gifted but learning disabled, group intelligence tests may be especially inappropriate. Their disabilities may make it impossible for these children to function at their full potential on a test that is usually primarily verbal and timed. The nature of the child's disability would need to be assessed to determine if this was a problem.

One argument against the use of intelligence tests for identifying academically gifted students is that although performance on an intelligence test may indicate academic potential, it doesn't provide enough information about specific abilities and achievements to plan programs for the child. For diagnostic and prescriptive purposes, therefore, batteries of aptitude and achievement tests may be more useful than intelligence tests for the nondisabled gifted child. With the learning-disabled/gifted child, however, the individual intelligence test may better assess the cognitive abilities that are not reflected on group tests because of the disability.

Models for Identifying 109

Aptitude and Achievement Tests

Standardized in-grade achievement tests are used by schools to determine the level of students' mastery over material to which they have been exposed and are often used as part of the screening process for gifted programs. When students fail to score well on a standardized achievement test, it is important to determine whether it is a result of inadequate learning because of a lack of effort or poor teaching, inadequate learning because of a learning disability, or the choice of the wrong test in light of the curriculum that was used with the students. Using achievement tests as part of the assessment procedure rather than as the sole instrument to measure performance would contribute to the reliability of the process.

With gifted students, a lack of test ceiling is often a problem on standardized group tests. Gifted students' scores frequently cluster near the top. Without additional information, discrimination among levels of giftedness in this population is difficult. For example, two students might both score at the 97th percentile on the in-grade mathematics achievement test but one might be a truly exceptional mathematical reasoner while the other has less aptitude but has mastered the in-grade course work. For the past several years, an annual Talent Search has been conducted at The Johns Hopkins University for seventh-graders. To enter the Talent Search, students must score at or above the 97th percentile on an in-grade achievement test. Their performance on the Scholastic Aptitude Test (SAT), a difficult test for high school seniors, varies enormously, ranging from the lowest to the highest possible scores. Thus, more difficult aptitude and achievement tests are needed for determining individual differences among upper ability youth.

There is little research on the long-term power of tests of specific aptitude and achievement to predict life accomplishments. However, the ongoing SMPY longitudinal study has found that scores on difficult tests of mathematical and verbal reasoning (SAT-M and SAT-V), taken in grades 7 and 8, correlate with aptitude scores and several measures of achievement in high school (Benbow, 1981). Stanley (1976) said, "For *appropriate criteria*, validity does not drop at the upper part of the score range of a test *that is difficult enough* for the persons tested" (p. 5).

With learning-disabled/gifted children, aptitude and achievement tests might predict ability in a specific area not affected by the child's disability. For example, a student with a specific reading disability might be gifted in mathematics. It is possible that the child who performs extremely well on a difficult test of mathematics might score

110   *Fox and Brody*

poorly on a test of reading comprehension. Most aptitude and achievement tests, however, are timed and material is presented in a written format, requiring a certain level of reading ability. Whether or not these factors would affect the child's performance depends on the nature and severity of the disability.

A test of abstract reasoning, such as the Raven's Progressive Matrices, may be helpful in identifying high ability in children who do not do well on verbal measures because of a learning disability. In a study of children attending a school for dyslexic children, Steeves (1982) identified a group of students who scored as well on the Raven's as a comparison group of selected private school students who had been identified as mathematically gifted. This suggests that the Raven's may be a useful tool in identifying good mathematical potential among a learning-disabled population, but more research is needed.

Teacher Nominations

There is little data with which to compare the predictive validity of teacher judgments versus standardized tests. Some studies have contrasted teacher nominations with the criterion of test performance. In the Terman study, teachers were asked to nominate the first, second, and third brightest children in their class and were also told to name the youngest. Nominations of the youngest child in the class produced more students who met the criterion of 140 or higher on the Stanford-Binet than did nominations of the brightest (Terman, 1925). It is important to recall, however, that the majority of the Terman sample was nominated in one of the categories by teachers. Terman estimated that, in some schools, 10–25% of the students who would have scored 140 or higher on the Stanford-Binet were not nominated by teachers. There is no way to know whether or not those students achieved as much in adulthood as the ones who were nominated by teachers.

Gear (1976) reviewed five studies in which students nominated by teachers were compared with a criterion of student scores 2 or more standard deviations higher than the mean of an individual test of intelligence, such as the WISC-R or the Stanford-Binet. In all five studies, teachers correctly identified less than half of the students and in one study, they only identified 10% (Jacobs, 1971). Teacher judgments were also inefficient in that they identified 10% or more of the nongifted students as gifted.

Because the vast majority of teachers have never been required to take courses in the area of education for the gifted, it follows that they may not be knowledgeable about the characteristics of such students. Many teachers may nominate dutiful students rather than those

Models for Identifying   111

who are brilliant but bored. Learning-disabled/gifted children who perform poorly in school are very likely overlooked. Gear (1978) studied how specific training on the characteristics of gifted children influenced teacher effectiveness and efficiency. Training increased effectiveness (the number of children nominated by the teachers who met the test criterion) but not efficiency (the proportions of truly gifted among the total groups nominated by the teachers).

In order to make teacher nominations more efficient, checklists have been developed to help guide teachers as to what characteristics to look for when nominating children for gifted programs. Examples of checklists that have been developed for gifted students include Renzulli and Hartman's (1981) and Alexander and Muia's (1982). Many school systems have developed their own. It is usually recommended that these checklists be used in conjunction with test scores. Besides providing additional information about behavior and achievement, the checklists are frequently used to identify children who do not test well as gifted. This may be important when identifying learning-disabled/gifted children. The characteristics of learning-disabled/gifted children listed by Tannenbaum and Baldwin in Chapter 1 of this volume formed the basis for a checklist used for screening in the program described by Baldwin and Gargiulo in Chapter 12.

Creativity Tests

Passow (1981) noted an increasing emphasis on creativity (defined in many ways) as either a component of academic and intellectual giftedness or as a type of giftedness itself. Guilford (1950, 1967) was the first to point out that there are some types of thinking involved in creative problem solving that are not assessed by typical achievement and aptitude tests. Eminent adults were not always obviously precocious in childhood (Cox, 1926) and may not necessarily score very high as adults on tests of intelligence (Albert, 1975; MacKinnon, 1965). The work of Getzels and Jackson (1958) and Torrance (1965, 1977) suggested that some children who score only moderately high on intelligence tests but high on creativity measures are capable of high levels of achievement. On some tests of creativity, there are few if any differences among cultural groups (Torrance, 1971). Torrance (1971, 1977) has recommended the use of the Torrance Tests of Creative Thinking instead of traditional intelligence measures to identify the disadvantaged gifted.

Whether or not it is possible to predict adult creativity from behaviors measured in childhood or adolescence is unclear (Crockenberg, 1972). An ongoing longitudinal assessment of the Torrance Tests of Creative Thinking (Torrance, 1977) soon may provide some data of interest. It has been argued also that creativity cannot be demonstrated prior to mastery of a discipline, and the ability to master a discipline is better measured by tests of aptitude and achievement than by tests of creativity.

Some of the controversy about the concept of creativity surrounds the question of the extent to which it is a personality trait, a specific cognitive ability, or a type of problem-solving strategy that might be learned (Michael, 1977). If it is the latter, there is less need to search for those who know the process than to teach the process to everyone.

Because there is controversy about the appropriateness and validity of creativity tests to identify giftedness, it is somewhat premature to recommend their use with the learning-disabled/gifted child. It is possible, however, that like the disadvantaged child, a learning-disabled child who does not score well on intelligence or achievement measures might do well on a creativity test. The Torrance tests, in particular, do not depend on proficiency in the areas of reading or spelling, but measure the quantity and quality of ideas that a child can generate. A high score on this measure might suggest potential that should be investigated further.

CONCLUSION

On the basis of existing research evidence, the most defensible approach for identifying the academically talented is the use of a variety of psychometric and nonpsychometric measures for initial screening. With learning-disabled/gifted children, multiple screening methods are particularly essential in order to identify a pattern of strengths and weaknesses and to reduce the risk that only one measure may not accurately reflect the child's ability. The information and methods used to screen a school population for giftedness should include: 1) evidence of high academic potential as assessed by standardized intelligence and aptitude tests; 2) evidence of specific academic achievement as measured by standardized tests and/or informal measures such as teachers' or experts' judgments about science projects, essays or poems; and 3) recommendations of teachers, counselors, reading specialists, or other educators who have observed a student's performance in a learning environment. Peer nominations, self-nominations and parent nominations, as well as tests of creativity and nonverbal reasoning, also should be considered and may be particularly important in identifying giftedness in a learning-disabled child. There is a need for measures that do not penalize the child because of problems in the areas of reading, spelling, and handwriting.

Models for Identifying 113

If this initial screening suggests a discrepant pattern of peaks and valleys, the child should be referred for a complete clinical evaluation, including an individual Intelligence Test and tests to assess specific learning disabilities. Decisions about placement in special programs for gifted and/or learning-disabled youngsters should be made on the basis of a clinical evaluation of the student and a careful analysis of the dimensions and requirements of the program.

Any problem of classification or selection requires that a value judgment be made about the problems of false positives and false negatives. In the case of learning-disabled/gifted students, it is advisable to risk identifying students as gifted even if this might not be the case. Give them the opportunities for special or individualized educational programs rather than err by possibly overlooking many talented students with high potential who are not achieving because of their disabilities. In Chapter 1 of this book, Tannenbaum and Baldwin suggest that students who are suspected of being gifted should be given the opportunity for enriching educational experiences; then, they should be further evaluated on the basis of their performance in these learning environments. This approach might encourage greater participation by learning-disabled/gifted children in programs for the gifted.

There might come a time when diagnostic assessment and prescriptive instruction will be developed for all children in keeping with their unique learning styles and instructional needs. Then there would be no need to try to predict whether or not a student is academically gifted because each student would automatically be continually directed to more difficult and challenging learning experiences. Until then, it is important to use carefully chosen measures to identify the unique patterns of abilities that learning-disabled/gifted children possess and to provide programs that will challenge them intellectually while remediating their weak areas.

REFERENCES

Albert, R.S. 1975. Toward a behavioral definition of genius. Am. Psychol. 30:140–151.

Alexander, P.A., and Muia, J.A. 1982. Gifted Education. Aspen Systems Corp. Rockville, MD.

Anderson, M. Kaufman, A., and Kaufman, N. 1976. Use of the WISC-R with a learning disabled population: Some diagnostic implications. Psychol. Sch. 13:381–386.

Bannatyne, A. 1974. Diagnosis: A note on recategorization of the WISC scaled scores. J. Learn. Disabil. 7:272–273.

Benbow, C.P., 1981. Development of superior mathematical ability during adolescence. Unpublished doctoral dissertation, The Johns Hopkins University, Baltimore.

Bloom, A., and Raskin, L. 1980. WISC-R verbal and performance I.Q. discrepancies: A comparison of learning disabled children to the normative sample. J. Clin. Psychol. 36:322–323.

Bruch, C.B. 1971. Modification of procedures for identification of the disadvantaged gifted. Gifted Child Q. 15:267–272.

Clements, S.D. 1963. The Child with Minimal Brain Dysfunction—A Profile. National Society for Crippled Children and Adults, Chicago.

Cox, C.M. 1926. The early mental traits of three hundred geniuses. In Genetic Studies of Genius, Vol. 2. Stanford University Press, Stanford, CA.

Crockenberg, S.B. 1972. Creativity tests: A boon or boondoggle for education? Rev. Educ. Res. 42:27–45.

Feldman, D. 1979. Toward a nonelitist conception of giftedness. Phi Delta Kappan. 60:660–663.

Fliegler, L.A., and Bish, C.E. 1959. The gifted and talented. Rev. Educ. Res. 29:408–450.

Fox, L.H. 1981. Identification of the academically gifted. Am. Psychol. 36:1103–1111.

Gear, G.H. 1976. Accuracy of teacher judgement in identifying intellectually gifted children: A review of the literature. Gifted Child Q. 20:478–490.

Gear, G.H. 1978. Effects of training on teachers' accuracy in the identification of gifted children. Gifted Child Q. 22:90–97.

Getzels, J.W., and Jackson, P.W. 1958. The meaning of "giftedness"—An examination of an expanding concept. Phi Delta Kappan 40:275–277.

Guilford, J.P. 1950. Creativity. Am. Psychol. 49:87–98.

Guilford, J.P. 1967. The Nature of Human Intelligence. McGraw-Hill Book Co., New York.

Jacobs, J.C. 1971. Effectiveness of teacher and parent identification of gifted children as a function of school level. Psychol. Sch. 8:140–142.

Karnes, F.A., and Collins, E.C. 1978. State definitions on the gifted and talented: A report and analysis. J. Educ. Gifted. 1:44–62.

Kaufman, A.S. 1975. Factor analysis of the WISC-R at eleven age levels between 6½ and 16½ years. J. Consult. Clin. Psychol. 43:135–147.

Kaufman, A.S. 1979. Intelligent testing with the WISC-R. John Wiley and Sons, Inc. New York.

MacKinnon, D.W. 1965. Personality and the realization of creative potential. Am. Psychol. 20:273–281.

Marland, S.P. 1972. Education of the gifted and talented, Report to the Congress of the United States by the U.S. Commissioner of Education, United States Government Printing Office, Washington, D.C.

Martinson, R.A., and Lessinger, L.M. 1960. Problems in the identification of intellectually gifted pupils. Except. Child. 26:227–242.

McCurdy, H.G. 1957. The childhood patterns of genius. J. Elisha Mitchell Sci. Soc. 73:448–462.

Meeker, M.N. 1969. The Structure of Intellect: Its Interpretation and Uses. Charles E. Merrill Pub. Co., Columbus, OH.

Meeker, M.N. 1977. Identifying gifted Navajo children in reservations. In: Interim Report from the SOI Institute. SOI Institute, El Segundo, CA.

Meeker, M.N., and Meeker, R. 1973. Strategies for assessing intellectual patterns in black, Anglo and Mexican-American boys—or any other children—and implications for education. J. Sch. Psychol. 11:341–350.

Models for Identifying 115

Mercer, T.B., and Lewis, J.G. 1978. Using the system of multicultural assessment (SOMPA) to identify the gifted minority child. In: A.Y. Baldwin, C.H. Gear, and L.J. Lucito (eds.), Educational Planning for the Gifted: Overcoming Cultural, Geographic and Socioeconomic Barriers. Counc. Except. Child., Reston, VA.

Michael, W.B. 1977. Cognitive and affective components of creativity in mathematics and the physical sciences. In: J.C. Stanley, W.C. George, and C.H. Solano (eds.), The Gifted and Creative: A Fifty-Year Perspective. Johns Hopkins University Press, Baltimore.

Newland, T.G., 1976. The Gifted in Socio-Educational Perspective. Prentice-Hall, Inc., Englewood Cliffs, NJ.

Oden, M.H. 1968. The fulfillment of promise: 40-year follow-up of the Terman Gifted Group. Genet. Psychol. Monogr. 77:3–93.

Passow, A.H. 1981. The nature of giftedness and talent. Gifted Child Q. 24:5–10.

Pegnato, C.W., and Birch, T.W. 1959. Locating gifted children in junior high schools: A comparison of methods. Except. Child. 25:300–304.

Renzulli, J.S. 1978. What makes giftedness? Reexamining a definition. Phi Delta Kappan. 60:180–184; 261.

Renzulli, J.S., and Hartman, R.K. 1981. Scale for rating behavioral characteristics of superior students. In: W. Barbe, and J. Renzulli, (eds.), Psychology and Education of the Gifted. Irvington Publishers, New York.

Richman, L., and Lindgren, S. 1980. Patterns of intellectual ability in children with verbal deficits. J. Abnorm. Psychol. 8:65–81.

Roe, A. 1952. The Making of a Scientist. Dodd, Mead and Company. New York.

Rourke, B., Young, G., and Flewelling, R. 1971. The relationships between WISC verbal-performance discrepancies and selected verbal, auditory-perceptual, visual-perceptual, and problem-solving abilities in children with learning disabilities. J. Clin. Psychol. 27:475–479.

Stanley, J.C. 1976. Use of tests to discover talent. In: D.P. Keating (ed.). Intellectual Talent: Research and Development. Johns Hopkins University Press, Baltimore.

Stanley, J.C. 1979. The second d: Descriptions of talent (further study of the intellectually talented youths). In: N. Colangelo and R.T. Zaffrann (eds.). New Voices in Counseling the Gifted. Kendall/Hunt Publishing Co., Dubuque, IA.

Stanley, J.C., Keating, D.P., and Fox, L.H. (eds.) 1974. Mathematical Talent: Discovery, Description and Development. Johns Hopkins University Press, Baltimore.

Steeves, K.J. 1982. Memory as a factor in the computational efficiency of dyslexic children with high abstract reasoning ability. Unpublished doctoral dissertation, The Johns Hopkins University, Baltimore.

Sternberg, R.J. 1981. A componential theory of intellectual giftedness. Gifted Child Q. 25:86–93.

Tabachnick, B. 1979. Test scatter on the WISC-R. J. Learn. Disabil. 12:626–628.

Terman, L.M. 1925. Mental and physical traits of a thousand gifted children. In: Genetic Studies of Genius, Vol. 1. Stanford University Press, Stanford, CA.

Thorndike, E.L. 1921. Intelligence and its measurement: A symposium. J. Educ. Psychol. 12:124–133.

Torrance, E.P. 1965. Gifted Child in the Classroom. Macmillan Publishing Co., New York.

Torrance, E.P. 1971. Are the Torrance tests of creative thinking biased against or in favor of "disadvantaged groups?" Gifted Child Q. 15:75–80.

Torrance, E.P. 1977. Creatively gifted and disadvantaged gifted students. In: J.C. Stanley, W.C. George, and C.H. Solano (eds.), The Gifted and the Creative: A Fifty-Year Perspective. Johns Hopkins University Press, Baltimore.

Vance, H., Gaynor, P., and Coleman, M. 1976. Analysis of cognitive abilities for learning disabled children. Psychol. Sch. 13:477–482.

Wechsler, D. 1974. Manual for the Wechsler Intelligence Scale for Children-Revised. Psychological Corp., New York.

Wechsler, D. 1975. Intelligence defined and undefined: A realistic appraisal. Am. Psychol. 30:135–139.

Whitmore, J. 1980. Giftedness, Conflict, and Underachievement. Allyn and Bacon, Inc., Boston.

Witty, P. 1958. Who are the gifted? In: N.B. Henry (ed.), Education for the Gifted: The Fifty-Seventh Yearbook of the National Society for the Study of Education, Part 2. University of Chicago Press, Chicago.

Chapter 6

Gifted Students
with Reading Problems
An Empirical Study
Lynn H. Fox

Although biographical and anecdotal accounts of eminent adults suggest that some of them had reading or learning problems, the learning-disabled/gifted child has never been studied extensively by educators. In the fall of 1979, the Spencer Foundation awarded a 3-year grant on learning-disabled/gifted students to four faculty members[1] in the Division of Education, Evening College and Summer Session, The Johns Hopkins University. The purpose of this grant was fourfold: 1) to study the problems of identification; 2) to explore ideas for educational intervention; 3) to develop a model for teacher training; and 4) to disseminate information in order to increase awareness in the educational community and general public. This chapter describes some of the research efforts related to the problems of identification.

The Johns Hopkins research team hypothesized that learning-disabled/gifted students might fall into three subgroups:

1. Subgroup 1 would include students whose learning problems were so severe that they would be identified as learning disabled. In the course of a complete clinical evaluation, some signs of giftedness, such as high scores on an individual measure of intelligence, might be found. The concern was that in the process of planning an appropriate educational program for the child, evidence of giftedness might not be taken into account.

2. Subgroup 2 would be comprised of children who were initially screened for gifted programs on the basis of some measure, such

---

[1] The faculty members included Dr. Lynn Fox, Dr. Gilbert Schiffman, Dr. Paul Daniels and Dr. Ronald Berk. The research associates on the project were Linda Brody and Dianne Tobin.

118   Fox

as an intelligence test, or high achievement in a particular academic area, such as mathematics, but who were not placed in a program. Also included would be those who failed to perform up to expectation in a program because their achievement did not correspond to their potential. In this instance, the concern is that these children would be viewed as false positives or errors of measurement instead of gifted children who have a learning problem and need further clinical evaluation and special adjustments to their educational program.

3. Subgroup 3 would include children who seemed to be functioning near grade level in class and/or on standardized tests but who in reality were well above average in intelligence and had some learning problems. These children seem to be average and performing near grade level and so they are rarely referred for clinical evaluation where the diagnosis of learning disabled/gifted could be made.

The rationale hypothesizing the existence of these three subgroups was based on the observation of students in clinical settings. These settings included the Kennedy Institute at The Johns Hopkins University, The Temple University Reading Clinic, and public school classrooms over a period of many years. Professors Schiffman and Daniels recounted numerous case studies in clinical situations and public school classes. They found that gifted children who had some learning problems were mistaken for hyperactive, emotionally disturbed, or simply poorly motivated. However, there seemed to be no systematic documentation in the research literature that such learning-disabled/gifted students existed.

In order to document the existence of children who could be considered both gifted and learning disabled, it seemed necessary to locate a sizeable number of school-age children who had been given a complete clinical (educational and psychological) evaluation. The Temple University Reading Clinic provided a unique situation in which such a population existed. The clinic, begun in 1946, had approximately 17,000 case histories of children on record. Mostly, they were between the ages of 6 and 15. Suspected to have reading disabilities, they had been referred by parents or schools for clinical evaluations. A decision was made to screen the 17,000 cases on record for examples of students who might be considered both gifted and learning disabled.[2]

[2] Graduate students at The Johns Hopkins University were invaluable in helping to collect and code the data from these 17,000 cases. The faculty would like to thank Virginia Berninger, Joyce Steeves, Wendy Bloomberg, Saralee Bernstein, Mary Ellen Lewis, Deborah Dolan, and Joanna Thomas.

Empirical Study 119

Because each of these children received an individual diagnosis, nearly all the files included a battery of tests and inventories based on a procedure called case-typing, which is described in Chapter 7 of this volume. The data available for the majority of cases included:

1. A Wechsler Intelligence Scale for Children (WISC or WISC-R)[3]
2. Subscales of the Detroit Test of Learning Aptitude
3. An informal word recognition inventory
4. An informal reading inventory
5. An informal spelling survey
6. A standardized achievement test
7. Tests of visual and auditory discrimination
8. Tests of associative learning ability
9. Assessments of personality
10. Measures of dominance and laterality

The following criteria were used to select the gifted population: a score of 125 or above on the Full-Scale (FS), Verbal Scale (V), or Performance Scale (P) of the WISC or WISC-R, and a chronological age below 15 years. For several reasons, the WISC or WISC-R was chosen as the intelligence test for screening the gifted population. First, it is a highly reliable, individually administered intelligence test. Second, it provides subscales scores that have been researched in relation to learning-disabled populations. Third, because it was used at Temple more often than any other single intelligence test, more cases could be screened.

Although definitions of academic giftedness vary, experts often recommend the use of scores of 130 or 132 on individual intelligence tests like the WISC. It was thought that learning disabilities might depress performance on intelligence tests; therefore, it was feared that a score cutoff of 130 would eliminate too many children who really were gifted. A score of 125 was chosen as one standard error of measurement below 130. Because learning-disabled youngsters often show discrepancies between their Verbal and Performance scores, the decision was made to screen all students who scored above 125 on the Verbal or Performance Scale as well as the Full-Scale WISC or WISC-R.

Of the 17,000 cases reviewed in 1952–1979, 432 (321 boys and 111 girls) met the criteria of scores on the WISC or WISC-R and the age criteria. In order to have a comparison group, the files of all students seen at the Temple Reading Clinic in the years 1956 and 1979 were studied. Students who did not meet the age criteria, or those without

---

[3] The WISC was used at Temple until the revised version appeared, at which time it was replaced by the WISC-R.

120   *Fox*

WISC or WISC-R scores were eliminated in order to provide comparability with the gifted population.

The first step was to determine which of the students in the two samples (the gifted group and the comparison years of 1956 and 1979) could be considered learning-disabled students. Several common criteria for such identification were considered:

1. The clinician at Temple made a diagnosis based on a procedure called case-typing. This is described by Rosner in Chapter 7 of this volume. Decisions were clearly based on the analysis of complex interrelationships among the various test scores, observations of behaviors during the testing, and case history information. Not all tests were given to each child, but most clinicians at the Temple Clinic administered an informal reading inventory (IRI). A discrepancy of 2 or more years between listening comprehension and instructional reading level on the IRI were viewed by many of these clinicians as one sign of potential learning difficulty. Thus, in the analysis presented herein, the results of the IRI are included in the discussions of the four samples.
2. Because some schools screen for learning-disabled students by looking for achievement on standardized tests of 2 or more years below grade placement, this analysis is provided for the four samples.
3. Some clinicians believe that a discrepancy of 15 or more points between the Performance and Verbal Scales of the WISC or WISC-R indicates a learning disability. This discrepancy is statistically significant at the 0.01 level (Wechsler, 1974). There is, however, considerable disagreement among experts about this issue (Kaufman, 1979). Although clinicians would not make a learning disability diagnosis based on the discrepancy of Performance versus Verbal or vice versa, such a discrepancy would be viewed as an indicator for further evaluation. Therefore, such analysis is reported for the four subgroups in this study.
4. A number of efforts have been made to consider the discrepancy between achievement and potential in terms of an expectancy formula based on mental age (MA) in conjunction with chronological age. Thus, a child performing at grade level might still show a discrepancy if the expectancy formula predicted achievement 2 years or more above grade level. Although the usefulness and validity of these formulas have been questioned (Hoffman, 1980; Berk, 1982), an analysis of the four samples in terms of the expectancy formula developed by Myklebust (1968) is included. In

Empirical Study   121

this formula, the expectancy age is the average of three ages—
MA, chronological age, and grade placement age.

THE GIFTED AND COMPARISON SAMPLES

Data for the gifted and comparison groups were analyzed separately by
sex. The decision to combine the subjects from 1956 and 1979 was
based on an analysis of the distribution of characteristics of the students for those 2 years. A distribution of students in each of the four
groups by age at the time of referral are shown in Table 6.1. The mean
scores on the WISC or WISC-R and the percentages of students who
qualified on the gifted criteria are shown in Table 6.2. An analysis of
selected years suggested an increase in the percentage of students who
scored 125 or higher on the WISC or WISC-R from a low of 1% in
the early years to 17% in 1979.

The number and percentage of cases who would meet selected
criteria for learning or reading disabilities are shown in Table 6.3.
These include clinical judgment, a discrepancy between listening comprehension and instructional reading level of 2 or more years, a reading
level below grade placement by 2 or more years on either an informal
or standardized test, a discrepancy between Verbal and Performance
Scales of the WISC or WISC-R, and the Myklebust expectancy formula. Descriptions of each group on these variables are provided in
the following sections.

Summary Profile of Gifted Boys

There were 321 boys in the gifted sample. Sixty-seven percent were
referred for testing before the age of 11, and the average grade placement was 4.6 for the 316 cases for whom grade was known. The majority (57.6%) were referred while in grades 2, 3, 4, and 5; 7.6% were
referred prior to grade 2; and 34.7% were referred after grade 7. The
mean WISC or WISC-R score was 125 for the group with a range from
104 to 154. The majority, 55%, had a total WISC or WISC-R of 125
or higher, and another 19% only qualified on the Verbal Scale while
26% met the 125 criteria on the Performance Scale only. The records
for 275 boys included the clinicians' judgment, and 89.5% of them
were diagnosed as having a reading problem.

Of the 251 gifted boys who had the complete IRI, 83.7% showed
a discrepancy of 2 or more years between listening comprehension and
instructional reading level. An additional 59 boys were tested for instructional reading level only. Of the 310 boys for whom instructional
level was reported, 50.3% scored 2 or more years below grade place-

122   Fox

Table 6.1.   Distribution of age, in percentages, by group and sex

| | Gifted | | 1956/1979 | |
Age	Boys $(N = 321)^a$	Girls $(N = 111)^a$	Boys $(N = 98)^a$	Girls $(N = 50)^a$
6	6.5^b	5.4	6.1	2.0
7	18.1	11.7	5.1	10.0
8	13.7	19.8	8.2	16.0
9	16.8	14.4	18.4	16.0
10	12.1	12.6	15.3	12.0
11	7.5	9.9	8.2	14.0
12	7.5	8.1	14.3	12.0
13	11.2	8.1	15.3	6.0
14	6.5	9.9	9.2	12.0

[a] Percentages do not add to 100 due to rounding.
[b] One gifted boy was only 5, but included with the 6-year-olds.

ment. A score of 2 or more years below grade placement was found for only 10% of the 261 boys tested on a standardized reading test. About one-fourth, 23.8%, actually scored 2 years or more above grade level on a standardized reading test.

In terms of discrepancy, about one-fourth (23.4%) had a Performance Scale score of 15 or more points higher than the Verbal Scale

Table 6.2.   Selected statistics on the WISC or WISC-R, by group and sex

| | Gifted | | 1956 and 1979 | |
	Boys $(N = 321)$	Girls $(N = 111)$	Boys $(N = 98)$	Girls $(N = 50)$
WISC—Full-Scale				
$\bar{X}^a$	125.03	125.94	102.56	103.18
SD	7.10	6.99	13.13	14.16
WISC—Verbal				
$\bar{X}$	122.93	123.33	101.60	101.78
SD	11.58	11.48	13.68	13.26
WISC—Performance				
$\bar{X}$	122.85	123.94	102.93	104.18
SD	10.73	11.79	14.48	15.00
Percentage who scored higher than 125				
Full-Scale	55	56	5	6
Verbal only	19	18	0	0
Performance only	26	25	5	4

[a] $\bar{X}$, mean.
[b] SD, standard deviation.

Empirical Study   123

Table 6.3.   Percentage of gifted and comparison groups, by sex, who were considered to have a reading problem by each of a variety of methods

Methods of determining problems	Gifted		1956 and 1979	
	Boys	Girls	Boys	Girls
Clinical judgment	89.5[a]	82.6	94.7	93.3
Listening comprehension exceeded instructional reading level by 2 or more years	83.7	77.8	72.1	58.1
Instructional level 2 or more years below grade on IRI	50.3	31.5	69.6	87
Achievement test score two or more years below grade	10.0	6.3	36.7	12.5
Discrepancy on the WISC				
V-P ≥ 15	22.7	25.2	15.3	10.0
P-V ≥ 15	23.4	27.9	17.3	16.0
Discrepancy by the Myklebust formula	35.2	30.5	60.8	35.0

[a] The number on which these percentages are based varies and are presented in the text.

score. Another 22.7% scored 15 points or more higher on the Verbal Scale than the Performance Scale. There were 261 cases for whom the Myklebust (1968) discrepancy formula could be computed. Of these, 35% met the criteria of learning disabled.

Summary Profile of Gifted Girls

Of the 111 girls in the gifted sample, 64% were referred for testing and evaluation before the age of 11. The average grade placement was grade 5 for the 108 cases for whom grade was known. The majority (52.7%) were referred while in grades 3, 4, 5, or 6; 16.7% were referred before grade 3; and 30.5% after grade 6. Girls comprised about one-fourth of all the gifted cases.

The average Full-Scale WISC or WISC-R was 125.9 with a range from 109 to 145. The majority, 56%, had a Full-Scale score of 125 or higher. Eighteen percent qualified on the Verbal Scale only, and another 25% on the Performance Scale. Ninety-two of the cases included

124   Fox

the clinician's judgment and of those, 82.6% were described as having a reading problem.

Of the 72 gifted girls who received the complete IRI, 77.8% had a discrepancy of 2 years or more between their listening comprehension and instructional reading level. The instructional reading level was available for an additional 36 girls. Thus, there were 108 who were tested for instructional reading level, and 31.5% of them were reading two or more grades below their grade placement. Of the 95 girls who had been given standardized reading tests, only 6.3% read below grade level by 2 or more years, and 27.4% actually scored 2 years or more above grade level.

Some students did have discrepancies between their Performance and Verbal Subscales in the WISC or WISC-R. Of these, 28% had a Performance score higher than the Verbal score by 15 points or more. Another 25.2% had higher Verbal than Performance scores. There were 95 girls for whom the Myklebust (1968) discrepancy formula could be computed. Of these, only 31% showed a discrepancy which, according to this method, indicated a learning problem.

Summary Profile of Comparison Boys

WISC or WISC-R scores were also available for 98 boys in the combined years of 1956 and 1979. Of these, 61% were referred for testing before the age of 12, and the average grade placement was grade 5 for the 95 cases for whom grade placement was known. The majority (54.8%) were referred while in grades 2, 4, 5, or 6; another 15.9% were referred before grade 3; and 29.5% were referred after grade 6. The mean WISC or WISC-R score was 102.6 with a range from 68 to 131. Only five cases scored above 125. An additional five cases scored 125 on the Performance Scale only. Records for 94 of the 98 boys included the clinical judgment, and 94.7% of these were classified as having a reading problem.

Of the 68 cases who had the complete IRI, 72.1% showed a discrepancy of 2 or more years between listening comprehension and instructional reading level. The instructional reading level of the IRI was reported for an additional 24 boys. For the total 92 boys tested for instructional level, 9.6% read 2 or more years below grade placement. A difference of 2 or more years between grade placement and reading level on a standardized test was found for 36.7% of the 79 boys who were tested.

In this group, only 17.3% had a Performance score of 15 or more points higher than their Verbal score. Another 15.3% scored higher on the Verbal than on the Performance Scale. There were 79 boys for

Empirical Study 125

whom the Myklebust (1968) discrepancy formula could be applied. Of these, 61% met the criteria of learning disabled by this method.

Summary Profile of Comparison Girls

There were 50 girls in the combined years of 1956 and 1979 for whom WISC or WISC-R scores were available. (Girls comprise about one-third of all comparison cases.) Of these girls, 70% were referred for testing and evaluation before their 12th birthday, and the average grade placement was grade 5 for the 48 cases for whom grade was known. The majority (60.5%) were referred while in grades 3, 4, 5, or 6; only 12.5% were referred in grades 1 or 2; and 27.1% were referred after grade 6. The average Full-Scale WISC or WISC-R was 103.2 with the range from 72 to 138. Only three cases had scores at or above 125. In addition, another two cases scored 125 or higher on the Performance Scale only. Records for 46 cases included the classification by clinicians, and 93.3% of those were described as having a reading problem.

Of the 31 girls who were given the IRI, 58.1% had a discrepancy of 2 years or more between their listening comprehension and instructional reading level. For those girls, the instructional level was 2 or more years below grade placement in 87% of the cases. A difference of 2 years or more between grade placement and scores on a standardized reading test was found for 12.5% of the 40 cases tested.

Of this group, 16% had a Performance score higher than their Verbal score by 15 points or more on the WISC or WISC-R. Another 10% scored higher on the Verbal Scale than on the Performance Scale by 15 points or more. There were 40 cases for whom the Myklebust (1968) discrepancy formula could be computed. Of these, 35% met the criteria of learning disabled by this method.

A COMPARISON OF THE GROUPS

The average age at the time of referral for the gifted students was a full year younger as compared with students in the control years. Distribution by grade level differed only for the gifted boys, who were likely to be referred at an earlier grade level than students in any other group.

In the comparison groups the percentage of students who were diagnosed by clinicians as having a reading problem was slightly higher than for the gifted sample. A discrepancy of 2 years or more between listening comprehension and instructional reading level, however, was found more often in the gifted groups. Students in the gifted groups were also more likely than the comparison groups to have a dis-

126   *Fox*

crepancy between their Verbal and Performance Scales of the WISC or WISC-R.

If students are viewed as having a reading problem only if they perform below grade level by 2 or more years, a far smaller percentage of gifted than comparison students would be identified. For example, less than one-third of the gifted girls, but 87% of the comparison girls, had an instructional reading level below grade level on an IRI. On the standardized reading tests, twice as many girls and three and a half times as many boys in the comparison groups than in the gifted groups read 2 or more years below grade level. This method would have identified only 6% of the gifted girls, 10% of the gifted boys, and a relatively small percentage of the comparison groups (12.5% of the girls and 36.7% of the boys).

Indeed, standardized test scores reflected that about one-fourth of the gifted group might have been identified as highly able readers because they scored 2 years ahead of grade placement. Only 3.8% of the boys and 7.5% of the girls in the comparison groups scored this high. The Myklebust (1968) discrepancy formula used the student's MA to adjust the expectation for achievement on a standardized test. This method would identify more gifted students than the straight grade discrepancy formula; however, the percentages it identified are still less than the percentages judged by clinicians.

STUDENTS WITH READING
PROBLEMS AS JUDGED BY CLINICIANS

Not all of the students in the sample populations were classified as having a reading problem. Separate analyses were done for those cases classified as having reading problems. The distribution of students by age are shown in Table 6.4. These distributions were essentially the same as for the total samples as were shown in Table 6.1.

The mean scores for the WISC and WISC-R and the percentage who scored above 125 on the Full-Scale, the Verbal Scale only, or the Performance Scale only are shown in Table 6.5. This data did not differ markedly from the data of total samples that were shown in Table 6.2.

One area of interest for this study was whether or not there would be a distinctive pattern of subscale scores for the gifted or the comparison populations. In Table 6.6 scores are shown for those cases who were tested on all the subscales. In the manual for the WISC-R (Wechsler, 1974), tables are provided to indicate the size of the difference between pairs of subscale scores that are considered signifi-

Table 6.4. Distribution of age by percentage for students who had a reading problem as judged by clinicians, by group and sex

| | Gifted | | 1956 and 1979 | |
| | Boys | Girls | Boys | Girls |
Age	(N = 246)	(N = 76)	(N = 88)	(N = 42)
6	4.5	3.9	6.8	2.4
7	17.5	13.2	5.7	9.5
8	15.0	19.7	6.8	19.0
9	18.7	15.8	17.0	19.0
10	13.4	13.2	15.9	9.5
11	7.3	10.5	8.0	11.9
12	7.3	6.6	14.8	9.5
13	8.9	7.9	15.9	7.1
14	7.3	9.2	9.1	11.9

Numbers do not add up to 100 due to rounding.

cant. For the gifted boys, the mean score on Digit Span (DS) was appreciably lower than all of the Verbal Subscales except Arithmetic (A), and the difference was greatest with Similarities (S). For gifted girls, the mean score on Digit Span was appreciably lower than scores on Comprehension (C) and Similarities. In the comparison groups,

Table 6.5. Selected statistics on the WISC or WISC-R, for students who had a reading problem based on clinical judgment, by group and sex

| | Gifted | | 1956 and 1979 | |
| | Boys | Girls | Boys | Girls |
	(N = 246)	(N = 76)	(N = 88)	(N = 42)
WISC—Full-Scale				
$\bar{X}^a$	124.61	125.13	101.90	101.48
SD[b]	6.82	6.45	12.79	13.01
WISC—Verbal				
$\bar{X}$	122.28	121.68	101.15	100.26
SD	11.48	10.81	13.72	12.61
WISC—Performance				
$\bar{X}$	122.76	124.22	102.23	102.57
SD	10.77	11.92	14.11	14.08
Percentage who scored higher than 125				
Full-Scale	54.5	55.3	3.4	2.0
Verbal only	18.7	15.8	0.0	0.0
Performance only	26.8	28.9	5.7	4.8

[a] $\bar{X}$, mean.
[b] SD, standard deviation.

128   Fox

Table 6.6.   Mean scaled scores on the WISC subscales for the gifted and comparison groups by sex who had a reading problem based on clinical judgment, and who had all the subscales

| | Gifted | | 1956 and 1979 | |
| | Boys | Girls | Boys | Girls |
WISC Subscales	(N = 91)	(N = 24)	(N = 83)	(N = 38)
Information	13.64	12.75	9.84	9.45
Comprehension	13.97	15.67	11.17	10.76
Arithmetic	12.30	12.83	9.43	9.37
Similarities	14.32	14.75	10.57	10.42
Vocabulary	13.98	12.83	10.49	9.97
Digit Span	10.84	11.88	8.70	8.74
Picture Completion	14.36	15.25	10.84	10.63
Picture Arrangement	13.53	12.88	11.37	11.05
Block Design	13.90	13.54	10.51	9.79
Object Assembly	13.03	13.83	10.10	9.82
Coding	11.66	13.88	8.58	9.95

Digit Span was the lowest subscale and Comprehension the highest, but the differences were not large enough to be significant. Differences were not sizeable among the Performance Subscales or between Performance and Verbal Subscales for any of the groups.

Scaled subscale scores for the gifted and comparison boys are plotted in Figure 6.1. In addition, Figure 6.1 shows profiles for a sample of gifted boys studied by Lucito and Gallagher (1960) and for a sample of boys of average ability who were judged by clinicians as reading disabled (Ackerman et al., 1971). In this study, the profile for the gifted sample differs from the profile of gifted who had no reading problems in several ways. First, the positioning of Information (I) and Comprehension on the Verbal Scale are different for the two groups. Second, the Digit Span score for the gifted students is considerably lower than all the Verbal Subscales except Arithmetic. This does not occur in the Lucito and Gallagher group. Third, Picture Completion (PC) and Coding (CO) have different relationships as compared with Block Design (BD) in the Performance Subscales.

When the profile for the comparison group of boys in this study was compared with that of similar students in the Ackerman et al. (1971) study, the profiles were very similar. The subjects in this study showed less elevation on the Vocabulary (V) Subscale and lower scores on the Coding Subscale, but not at a statistically significant level.

The intercorrelations of the WISC or WISC-R subscales are shown in Table 6.7 for the gifted samples and in Table 6.8 for the comparison groups. Correlations for girls are shown above the diagonal

Empirical Study 129

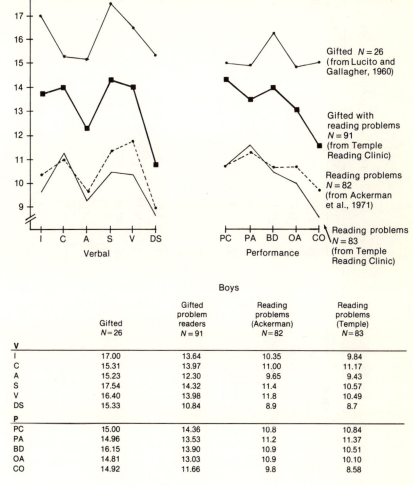

Figure 6.1. WISC profiles for four groups of boys.

and those for boys are below the diagonal. For gifted boys, the subscales which correlated most highly with the Full-Scale score are Information, Arithmetic, and Block Design; for gifted girls, it is Similarities and Block Design.

For comparison boys, the correlations with the Full-Scale score were highest for Information, Similarities, and Block Design; for the girls, they were highest for Similarities and Block Design. Normative data for the sexes combined is provided by the WISC-R manual

Table 6.7. Intercorrelations of the WISC subscales for the gifted group, by sex, who had a reading problem based on clinical judgment

	FS	V	P	I	C	A	S	V	DS	PC	PA	BD	CO
FS	1.00	0.48	0.54	0.30	0.26	0.38	0.40	0.25	0.25	0.35	0.15	0.46	0.19
V	0.65	1.00	−0.48	0.72	0.50	0.68	0.62	0.75	0.47	−0.27	−0.42	−0.09	−0.25
P	0.39	−0.42	1.00	−0.39	−0.21	−0.27	−0.20	−0.47	−0.19	0.62	0.55	0.56	0.42
I	0.40	0.66	−0.32	1.00	0.25	0.51	0.24	0.61	0.25	−0.20	−0.26	−0.10	−0.32
C	0.37	0.59	−0.27	0.27	1.00	0.15	0.29	0.16	0.08	−0.07	−0.19	−0.15	−0.09
A	0.40	0.52	−0.15	0.32	0.08	1.00	0.24	0.56	0.26	−0.21	−0.20	−0.04	−0.19
S	0.38	0.65	−0.33	0.37	0.42	0.27	1.00	0.45	0.09	−0.19	−0.30	0.08	−0.09
V	0.35	0.61	−0.33	0.46	0.41	0.12	0.45	1.00	0.21	−0.39	−0.23	−0.16	−0.31
DS	0.25	0.41	−0.19	0.21	0.05	0.20	0.05	0.11	1.00	−0.03	−0.34	0.00	0.02
PC	0.23	−0.17	0.49	−0.16	−0.10	−0.14	−0.19	−0.11	−0.10	1.00	0.19	0.17	0.04
PA	0.05	−0.28	0.41	−0.24	−0.03	−0.25	−0.17	0.02	−0.19	0.06	1.00	0.03	0.01
BD	0.24	−0.17	0.52	−0.18	−0.22	0.04	−0.14	−0.24	−0.10	0.16	−0.10	1.00	0.04
CO	0.22	0.01	0.26	0.00	−0.01	0.09	−0.06	−0.11	−0.05	0.02	−0.07	0.08	1.00

Correlations for girls are shown in the upper right diagonal of the table, and correlations for boys are shown in the lower left diagonal. The number of cases for girls is 69 and the number for boys is 233.

Table 6.8. Intercorrelations of the WISC subscales for the comparison group, by sex, who had a reading problem based on clinical judgment

	FS	V	P	I	C	A	S	V	DS	PC	PA	BD	CO
FS	1.00	0.88	0.88	0.65	0.64	0.64	0.72	0.59	0.20	0.46	0.47	0.78	0.48
V	0.83	1.00	0.57	0.76	0.76	0.68	0.76	0.73	0.29	0.32	0.30	0.57	0.31
P	0.81	0.37	1.00	0.39	0.39	0.47	0.49	0.33	0.09	0.50	0.53	0.80	0.57
I	0.66	0.80	0.27	1.00	0.43	0.58	0.49	0.46	0.31	0.19	0.16	0.42	0.20
C	0.54	0.63	0.26	0.45	1.00	0.43	0.50	0.56	0.14	0.29	0.23	0.39	0.14
A	0.65	0.74	0.32	0.53	0.29	1.00	0.27	0.25	0.31	0.44	0.23	0.45	0.25
S	0.66	0.81	0.27	0.64	0.41	0.50	1.00	0.62	-0.05	0.17	0.34	0.49	0.23
V	0.65	0.79	0.28	0.59	0.54	0.56	0.58	1.00	0.05	0.10	0.15	0.19	0.44
DS	0.50	0.55	0.28	0.37	0.06	0.53	0.38	0.22	1.00	0.09	0.11	0.31	-0.02
PC	0.60	0.26	0.74	0.20	0.18	0.13	0.19	0.28	0.23	1.00	-0.02	0.36	-0.01
PA	0.56	0.32	0.62	0.21	0.30	0.19	0.25	0.28	0.06	0.41	1.00	0.38	0.21
BD	0.66	0.32	0.78	0.25	0.07	0.43	0.22	0.22	0.34	0.46	0.33	1.00	0.24
CO	0.48	0.23	0.58	0.14	0.15	0.28	0.19	0.14	0.25	0.29	0.20	0.30	1.00

Correlations for girls are shown in the upper right diagonal of the table, and correlations for boys are shown in the lower left diagonal. The number of cases for girls is 39 and for boys is 86.

132   Fox

Table 6.9.   The Bannatyne recategorization of WISC subscale scores for students with a reading problem as judged by clinicians, by group and sex

WISC subscale categories	Gifted		1956 and 1979	
	Boys (N = 91)	Girls (N = 24)	Boys (N = 83)	Girls (N = 38)
Conceptual	14.09	14.42	10.74	10.38
Spatial	13.76	14.21	10.48	10.08
Acquired	13.31	12.80	9.92	9.60
Sequential	11.60	12.86	8.90	9.35

(Wechsler, 1974). Among the Performance Subscales for this normative group, Block Design correlated most highly, and the Verbal Subscales that most correlated with the Full-Scale were Vocabulary and Similarities.

Several researchers have attempted to compare children who have reading problems with those who have no problems by using a recategorization of the WISC subscales first developed by Bannatyne (1968) and revised in 1974 based on the work of Rugel (1974). In this scheme, there are four clusters as follows:

1.   Acquired Knowledge = Information + Arithmetic + Vocabulary
2.   Spatial = Picture Completion + Block Design + Object Assembly
3.   Conceptual = Comprehension + Similarities + Vocabulary
4.   Sequencing = Digit Span + Arithmetic + Coding

The pattern most often associated with reading problems is high spatial and low sequencing with conceptual in between. Normal readers are often described as highest in conceptual and lowest in sequencing with spatial in between (Rugel, 1974). Table 6.9 shows the scores on these clusters for the samples in this study. All the groups have the pattern associated most often with normal rather than disabled readers.

In Table 6.10, the four groups are characterized by the degree to which they meet the criteria for several common discrepancy formulas. For the gifted boys and girls and the comparison boys, the difference of 2 or more years between listening comprehension and instructional reading level as measured by the IRI is highly related to clinical judgment. Very few students in any of the four groups showed a difference of 2 or more years between their grade placement and standardized test scores for reading comprehension. Adjusting this for MA, as in the Myklebust (1968) formula, increased the relationship to clinical judgment. This method, however, still does not agree highly with clinical judgment, especially for the gifted group. In these analyses, MA was based on the results of the WISC or WISC-R. If a group test had been used instead, the percentage identified would probably have been even smaller.

Discrepancies on the WISC or WISC-R subscales were found in the gifted samples more often than the comparison group. Clinicians, however, judged many students who differed by less than 15 points between the Verbal and Performance Scales to have reading problems. This was especially true for the 1956 and 1979 groups. Specific differences between Similarities and Digit Span of three or more scaled score points were found for a sizeable number of gifted students.

The case reports for most students included a judgment by clinicians as to whether or not specific perceptual or information-processing problems existed. This was based on a variety of measures. The percentages of students in each group that were rated unsatisfactory with respect to these processes are shown in Table 6.11.

Table 6.10. Numbers and percentages of students judged by clinicians to have a reading problem and who also met the criteria for a variety of discrepancy formulas, by group and sex

Methods of determining problems	Gifted		1956 and 1979	
	Boys	Girls	Boys	Girls
Listening comprehension exceeded instructional reading level by 2 or more years	174 of 200 (87.0)[a]	42 of 51 (82.4)	49 of 63 (77.8)	17 of 28 (60.7)
Achievement test score 2 or more years below grade	21 of 205 (10.2)	5 of 64 (7.8)	27 of 71 (38.0)	4 of 36 (11.1)
Discrepancy on the WISC				
V-P $\geq$ 15	55 of 246 (22.4)	18 of 76 (23.7)	14 of 88 (15.9)	4 of 42 (9.5)
P-V $\geq$ 15	62 of 246 (25.2)	25 of 76 (32.9)	15 of 88 (17.0)	7 of 42 (16.7)
S-DS $\geq$ 3	154 of 235 (65.5)	42 of 71 (59.2)	40 of 86 (46.5)	14 of 41 (34.1)
Discrepancy for Myklebust formula	78 of 205 (38.0)	22 of 64 (34.4)	43 of 71 (60.6)	14 of 36 (38.9)

[a] The number refers to the number of cases for whom analysis was possible, and the percentage is the percentage of those who met the criteria.

134   Fox

Table 6.11.   Percentages of students judged by clinicians as having a
reading problem who were rated unsatisfactory on factors to perception and
processing information, by group and sex.

	Gifted		1956 and 1979	
	Boys (N = 245)	Girls (N = 75)	Boys (N = 84)	Girls (N = 40)
Vision	30.6	32.0	21.4	37.5
Visual discrimination	16.7	8.0	25.0	12.5
Hearing	9.0	5.3	12.0[a]	15.0
Auditory discrimination	11.8	1.3	20.5[a]	10.0
Laterality	8.2	4.0	7.1	5.0
Reversals	11.9[b]	13.3	32.5[a]	10.0
Language development	14.0[c]	09.3	13.3[a]	12.5
Speech	6.6[c]	6.7	2.5[d]	5.1[e]
Personality	51.9[b]	41.3	57.8[a]	45.0

[a] Based on 83 cases.
[b] Based on 243 cases.
[c] Based on 242 cases.
[d] Based on 81 cases.
[e] Based on 39 cases.

Information about such problems as vision, hearing, and reversals was included. For example, visual discrimination and auditory discrimination problems were reported more frequently for boys than girls and for the comparison groups than the gifted.

In many cases, tests of personality were also administered. The clinicians combined that information with interview data for an overall rating of satisfactory or unsatisfactory on personality. The percentages of children judged to have some personality problems are shown in Table 6.11. It can be speculated that behavior problems in the home or school rather than the recognition of a problem in learning and school achievement led some parents or teachers to suggest clinical evaluation.

IDENTIFYING THE LEARNING-DISABLED/GIFTED CHILD

Although the number of students who scored 125 or higher on the Verbal, Performance, or Full-Scale WISC or WISC-R in the Temple University Clinic population was as high as 17% in 1979 and 10% as early as 1956, no generalizations about the actual incidence of gifted among the learning-disabled students in the general school population can be made. It can be speculated that the numbers would be higher

Empirical Study 135

in the schools than in the Temple population. Of the gifted cases that were judged by the clinicians to have a reading problem, only 10% performed 2 or more years below grade placement on a standardized reading test, a discrepancy most likely used for school screenings. Thus, a far larger percentage scored at or above grade level making it unlikely that schools would refer students for evaluation. Even formulas which adjust for MA and achievement discrepancies as opposed to chronological age and achievement differences would identify only one-third of the learning-disabled/gifted youngsters in the Temple population. If group measures of MA were used in school settings, the proportions probably would be even smaller. It seems logical to conclude that the vast majority of students who might be judged by clinical evaluation to be learning-disabled/gifted students would seem to be nongifted and nondisabled in most settings.

It is also interesting to note that there was a 2–1 ratio of boys to girls in the comparison years. Among the gifted, there was a 3–1 ratio of boys to girls. Are learning problems more common for boys, especially among the most able? A rival hypothesis might be that there are nearly equal numbers of boys and girls in school settings; but girls who do not perform as well as they are capable of performing are simply less likely to vent anger or frustration in ways that will lead parents or teachers to notice them. Thus, girls are less likely to be referred for clinical evaluation.

It is clearly desirable to determine the following: 1) ways to notice giftedness among learning-disabled populations; 2) ways to screen for learning or reading problems among those identified as gifted; and 3) ways to screen for both learning problems and giftedness in the general population. Ideally, there should be techniques that classroom teachers, school psychologists, and reading specialists could use to initially screen for referral and subsequently, more in-depth clinical assessment.

Academically gifted youngsters are typically described in terms of their wealth of information and extensive vocabularies; however, it seems that the strength of gifted children with reading problems lies more in verbal reasoning abilities as assessed by the Similarities and Comprehension Subscales of the WISC or WISC-R than in accumulated knowledge. This seems true most frequently for those who are identified as gifted based on their Full-Scale or Verbal Scale scores as compared with those who qualified as gifted based on the Performance Scale only.

Table 6.12 shows that in the total samples, the percentages of students who had a scaled score of 15 or higher (equivalent to 125 on

136   Fox

Table 6.12. Percentages of students scoring higher than 15 on selected WISC subscales by group and sex.

| | Gifted | | | | 1956 and 1979 | |
| | 125 on Total or V | | 125 on P only | | | |
WISC subscales	Boys (N = 241)	Girls (N = 84)	Boys (N = 80)	Girls (N = 27)	Boys (N = 98)	Girls (N = 50)
Information	54.2[a]	42.9	5.0	3.7	4.1	6.0
Comprehension	58.6[b]	61.9	11.3[c]	18.5	13.3	8.0
Arithmetic	33.8[a]	32.1	3.8[c]	3.7	6.1	8.0
Similarities	76.7	76.2	24.1[c]	18.7	10.2	2.0
Vocabulary	58.5	58.3	7.6	3.7	9.4[d]	0.0
Digit Span	10.7[e]	18.2[f]	2.5[c]	0.0[g]	3.1	4.2[h]
Picture Comprehension	35.7	35.7	51.3	44.4	11.2	10.0
Picture Arrangement	26.7[a]	23.8	46.3	21.3	21.4	10.0
Block Design	41.0[b]	33.3	42.5	29.6[g]	9.2	14.0
Coding	13.8[a]	29.3[j]	20.0	48.1	2.1[i]	14.3[k]

[a] Based on 240 cases.
[b] Based on 239 cases.
[c] Based on 79 cases.
[d] Based on 96 cases.
[e] Based on 225 cases.
[f] Based on 77 cases.
[g] Based on 26 cases.
[h] Based on 48 cases.
[i] Based on 82 cases.
[j] Based on 97 cases.
[k] Based on 49 cases.

Empirical Study   137

the Full-Scale) on each subscale are shown. About three-quarters of the gifted boys and girls who scored 125 on the Full-Scale or Verbal Scale also scored 15 or higher on Similarities. Those who qualified only on the Performance Scale tended to score highest on Picture Completion (PC), followed by Block Design for boys and Coding for girls. Only a relatively small percentage of the comparison groups scored this high. Thus, it would seem desirable to study further ways to investigate the use of selected WISC-R subscales to identify giftedness among learning-disabled children and also to try a group test like the Raven's Progressive Matrices, which measures abstract reasoning but not vocabulary and information.

The analysis of data for the gifted and comparison groups suggested no definitive profile on the WISC-R that could be used for quick screening, although a significant discrepancy between Similarities and Digit Span did appear frequently in the gifted groups. Perhaps the most promising avenue of research is for teachers to use an IRI for quick screening with emphasis on the discrepancy between listening comprehension and instructional level, even if the child is reading at grade level. More validation of the IRI technique is needed.

CONCLUSION

On the basis of the analyses of the files at the Temple University Reading Clinic, it seems safe to conclude that learning-disabled/gifted children do indeed exist. Furthermore, it seems likely that the vast majority are unrecognized as such because their disability is not severe enough for their performance to be noticeably below grade-level expectations on standardized tests or in normal classroom functioning. Many interesting questions are suggested from the analyses of this very special sample drawn from an independent clinic.

If learning-disabled students are defined as those with average to above-average intelligence who show a sizeable discrepancy between performance and potential, this data suggests most of the brightest children with problems will not be identified by the types of screening techniques commonly used by schools. Clearly, a thorough screening and clinical evaluation of all children in a school system would be necessary to determine the exact numbers of learning-disabled students and the percentage of those who could also be described as intellectually gifted. Such an undertaking would be costly. Thus, other means must be established. Data analysis herein suggests that an initial screening by classroom teachers on the IRI might be efficient and effective, and it would require little time or money. This approach

138   *Fox*

seems likely at least to identify more children who would be judged learning disabled/gifted by clinicians than discrepancy formulas that involve standardized group test data. Nor does continued search for a quick screening on selected WISC-R subscales seem the optimal strategy.

Considerably more research, however, is needed to describe better the various patterns of strengths and weaknesses that might be found among this population so that better educational prescriptions and techniques can be devised. Some thorny issues have yet to be confronted. For example, should children with high Performance Scale scores but more nearly average Verbal and Full-Scale scores be judged as learning-disabled readers if they perform at grade level? Does their pattern simply suggest that their giftedness lies elsewhere?

If most learning-disabled/gifted students function near grade level, they may not require extensive remedial reading programs; but they can benefit from small modifications or adaptations (described in Chapter 10) in order to function in classes designed for the intellectually able. The fact that some students may be experiencing frustration and developing poor self-concepts and even more severe emotional reactions suggests that some intervention is necessary indeed. All children should be treated in the classroom as individuals with unique patterns of strengths and weaknesses. This will require some individualized prescription to maximize the full development of all of their intellectual abilities. Until such a time, society is likely to fail to identify and nurture many potentially gifted people.

REFERENCES

Ackerman, P.T., Peters, J.E., and Dykman, R.A. 1971. Children with specific learning disabilities: WISC profiles. J. Learn. Disabil. 4:150–166.

Bannatyne, A. 1968. Diagnosing learning disabilities and writing remedial prescriptions. J. Learn. Disabil. 1:242–249.

Bannatyne, A. 1974. Diagnosis: A note on recategorization of the WISC scaled scores. J. Learn. Disabil. 7:272–273.

Berk, R.A. An evaluation of procedures for computing an ability-achievement discrepancy score. J. Learn. Disabil. In press.

Hoffman, J. 1980. The disabled reader: Forgive us our regressions and lead us not into expectations. J. Learn. Disabil. 13:7–11.

Kaufman, A. 1979. Intelligence Testing With the WISC-R. John Wiley and Sons, Inc., New York.

Lucito, L., and Gallagher, J. 1960. Intellectual patterns of highly gifted children on the WISC. Peabody J. Educ. 38:131–136.

Myklebust, H.R., (ed.) 1968. Progress in Learning Disabilities, Vol. 1. Grune and Stratton, New York.

Rugel, R. 1974. WISC subtest scores of disabled readers: A review with respect to Bannatyne's recategorization. J. Learn. Disabil. 7:57–64.

Wechsler, D. 1974. Manual for the Wechsler Intelligence Scale for Children-Revised. Psychological Corp., New York.

Chapter 7

Diagnosis
A Case-Typing Approach
Stanley L. Rosner

The reasoning process that a clinician uses to evaluate a youngster with a learning problem is complicated. Conclusions are based on a web of evidence of mutually confirming data. David S. is an example of such a case. In Figure 7.1, a completed case-typing sheet shows the results of a clinical evaluation of David S. The graphic presentation of a case-typing sheet helps the clinician get a total picture of the child's functioning. This Chapter explores the steps taken by a clinician in making a diagnosis about a child. Specific references are made to the case-typing approach and how it helps the clinician reach a conclusion. Although it is presented as an individual effort in this case, discussions such as those that follow are usually team efforts, with the team working together to understand the child's problem.

EVALUATION OF DAVID S.

David S. was 8 years old when his mother brought him in for evaluation. Although he was doing average work in school, Mrs. S. sensed that David had greater ability than he was utilizing. She also seemed troubled by his tendency to function in a highly inconsistent manner from day to day.

Case History

The first major area of information which was examined was case history. This would be summarized in the lower right corner of the case-typing sheet. Mrs. S. said that basically, the family was stable and happy. David's father is a physician and his mother, who earned a bachelor's degree in college, is occupied full-time as a homemaker. There are five children in the family: George, age 13; Steven, age 12;

141

Client David S.
Case no. I Grade 3
Date of birth ______ Age 8-6 Mental age 11-2

Date ______
Clinician ______

Parent ______
Address ______
Phone ______

Profile Section

Intellectual functioning	Informal Word Recognition Inventory: Level	Flash	Unflash	Spell	IRI	Standardized achievement tests	Discrimination: Auditory	Visual
Vocabulary 18 Similarities 18 Comprehension 18 Block Design 17 Picture Completion 16								
Verbal 135 Full-Scale I.Q. 132							Adequate	
Performance 123 Arithmetic 12	Preprimer Primer 1 2 3	100 85 75 55 50	100 85 75 60 55	I 80 II 40	Independ. 1 Instruction 2 Frustration 4	Arithmetic Computation 4.2 Word Recognition 2.8		Slow in making discriminations
Picture Arrangement 11 Object Assembly 11 Digit Span 11 Coding 11						Paragraph Meaning 1.7		

Associative learning	Memory span	Language and conceptual development	Lateral and perceptual motor	Social and emotional adjustment	Screenings
					Vision ✓
(Gates) Visual/Visual Geometric (A-1) 7+ Visual/Auditory Geometric (B-1) 6.0	(Detroit) Oral Directions 11-9 Auditory Related 11-3	Verbal Opposites 12-0	Bender Gestalt	High goal setting	Hearing ✓
Visual/Auditory Word like (B-2) 3.0 Visual/Visual word like (A-2) 2.0	Auditory Unrelated 9-0 Visual Objects 7-0			Anxious	Neurological ✓
	Visual letters 5-9			Regressive	Speech ✓

Case-typing: Learning disabled/Gifted
Recommended instructional setting: Regular classroom (gifted programming–reading help)
Psychological approach: Multisensory word learning
Pedagogical approach: Experience approach
Referrals: ______
Prognosis: Good
Parental reaction: ______

Alternative recommendations:

Case history:
Somewhat slow in motor development
Age 3½, clumsy and incoordinate–vision problem corrected by glasses
Tends to overeat—fussy after school
Bladder training late
School learning uneven and inconsistent
In Reading Resource Program
Sibling conflict

Figure 7.1. Case-typing sheet.

Figure 7.1. Case-typing sheet.

David, age 8; Jessica, age 5; and Matthew, age 3. Mrs. S. indicated that all of the school-age children have been doing very well academically. In discussing developmental factors, Mrs. S. noted that there were no difficulties with pregnancy or birth although David was born unusually large, weighing 10 pounds. In reviewing the various developmental milestones after birth, Mrs. S. indicated that David seemed within normal limits. She said that except for somewhat slower development of motor behavior, he progressed much like the other children. It seemed to her that he walked somewhat later than the other youngsters and was not nearly as interested in manipulative kinds of activities. It was also noted that David's apparent clumsy and uncoordinated behavior at about the age of 3½ was related to a visual problem, which was corrected with glasses. He has been wearing them since then, and his vision now is at the normal (20/20) level. Regular contact with physicians and specialists has suggested nothing unusual about David's physical or health development.

In fact, David's health history was reported to be excellent. His mother noted that his excellent appetite at times causes him to overeat somewhat, and in spite of her attempts to downplay the importance of food, he has gained 15 pounds in the past year. She also indicated that when he comes home from school, he frequently is rather "out of sorts" and quite hungry. Significantly, David mastered most socialization activities at the appropriate time with the exception of toilet training. Until about age 7, he had several occasions of wetting himself. This would happen most frequently when he was out playing rather than when he was in school or at home.

David entered nursery school at about age 4½. He had no difficulty being apart from his mother and got along very well with the other children. He was characterized as bright and active, but Mrs. S. noted that he had considerable difficulty learning the names of colors. He entered kindergarten at the age of 5½, continued to have an excellent adjustment, and was well-accepted by both other youngsters and his teacher. However, the kindergarten teacher noted that he had difficulty settling down to work. Reports from grades 1 and 2 continued to suggest a good adjustment, but indicated further that David was quite uneven in his performance and often had trouble sitting still or concentrating for extended periods of time. Because of this inconsistency, he was enrolled in grade 2, in the Reading Resource Program and moved from the lowest to the middle reading group.

In describing David from a checklist of adjectives, Mrs. S. suggested that he was impulsive, easily frustrated, distractible, and had a short attention span. She felt that he was poorly organized, restless,

144   *Rosner*

and often daydreamed. Furthermore, she felt that he very frequently needed to have directions broken into individual steps in order to deal with them effectively.

Within the family, David is often the target for his two older brothers. Particularly when he tries to act like a "big guy," they have to "knock him down a peg." He is very active, participates in a number of sports, and is characterized as a youngster who keeps himself rather busy. He is seen as a leader in many social situations and gets along very well with both children and adults. Mrs. S. noted that she found David to be a friendly child with a nice sense of humor and indicated that for the most part, he was able to be helpful and responsible.

As with many youngsters who have learning problems but are gifted, the data from the case history does not contain large, obvious "red flags" to draw attention to particular areas. There is some suggestion of developmental slowness in the motor area, a visual problem which was corrected early, some suggestion of psychological immaturity because of the extended period of time necessary for David to stop wetting himself, and some indication that perhaps he is a target for his siblings' anger. The case history does not present a significant collection of data in any single area sufficient to allow a strong hypothesis about David at this time. However, additional evidence may help to pull some of the case history data into focus.

Intelligence

The next area to be considered is intelligence. The results of the Wechsler Intelligence Scale for Children-Revised (WISC-R) can be found in the column entitled Intellectual Functioning (the extreme left-hand side of the case-typing sheet). David's Full-Scale intelligence test score is represented across the case-typing sheet by the central horizontal line. This sets up the standard for assessing the relative adequacy or inadequacy of each of the areas evaluated. Scores found above this line indicate a level of functioning at or above intellectual functioning in those areas. Scores which appear below this line indicate the areas in which the child is performing below intellectual capacity. In David's case, there is a discrepancy between the verbal and performance functioning in favor of the verbal scores. This is not unusual in bright youngsters who come from culturally enriched homes. It is frequently seen in an even more dramatic fashion when they are younger. In David's case, however, it is important not to stop at the comparison between Verbal and Performance scores; rather, the individual subscales should be examined to see if it can be confirmed or refuted that David is a youngster who, in spite of being gifted, has a learning disability.

About one-half of the subtests that were administered point very dramatically to David's giftedness. In the measures of Vocabulary, Similarities, and Comprehension, he scores very close to the upper limits of the test. All of these involve mastery of oral expression, sensitivity to information available in the environment, and an ability to think in a high-level fashion. David also scores quite well on two subscales which are not verbal in nature—the Block Design measure and the Picture Completion measure. The Block Design performance indicates a youngster with good problem-solving ability, and Picture Completion suggests sensitivity to detail. As with most youngsters, the quality of David's responses indicates as much about the nature of his intelligence as the quantitative score. In David's case, verbal responses were elaborated without much questioning, and his problem solving was quick and systematic.

In examining David's lowest scores, it is important to note that first, nothing is below the high part of the average range; second, if there is a thread which unifies all of his less adequate subtests, it is that they all involve the ability to attend and concentrate. In addition, the Coding Subtest involves perceptual motor coordination. Thus, there is some confirmation from the intelligence test results for what was noted in the case history. David is indeed a youngster who seems less adequate in focusing his mental energies than his overall intellectual endowment would suggest, and he seems to have somewhat greater difficulty with fine motor coordination than would be expected given his potential. At this point, there is good reason to believe that David is a gifted youngster, as this term is operationally defined, but additional information is required to be certain that his mother's perception of underachievement is accurate. He does show some of the characteristics of youngsters who have learning problems because of his consistent difficulty in approaching his potential on measures which involve focusing his mental energies.

Word Recognition and Spelling

The results of the Informal Word Recognition Inventory (IWRI) are shown in the second column of the case-typing sheet. These results suggest that David's ability to comfortably recognize words begins to break down at grade 2 level and becomes quite deficient at grade 3 level. More important than the simple level of competence in isolation, however, is the virtual lack of difference between his scores on the flash part of the test, which assesses sight vocabulary, and his scores on the untimed part of the test, which assesses word analysis skills. David shows a typical pattern for a gifted youngster with some learning difficulty; that is, a tendency to memorize as much as possible. The IWRI results indicate that David has memorized a good number of words; but if words are not a part of his sight vocabulary, he has not mastered the skills necessary to figure them out. This impression is reinforced by his performance in spelling, shown in the third column on the case-typing sheet. Here, he either knew the words or devised a series of letters which frequently bore little resemblance to the word. It is important again to point out an area in which confirmation of other data is gained—that David's handwriting and spelling were extremely poor. This confirms his difficulty with perceptual motor coordination, noted on the intelligence test, as well as his mother's report that he had difficulty with fine motor coordination as a youngster.

Reading

The informal reading inventory (IRI) is an instrument designed to help assess David's overall level of competence in reading. The results of David's IRI are shown in the fourth column of the case-typing sheet. They suggest that David is able to profit from instruction as high as grade 2 level. Grade 3 material does not frustrate him, but neither is he able to utilize it for instruction because he approaches a level of frustration. It must be emphasized that the standard for adequacy for David should not be grade level but should be based instead on his intelligence, which is significantly greater than his current placement. It should be noted also, that on the IRI, David frequently was able to answer questions following selections that he had found difficult to manage in terms of word recognition. Again, his basic brightness allowed him to utilize whatever information he received from reading the words; he coupled this with some of the clues that are implicit in the questioning process at lower levels. As a result, a youngster like David can "fake out" the teacher even in fairly carefully structured reading lessons. The impact of David's deficit in reading on his ability to understand what he had read can be seen only as the demands for higher level comprehension and more independent functioning are increased.

Achievement

The results of standardized achievement tests that were administered to David are shown also on the case-typing sheet. He received a grade equivalent score of 4.2, which was reasonably close to his potential. He also was able to demonstrate the ability to do better on brief word recognition measures than on the subtest which required him to read short selections and then pick out a correct answer to fill in a blank. While taking this test, it was noted that he had real difficulty adhering to its demands, and toward the end of the test, he seemed to be guessing in a rather random fashion.

Readiness

The area labeled auditory and visual discrimination on the case-typing sheet represents the readiness skills that are necessary for a youngster to deal successfully with reading instruction. As indicated on the case-typing sheet, David had some difficulty with the measures of Visual-Perception and Discrimination. This coupled with problems he had in comprehending words that he could not immediately recognize and the early visual difficulty noted in the case history seems to develop another thread of evidence composed of several strands of information.

Associative Learning

Moving across the case-typing sheet to the associative learning area, it can be noted that only two of his scores on the Gates Associative Learning Test are above the expected level of functioning. This test measures the ability to make associations with geometric designs or wordlike patterns and visual or visual/auditory input. It is also significant, however, that on this measure, David did less well on the symbol-learning task. The relative position of these scores continues to give a sense that David is a youngster with a possible deficit in terms of processing wordlike symbols. The Associative Learning Test usually is utilized to help distinguish between youngsters with a primary reading disability and those with more secondary or symptomatic problems. In David's case, he does not seem to have a clear-cut primary reading deficit, but certainly has enough interference for concern about not reaching his potential.

Memory Span

The Memory Span battery, which is taken from the Detroit Tests of Learning Aptitude, provides additional information along the same lines. Simply examining the range of scores confirms Mrs. S's impression of David's inconsistency and the difficulty in consistently attending and concentrating that was previously noted. Additionally, there seems to be some tendency for David to do less well with some tasks that require visual attention and concentration than on tasks which are either multisensory or auditory in nature.

148   *Rosner*

Language and Conceptual Development

The data on language and conceptual development which is generated from the Detroit Verbal Opposites Subscale simply replicates what had been noted previously in discussion of the intelligence test. It is also further confirmation of David's basically good intellectual potential, indicated by his excellent score on the Verbal Opposites Subscale.

Developmental Skills and Personal Adjustment

Information related to developmental skills and personal adjustment is included in the columns labeled Lateral and Perceptual Motor and Social and Emotional Adjustment, to be found at the right on the case-typing sheet. No indications of difficulty were noted in either laterality or perceptual motor development, and although David's performance on the Bender Gestalt was not an elegant copy of the designs, it did represent an age-appropriate performance. In the social and emotional adjustment area, it is possible to note the presence of some anxiety coupled with a rather high-level set of goals that David has for himself. He seems to enter the learning situation much as his mother describes him in interaction with his brothers; that is, he attempts to meet their level of competence rather than tailor his goals to his own level of skill and ability. He also seems to be a youngster who uses some regressive tendency, such as becoming overly involved in nurturance (overeating) when frustrated.

Screenings

David was screened in the areas of vision, hearing, neurological functioning, and speech. The results appear in the far right column on the case-typing sheet. David showed no problems in any of the screening areas.

CONCLUSION

An overview of the data presented, then, can be viewed either quantitatively or graphically on the case-typing sheet. First, it seems that David really is a gifted youngster based on the upper limits of his functioning and his intelligence test scores. Second, it is obvious that David's giftedness is not completely obvious in day-to-day situations because of the inconsistent nature of his functioning and his failure to demonstrate his level of potential in the achievement area. Indeed, in many teachers' minds, a youngster who does not perform at a gifted level is not really gifted, regardless of the other indications of potential.

Diagnosis 149

David shows a mild but rather persistent set of deficits in terms of visual input of information. There were deficits in a number of the discrimination tests as well as in Associative Learning and Memory Span. In addition, although David's copying of the Bender Gestalt design was a reasonably adequate performance for someone his age, his ability to recall and reproduce any of the designs after the copyface had been finished was clearly inadequate. With David, it is possible to see not only the impact of some developmental needs on his learning but also the impact on his overall personal adjustment. He operates at a level consistent with his potential when talking to others and thinking about his own goals, but becomes frustrated and anxious when he perceives his own inability to function at the level which he deems appropriate for himself.

A youngster like David requires very careful programming in a school situation. He should have access to all of those opportunities available to gifted youngsters; at the same time, he should be provided with supportive, tutorial work in areas such as reading and writing so that he can fully realize his potential before the increased frustration overwhelms his basically good learning skills. Prognosis for David would be good provided his needs are met both educationally and psychologically within the school and within the family.

PART **III**

PROGRAMMING

Chapter 8

Teaching the Learning-Disabled/Gifted Child

Paul R. Daniels

There seems to be no doubt that a group of children can be identified as basically gifted yet learning disabled. However, efforts to meet the rather specific needs of these children have been minimal at best. Unfortunately, when attempts have been made, the emphasis has been on the remediation of the learning disability, excluding the needs brought about by the giftedness. This is perhaps because the learning disability is so often much more observable than the giftedness.

Essentially, the learning disabilities must be dealt with if the giftedness is ever to be of value to the children. In many remedial programs for learning disabilities, however, the gifted children would actually suffer rather than prosper. Therefore, it is important to note what basic modifications of learning disability programs must be made to accommodate gifted children. On the whole, however, this is seldom done.

Children's needs that are generated by their giftedness should be addressed. These children often bring intense interest and high levels of information to the learning situation as well as elements of academic sophistication to the planned activities. When these aspects of their personalities are thwarted by highly structured remedial programs, negativism and behavior difficulties are often forthcoming.

ADMINISTRATIVE CONSIDERATIONS

If learning-disabled/gifted children are going to receive the services they need, certain current practices in education need to be reevaluated and changed. It must be recognized that the population being addressed is small which, in and of itself, puts a burden on the school

153

154   *Daniels*

and the teacher. It becomes very difficult for a teacher to deal with the unique problems of a single child in the context of dealing with a class that is too frequently too large. Therefore, in order to address the needs of these children, changes must begin at the administrative level of the local school district.

Placement

PL 94-142 never mentions mainstreaming, but instead requires the least restrictive environment. This concept unfortunately has often been misinterpreted to mean that normal classroom placement is always the least restrictive environment. For many learning-disabled students, especially those that are also gifted, that concept is patently untrue.

Many of these children might be better served in a full-time special education class, with or without mainstreaming in different academic areas. The frustration of children in trying to understand and deal with both abilities and disabilities might well lead to a fight or flight reaction. For a child to know that in the areas of knowledge, concepts, and interests, he or she is superior to most other classmates but lags seriously behind them in processing abilities must lead to confusion and self-doubt. Peer ridicule also could be a logical by-product of an incorrect placement.

Placement which will meet the needs of the learning-disabled/ gifted child then becomes one of the most important aspects of the overall program. Therefore, the concept that learning-disabled/gifted children should receive their instruction together is advocated. If it is impossible to develop an entire class or group, then a small group within another group is preferable. The concern over elitism must be shunted aside as a detrimental factor in the education of very bright children with learning problems. The banner of egalitarianism has led these children to a point where in many cases they have been deprived of the possibilities of living to their full potential.

Several alternatives to consider might be:

1. A total program of instruction in a self-contained classroom for some of the learning-disabled/gifted children
2. Basic placement in the self-contained classroom for appropriate subject matter and a pull-out program into regular classrooms or gifted and talented classrooms, whichever would be most appropriate for some of the children
3. Regular or gifted and talented placement and pull-out into the learning-disabled/gifted classroom for special education placement for other children.

Teaching Learning Disabled/Gifted   155

All of these alternatives provide learning-disabled/gifted students with some interaction with other learning-disabled/gifted peers for at least part of the day.

Although part-time special educational placement for learning-disabled/gifted children is the least satisfactory organizational plan, it can be effective if there is a strong organizational system to guarantee that the children will not be lost in a confusion of adult assignments. First, there must be an understood, and probably written, agreement concerning which teacher will have the basic responsibility for developing and carrying out the instructional program. Second, someone must assume the role of case manager. A child should not be lost because no one is monitoring the instructional program.

To develop a separate total class of learning-disabled/gifted children by school grade is probably impossible, but serious thought should be given to a special education placement class—probably a primary (grades 1–3), intermediate (grades 4–6), and middle (grades 5–8) placement opportunity. This classroom placement would allow the best opportunity to meet the requirements of the least restrictive environment. If this is not possible, a grouping of grades 1–5 or 6 could be investigated. In addition, districts might combine their children to provide this needed instruction. Mutually accepted financial arrangements for housing, teachers, and materials could surely be made. It also seems reasonable that the parents of these children would be grateful and appreciative of the effort and concern of school personnel, who would invest so much of their time and energy for such a program. Goodwill would almost surely replace the hostility so obvious in the parents of many of these children.

Teacher Characteristics

If a separate multiage, multigrade level class for learning-disabled/gifted students can be organized in a school, clinical, or university setting, one teacher should be assigned to work with them. Preferably, the teacher should be trained in learning disabilities and also have experience with gifted children. Such teachers should have a number of important personal characteristics and learned behaviors. For example, teachers of the learning-disabled/gifted need to be well-adjusted to recognize that a child's negative behaviors represent nothing personal at all. These teachers should be able to deal with such behaviors constructively. They must also be able to accept and use the anger and hurt of these children's parents to help establish an educationally supportive home environment. They must sense when scheduled activities need to be terminated and different activities introduced, and

156   *Daniels*

must be adaptable yet not be caught up in the diversionary techniques of the children. If teachers become so rigid that necessary adjustments are precluded or if they become so flexible that they are manipulated by the children, then the necessary support structures that the children need in order for learning to occur are never erected in the program. Finally, learning-disabled/gifted teachers must develop enough ego to value their skills, competencies, and knowledge when dealing with other professionals. The teachers should not hold other professionals, such as physicians, psychologists, or social workers in awe. They must have enough self-respect to deal with other professionals as different but equal contributors toward a program that will benefit the child. Essentially, personal professional narcissism is needed to counter impractical or unrealistic suggestions and demands. Many educators have difficulty reaching this awareness and so their important contributions are diminished.

Learned skills or characteristics are also important. Of particular importance is the ability to know and use a number of pedagogical approaches in the instructional setting. The teacher who can use only one approach to address a child's problem will probably not be helpful. Adaptability will only be useful if a variety of approaches is available from the teacher.

The teacher of learning-disabled/gifted students also needs to have an excellent understanding of human growth and development. This understanding is important in the child's physical and psychological world. Decisions must be made, and sometimes rather quickly, as to whether a behavior is developmental or abnormal. Growth and developmental sequences and milestones must be understood and appreciated if organizing systematic evaluations are to be carried on.

Child and family counseling techniques are vital tools for special educators, who must carry out immediate interventions at times and provide guidance for improved child-family interactions. The consequences of a home or family problem will often completely disrupt an educational program. When these events occur, the special educator often may be the only professional available to interact in a positive, constructive manner.

Finally, the teacher of learning-disabled/gifted students must be able to communicate at a level appropriate to the person being addressed. Children need to be involved in their education. They must understand the goals and objectives of the program, evaluate their progress, and suggest other courses of action or interest areas. Teachers must listen to them seriously and respond to them honestly. Parents need the same forthrightness. Concepts and procedures should be made clear to them, and understanding of the reasons for the program should be presented. Their fears and doubts should be accepted and plans to deal with these problems formulated. However, if the plans are overly technical, or seem to be pedantic, the necessary family-child-teacher understandings that are so crucial for child improvement probably will not develop. The act of direct, honest communication in words or in print is a cornerstone in a clinical educational setting.

Related Services

Related services are more often available in a clinical setting than in a public school; but, to the extent that it is possible, the following support services are recommended. First, most special educational settings would profit greatly from the availability of a well-trained clinical psychologist. However, such a psychologist must have a background for dealing with exceptional children and their families. This does not suggest that individual child psychotherapy is unimportant. Often, it is vital. But, it is very important to have a trained person who is equipped to deal with the child and family dynamics. At times, a well-trained special education teacher, as well as a psychologist, might be able to intervene in a situation. However, in certain crisis situations, the need for a psychologist with very particular skills and insights becomes almost mandatory.

There is often a need for a psychologist who is trained in group management to be available on a regular basis during the school week. Many of the problems of the learning-disabled child can be better treated initially in a group. The spacing of therapeutic sessions should be arranged by consulting with the whole staff, and the possible consequences of therapy must be understood by all. However, a well-trained psychologist with an understanding of exceptional children will recognize these consequences and can help the teacher to plan for them.

Personality assessment often lacks clinical evaluation for learning-disabled children. Detailed assessments of physical factors, potential, and achievement are carried out; yet, the aspect of human beings that brings about or avoids the necessary and appropriate interactions with the environment that learning requires goes unevaluated. The psychologist should use projective techniques and observation to help the teacher and staff recognize and understand behaviors of the children within themselves and with others. These evaluations need to be ongoing. The communication skills of the psychologist and staff must be sharpened to foster understanding for the benefit of the children involved.

158   *Daniels*

In certain instances, a social worker should be available at the school's request. Many problems that are transferred from the home to the learning situation are better understood and addressed by direct contact with and in the home. Familial problems, such as alcoholism, drugs, and extended family members must be discovered and, if possible, treated. However, the real value may be achieved when a social worker's perceptions make it clear that family problems cannot be ameliorated—that the school and therapist must help the child learn to cope and live with the problem in the least damaging way. The social worker needs to share basic insights with the professional team trying to help the child. The team must function as a multidisciplinary unit in which they can weigh all contributions and agree upon the best course of action.

Paraprofessionals can be important in a special education setting if used correctly. Without adequate preparation and supervision, however, paraprofessionals can often become a disrupting element. Aides should be used to support the teacher's programs and to support the children. However, they should not be asked to assume the teacher's role. Children with severe learning problems need consistency in terms of authority figures, procedures, and techniques. Paraprofessionals should support programs—not direct them.

Aides can be effective in supplying immediate guidance and feedback for individual children and small groups. They can help develop enrichment and practice activities required by the teacher. They often can provide clerical assistance to permit the teacher more time to focus on educational matters.

Teachers and aides must see themselves as a team. Teachers must find time to share their goals and objectives with aides and to communicate with them specific courses of actions. Aides must know as nearly as possible how the teacher wants a particular course of action to be handled or followed. In developing a schedule, an administrator must build in meeting and planning time for the teacher-aide teams.

Peer tutors can be an important element in a special education program. If handled properly, the interaction of peers should be beneficial to both. The tutee should profit from the help provided because in many instances, it can be much more immediate than that from a teacher or an aide. In some instances, children feel more comfortable with peers than with adults. This is often true for children who are new to the program or just beginning a new procedure. For the tutor there is often increased self-esteem as a result of knowing something another does not. The tutor must often strive for better organization

Teaching Learning Disabled/Gifted 159

in the help provided and exact vocabulary. For learning-disabled/gifted children these strivings are important ingredients in their own development.

It is often helpful to have student committees in a classroom. Groups of children who do better than others in specific areas can be designated as helpers. One child might do well in arithmetic and help others who are less able; another child might be able to spell well enough to help others who are having trouble. A number of children designated as a specific subject committee works best because in most instances, a child would not have to be disturbed in the middle of an important activity because someone else will probably be available. Once again, the key is planning and support with and for the individuals.

DIAGNOSIS AND EVALUATION

It seems rather obvious that some standards for placement in a learning-disabled/gifted program need to be developed and maintained. Screening for giftedness may include a strict cut-off score on an intelligence test, a measure of academic achievement, teacher judgment, and/or parent determination. If it is suspected that a child is learning disabled, all those children who seem to be gifted on any of these measures should be tested with a respected measure of intellectual potential. This measure should consist of an individual intelligence test, such as the Wechsler Intelligence Scale for Children-Revised (WISC-R) or the Stanford-Binet. If no detailed analysis of achievement and process abilities has been made previously, then this should follow: 1) evaluation of depth and breadth of vocabulary; 2) tests of memory, memory span, learning modalities, discrimination tasks, and adjustment; and 3) physical examinations for vision, hearing, and neurological functioning. Overall physical development should be evaluated. The whole child, that much abused term, must be seen because the child functions in psychological, physical, and sociological realms, all of which are interrelated. What frequently happens is that little pieces of the mosaic determine the whole picture. With learning-disabled/gifted children, one piece, learning disability, too often distorts the picture so much that the children's real needs never are perceived and therefore, are never met.

However, this intensive clinical diagnosis should not be considered as an end unto itself. Rather, it should be looked upon as a means for providing directions and guides for the very crucial next step—

160   *Daniels*

diagnostic observation and diagnostic teaching. These depend on the talents and insight of the teachers. As noted earlier, there is really no substitute for a well-trained, dedicated teacher.

The teacher with whom the prospective learning-disabled/gifted child will work should be provided an opportunity to observe the child in the present teaching situation in order to evaluate the influence of this situation as negative or positive factors. The observation also should be channeled toward specific behaviors that the original diagnosis stated as positively or negatively important. Objective judgments tempered with subjective evaluations should begin to develop a possible plan of action.

Once a possible plan of action has been developed by the learning-disabilities/gifted teacher, some diagnostic teaching should be employed prior to placement into an appropriate group. This procedure will provide enlightenment about the child's reactions; it will also help the teacher to refine the instructional plan so that the first days of instruction in the new placement will be as rewarding and satisfying as possible. In this way, confusion can be minimized and order provided. For most learning-disabled/gifted children, order is something that is needed desperately.

Ongoing Diagnosis

Ongoing diagnosis should be the hallmark of any program for learning-disabled/gifted children. In effect, the original diagnosis developed a number of hypotheses about the child's problem. The ongoing diagnosis is where these hypotheses are accepted or rejected and because verification can occur for only a few of these at any one time, the process must be continuous. The initial and certain subsequent phases of programming must be viewed as extensions of the diagnosis; those making diagnoses must indicate in their reports that this is an important element in their view.

The teacher in the initial programming must provide instruction, which grows from the diagnostic recommendations. However, the teacher must not be overawed by these. If the recommendations are beneficial and progress is apparent, then the diagnosis was probably valid. If, however, the teacher is able to show that the recommendation has not worked out, the teacher should not be afraid to note this and then either ask for further help or strike out independently by using a different approach.

Priorities must be set, usually by the diagnostic team, as to the instructional recommendations that should be addressed first. For instance, if a program of psychotherapy has been recommended, a decision must be made as to whether it should be provided prior to, during, or after the initiation of the instructional program. The ongoing diagnosis could be thoroughly distorted if the proper judgment in such a situation is not made. In most cases, the setting of priorities for which recommendation should be carried out first will often determine the effectiveness and value of the ongoing diagnostic approach.

Although the ongoing diagnosis is often left to a teacher, it is better done as a team. Multiple views of behavior often provide greater and more useful insight. The team approach also means that responsibility is shared and in this sharing, the teacher may become more venturesome and creative. This instructional creativity is often a prime necessity in helping learning-disabled/gifted children solve their problems.

Evaluation

Although diagnosis and evaluation are integrally linked, it is often helpful to view diagnosis and evaluation as separate entities. Diagnosis can be seen as the attempt to see what is wrong and why. Evaluation may be viewed as the determination of the present state of development of achievement.

A good diagnosis should begin with an evaluation to determine where the child is in relation to self and others. At this point, learning-disabled/gifted children are often missed; that is, unless the teacher knows that grade level criteria are inappropriate because standardized test scores often approach or exceed grade level norms. When reading achievement is measured against listening achievement, serious retardation often is found. The results of an informal reading inventory can be used to give this information. Criterion-referenced inventories often highlight skill deficits that are otherwise masked by intelligence.

Periodically, an audit needs to be carried out. Has progress been made? Informal measures are very useful and informative, but in many instances, political and institutional demand must be met through standardized tests. The best auditing procedure for standardized tests is pre/post over a sensible period of time. Pre-/post-testing should not be closer than 5 months apart. The audit should be based on comparing two forms of the same level of the test. In reporting, the form and level should be clearly indicated.

The simple grade-level scores generated are useful for group comparisons but will not really provide much insight for individuals. For example, the lack or use of guessing should be studied. Sometimes, children who have problems but receive good remedial instruction

162   Daniels

actually score lower on post-test evaluations. When the performance is analyzed, it is obvious that the children have become more careful and thoughtful and have guessed less. The depressed score, in effect, may be an extremely encouraging sign that progress is being made. Often, the number of items attempted on a post-test will be fewer than on a pretest; yet when the percentage of success is computed, the converse is true.

Finally, when evaluations use standardized tests, it must be remembered that the scores obtained are usually grade-level scores. These scores should not be extrapolated to reader-level or arithmetic-level scores for instruction. Instead, the teacher must evaluate yesterday's learning, last week's learning, and last month's learning in order to provide information concerning the amount of repetition needed by the child. Without daily, weekly, and monthly evaluations, these crucial factors in the child's problem often go unappreciated, resulting in the lack of progress and sense of failure. In such cases the child, parents, and staff can become disillusioned.

The instructional program needs an ongoing diagnostic and evaluation phase if it is to be effective. However, it should not become so formalized or structured that nothing is left to the teacher's discretion. Teachers must become experts in evaluation and diagnosis.

PROGRAMMING

In order to be effective with the learning-disabled/gifted child, the teacher must understand the child's needs and possess a broad repertoire of curricular approaches and pedagogical procedures. The teacher must understand that the learning-disabled/gifted child evidences two exceptionalities, and in many instances, these are antagonistic. Very bright children know that they are brighter than others; yet, they also know that they cannot succeed in important academic areas where others do. Self-doubt and lowered self-esteem are generated, which can, in turn, feed into greater failure. This vicious cycle can only be broken by success in the areas where failure initiated the cycle.

If the giftedness is to be fostered, the teacher must believe that the learning disability needs to be ameliorated. First, however, his or her attention must be directed toward the children's abilities. In planning the prescribed program, grade level curriculum, in most cases, should be ignored. The interests of the children should be used as the curriculum materials for oral and written language instruction. After this initial approach, the teacher can elaborate on group interests and develop interests which can be integrated into future curriculum demands—demands that the children will face in a conventional classroom. For example, if they soon will be dealing with American history, an interest in the Constitutional Convention might be cultivated from current affairs that are reported on television or in the newspapers. The Connecticut Compromise and the Three-Fifths Compromise could be developed and explained in readiness for not only early Constitutional development but also the Civil War. Science principles and vocabulary could be developed to permit these children to feel good about themselves among their nondisabled peers. There is no better way to foster self-esteem than success. For learning-disabled children, especially gifted ones, the personal recognition that they are no longer at the bottom of the list is quite stimulating.

Teachers of learning-disabled/gifted students must be willing to take some professional risks. Conventional remedial programs might be tempting because they are easy to use. These programs, however, will seldom be satisfying to the teacher. The satisfaction that is found in producing positive, rewarding changes in children will probably not be forthcoming in learning-disabled/gifted children if these programs are used. Many remedial programs obviously are not stimulating to the bright child. They lack real content because their goals are almost always skills-related. Unfortunately, the same can be said about the skills program. Too often, these programs are designed to proceed more slowly, or skills are repeated excessively as an intensive reinforcement technique. These are not the basic pedagogical changes required for gifted children who need clinical instruction.

The first element that must be changed is the approach to the children's learning styles. Almost by definition, learning-disabled children cannot learn by conventional visual/auditory means. Changes of materials will avail nothing if visual/auditory learning is still the required learning model. Teachers of learning-disabled children should be taught to use a multisensory approach. It is interesting to note how frequently this obvious need is ignored in commercially prepared remedial programs. The use of multisensory learning is appropriate if there is an associative learning difficulty, short-term memory problem, or problems with concentration. A language experience approach, using a modified Fernald Visual-Auditory-Kinesthetic Tactile (VAKT) procedure, may also be valuable. For children with an associative learning problem, it is important to use materials that are of interest and reflect a strong experiential background. This will help with recall of the learned material.

Concentration problems can be insidious because they can be reflected in a wide range of behaviors. The teacher must not focus on the behavior problems in a vacuum, but instead must see them as a reflection of the problems in concentration. Children must not be mistakenly labeled as unable to learn or as having problems with the central nervous system because they failed to respond to the presented visual/auditory stimuli. In reality, the problem might be a lack of concentration. Multisensory learning is important for helping these children. When this type of learning is used correctly, problems in concentration will be eliminated. The procedures must be followed exactly; failure to do so would be immediately conveyed to the learner. Multisensory learning really can work because it forces concentration rather than the obvious employment of three or more senses.

The multisensory approach also is useful diagnostically. Children with certain types of emotional problems will not find it possible to learn even with this approach, and they should receive an intensive psychological evaluation to determine the best course of action. Usually, these children need psychotherapeutic intervention before academic progress can be expected. Sometimes, intervention can be provided while academic instruction is carried on. However, the teacher must realize that this dual approach is not always feasible.

With certain children the short-term memory problem is the major disability. Again, a multisensory learning approach can be very successful with many of these children. Yet, the success is limited sometimes to such a degree that satisfactory rewarding progress cannot be obtained. This is especially true with many of the children who demonstrate learning disabilities in mathematics. At this time, it should be apparent that these children should not be made to suffer blows to their self-worth. Because of the electronic evolution, these children can be provided with hand calculators and have access to microcomputers. The child who cannot retain number facts should be allowed to retrieve them electronically. Learning-disabled children, in particular, should be allowed to use such adaptive means with no reservations, recriminations, or shame.

An important factor in learning is recall, which is facilitated by indexing. This skill entails relating new learnings to old learnings. New learnings that are unrelated to past learnings must be based in rote memory components, which are notoriously weak in learning-disabled children. Once again, gifted youngsters, whose information and ideas are often sophisticated, receive instruction with material that cannot be related to their backgrounds of experience in any way.

An additional vital factor is time. Children need time on task in order to learn. Yet, it seems that time on task is being diminished in increasing degrees as children jump or are pushed from one task to another. This curriculum and instructional variability seems to be a direct reflection of the adult concept that variety is the spice of life. This may well be true, but it is not the spice of learning. Consistency is the basis for learning. To foster retention, repetition is needed, and repetition requires time. It should be obvious that learning-disabled children need even more repetition and, therefore, even more time.

The teacher needs the freedom to select broad generic areas of the curriculum. In this approach, content units become particularly useful. For example, a teacher might have a unit on meteorology in winter, botany in spring, and simple machines at another time. It often is better to stay with those subjects that basically are cognitively oriented for instruction. This in no way diminishes the realm of literature. However, it does suggest that literature should be viewed as the humanizing component of the curriculum and might be handled better from the aural language approach rather than reading. As progress is made, independent reading can be fostered.

The teacher must also maintain certain attitudes and skills regarding the variability of concepts and skills that a single group of learning-disabled/gifted children might bring to a particular content unit. First, he or she must know the needs of the children and which needs must be dealt with first. Second, the teacher must be aware of the variety and level of concepts available in the curriculum area to be used. Third, the teacher must know which materials are available in the school, and how they pertain to the goals developed and the needs to be met. Instructional strategies must be viewed in light of these factors.

For example, in a unit on meteorology, a teacher might develop three instructional groups, each with a different level of competency in reading. Each group then would deal with an aspect of the science— one might work on the concept of pressure systems and fronts; another on types and formations of precipitation; and the third on weather instruments. Then, each group would investigate a topic unique to the unit and would be required to develop a culminating activity to share with the other groups so that information is disseminated to all. A botany unit might entail the detailed study of a plant mitosis and meiosis, plant structures and their variability, and basic plant needs.

For meteorology, the following instructional groupings might be developed:

1. *A group with problems in visual/auditory learning* These children might use weather instruments as a vehicle for learning. The instructional goals might include increased sight vocabulary and the ability to follow simple directions. Through the use of a modified

166   *Daniels*

Fernald approach, involving kinesthetic or haptic stimulation, the words of the necessary directions and the specific vocabulary of the unit could also be taught. The unit might culminate in a demonstration of the machines and their use. The sight vocabulary would be incorporated into a word bank that would be the source for skills development. If a child knows some words with the same necessary precepts, then those words can be used to develop the desired concept.

2. *A group with difficulties in organization skills* These children might be instructed with teacher-prepared materials concerning the theory of fronts and weather maps. The teacher material would be designed so that the variability of topic sentences, the statement of main ideas, and the varied order of details and paragraphs would be emphasized. A directed reading approach could well be the best instructional procedure, allowing enough time to foster the appropriate understanding. The curriculum becomes the vehicle for the skills, and the mindless "covering of material" is unnecessary. The culminating activity could be a presentation of the ideas through the use of a series of weather maps with appropriately written paragraphs providing detailed information. Members of the presenting group could read to the children in another group who are unable to read the materials for themselves.

3. *A group of verbalizers* These children can "read" anything if reading means word-calling. However, they lack overall comprehension abilities and study skills. For this group, a teacher might use commercially prepared science materials and a combination of directed reading and independent research. Their goals might include setting and reading for a purpose, constructing outlines, preparing summaries, comparing sources, and library skills. Their curriculum task might be to develop a paper on the history of weather forecasting. Surely, this would require work in history, geography, and folklore as well as meteorology. The culminating activity might involve a paper to be posted in the school or class library and a series of vignettes about folklore forecasting.

If such a regime were set up, all the learning-disabled/gifted children would be challenged but not frustrated. Goals could be developed with the children and the attainment of the goals could be evaluated. Such a program must be based on the interests and better than average ability of these children.

The acquisition of independence should emerge from a sound program for learning-disabled/gifted students. These students often

Teaching Learning Disabled/Gifted 167

will have to fend for themselves in areas of high interest or sophistication. They will have to use highly individualized learning procedures. Learning-disabled/gifted children must learn that they can be successful if they master what they know and need and can function in an independent manner. The teacher of these children must provide activities for independent behavior and value their growth.

Although academically gifted children are usually capable of mastering a greater amount of material at a higher level than average children in the population, learning-disabled/gifted children may not be able to get the information easily from printed matter. The emphasis on content instruction as the vehicle for skills development is one way to compensate for this problem. However, to develop feelings of success and stimulation from their greater potential, activities other than reading should be employed. Contacting and working with higher level concepts can be accomplished by using simulation activities or problem-solving activities in a specific content area or in an area of interest. These activities may fall under the title of kits, games or gadgets, or may involve microcomputers. The important element, however, is the presentation of information and the challenge of ideas in a form other than written. The age of the microcomputer shows promise for learning-disabled/gifted children. These ideas are further elaborated in Chapter 11 of this volume.

COUNSELING SERVICES TO STUDENTS AND PARENTS

Learning-disabled/gifted students often need more help in the adjustment areas than do students who exhibit only one exceptionality. It is usually difficult for bright children to use and accept their intelligence while recognizing that they are less capable in academic areas than their less endowed peers. The major impact of this apparent paradox is on self-esteem. Therefore, the educational program must become, in effect, a counseling program, the cornerstone of which must be the development of successful experiences. Goals must be kept short-range and precise enough that each child individually can recognize success and specific future needs. The long-range picture should be minimized until the children are able to face a future of success growing out of short-range sets of goals.

Teachers must feel free to deal with negative-affect problems when they arise. Rigid adherence to academic programs usually means that counseling opportunities are lost. An academic activity should be held in abeyance until emotional overtones or barriers are removed from the learning situation. Many small group instructional sessions

168   *Daniels*

can become effective group counseling sessions if the problems are perceived and handled sensitively. Individual conferences, an important part of any good instructional program, might be more advantageously used to address feelings, emotions, and worries than academic problems. The teacher of learning-disabled/gifted children must be free to be versatile and adaptive.

A teacher must assure the students of confidentiality. This relationship is important. Permission to discuss certain things with parents should be a trust between the child and teacher and should be done only if the child agrees. If the child refuses permission, the teacher should elaborate on the value or necessity of the communication. If the child still refuses, ask for further thought and pursue the point at a later time. If a factor of health or safety is to be communicated the child should be told why the teacher must break the confidence and again ask for the child's agreement. Remember that in many states, the law requires a teacher to report certain elements in a child's existence, even if the child does not want these elements reported.

Parents need to be helped in order to accept realistically their children's learning disabilities as well as the giftedness. Many learning-disabled/gifted children view the emphasis on their giftedness as a way of shaming them into better performance, which they feel they cannot accomplish. Too often, this use of giftedness does become a kind of a tension-relieving weapon for an angry, hurt parent who cannot understand why a bright child is failing. In this situation, as with all learning-disabled/gifted children, a teacher must delineate the concepts behind giftedness and learning disability. Only in this way can the confusing apparent paradox be resolved. These exceptionalities must be viewed as separate entities—not a cause-and-effect relationship.

Parents of these children must have an opportunity to share their feelings and especially their frustrations at special parent meetings, planned for that purpose. Where appropriate, both parents should attend. The school psychologist, social worker, and principal can be extremely supportive and should be approached to help conduct these meetings. Program presentations must be consistent with the teacher's goals for the program in order to enhance parental confidence in the program. Without this confidence, the progress of the students will be diminished or lost, and their ego and self-esteem will receive another damaging blow. This can lead many children to withdraw totally from learning and never even reach the potential placed upon them by their disability.

Teaching Learning Disabled/Gifted   169

Parent and child counseling should be a part of the regular program for learning-disabled/gifted children. It cannot and should not replace or intrude upon a professional counseling or psychotherapeutic program. It should, however, be available as an adjunct or supplementary program and for some, it may well become their major source of emotional support. A program which does not recognize the counseling element as an important component of the program will probably not meet the needs of these children as well as could be anticipated.

CONCLUSION

Because nearly all school systems have programs for the learning-disabled children, the integration of gifted children would seem to be an obvious step. Unfortunately, this does not seem to be advisable at this time because learning disabilities programs are often devoid of a conceptual base. They overemphasize skills development and are often noncategorized in nature so that no matter what the "learning disability" is, a child fits. The lack of stimulation can be deadly to most children, but to a gifted child, such programs can become an anesthetic.

As noted earlier, there is no real administrative reason not to have learning-disabled/gifted children work with each other in groups or classes. Schools must commit time, energy, and money to make a learning-disabled/gifted program function. Teachers must commit themselves to a task involving more than a little extra study and work. Finally, there must be a community commitment to justify the existence of such programs.

This concept has always been a major source of difficulty because commitment has been diluted by generalities. In many schools, it will be necessary to start from the beginning. Deliberate action must be taken to identify the gifted child with learning disabilities. These children should have a program to provide maximum growth. Otherwise, they will be lost to the future of society. If commitment is forthcoming, the learning-disabled/gifted child will be able to thrive.

Chapter 9

The Adaptation of
Gifted Programming for
Learning-Disabled Students

James J. Gallagher

Practitioners who are experienced in the field of exceptional children are well aware that children do not come in neat packages to be pigeonholed into arbitrary classifications. Many if not most exceptional children have some combination of exceptionalities. These commonly have been viewed as collections of disabilities and form a growing category called multiple handicaps; it has become evident, however, that a child could have a specific learning problem and be outstanding intellectually at the same time. Gifted youngsters who have advanced talent in many areas also may have specific learning deficits that will keep them from realizing these substantial talents (Maker, 1977). Five years ago, there would have been no real discussion of learning-disabled/gifted children. Consequently, society is on the threshold of considering a problem that previously received little or no systematic attention in education.

The biographies of many famous individuals (Leonardo da Vinci, Albert Einstein, Woodrow Wilson, etc.) have revealed that in their early lives, some special learning problems caused substantial educational difficulties (Elkind, 1973). Winston Churchill, for example, had a variety of problems that suggested early perceptual handicap and hyperactivity. These problems caused much dismay and concern in his family and consternation in a variety of English schools.

Nelson Rockefeller, former New York governor, was known widely to be dyslexic, and was almost a nonreader because of some suspected perceptual problems. Naturally, these noted people were successful in adapting to their problems and eventually overcoming them so that their gifts and talents were able to flourish. The interesting and dis-

172   Gallagher

turbing question is: How many other children are similar to these noted individuals in that their learning difficulties and disabilities may be severe enough to prevent full utilization of their other talents? The loss of one such talent is too many, but there is no way of accurately assessing the number of youngsters who might fall into this dual category.

DEFINITIONS OF GIFTEDNESS AND LEARNING DISABILITIES

There are dual problems connected with the identification of such youngsters in the first place. These problems are associated with the fundamental definitions of each of the components—gifted and learning disabled. Both of these concepts have evolved in rather striking fashion over the past quarter of a century. Prior to the 1960s, the definition of gifted was limited to academic and intellectual talents and even then was widely thought to be predominantly genetically determined (Pressey, 1955). In the 1970s, there was a major attempt to reconceptualize the definition in order to incorporate aspects of creativity, leadership, and the visual and performing arts.

The definition that was eventually codified in federal legislation was originally proposed in the Marland Report (Marland, 1972) on the status of gifted education in the United States (see Introduction). The federal definition reflects fairly well the definitional shift that preceded it. Although it clearly intended to broaden the concept, stating a definition is one thing; making it operational is quite another. Most school systems still rely heavily upon intelligence and achievement tests in their identification processes.

Defining learning disabilities has been more difficult than defining the gifted. Essentially, the concept of learning disabilities emerged out of an interest in children with brain damage. Some of the early work done by Strauss (Strauss and Kephart, 1955) was continued by special educators Cruickshank and Kirk (Cruickshank et al., 1961; Kirk, 1966). The term "minimal brain damage" was used to identify a category of youngsters whose developmental patterns were such a unique or bizarre blend of strengths and weaknesses that a presumption of neurologic impairment was made even in the absence of positive or definitive neurological signs.

A new set of discoveries concerning brain function was revealed through the medical treatment of intractable epilepsy. This treatment consisted of cutting the fibers of the corpus callosum and thus separating the two hemispheres of the brain. Once the connecting fibers were separated, the epileptic seizures were markedly reduced. This,

Adaptation of Programming 173

however, also tended to allow a sharp contrast to be drawn as to which functions are controlled by which hemisphere of the brain. Apparently, visual material projected to the right visual field and thus ending in the left hemisphere could be described in speech and writing; material projected to the left visual field, which connects to the right hemisphere, would not receive meaningful information—only a flash of light when the connecting fibers were cut.

Lerner (1976) reported an experiment in which a split-brain patient was asked to identify objects put in his hand. When the object was placed in his right hand, he could name the objects in speech and writing; but when the same objects were placed in his left hand, he would make only wild guesses to identify the object. Also, when a picture of an object was exposed to his left visual field, he had no trouble identifying the same object by touching it with his left hand; however, when the picture was seen with the left visual field, the patient could not match the objects by touching them with his right hand. It seems likely that as more is learned about the differential functions of the two hemispheres of the brain, greater insight into the etiology of certain learning disability problems will become more understandable.

The federal definition of a learning disability in the 1980s intended to change a biological or neurological concept into an educational concept, because the predominant mode of treatment for youngsters with these problems was education. This definition, shown in the Introduction to this book, probably demonstrates the confusion within the field more than it brings clarity to the definition of a learning disability.

Another approach to describing the learning-disabled child has been to conceptualize the problem in terms of an information-processing model. In this view (Bryan and Bryan, 1980), there were fundamental defects in information reception (visual or auditory reception), in information synthesis and reasoning, in information expression, and/or in the *executive function* (controlling attention, cognitive strategies, etc.). These information-processing defects then result in an unusual pattern of measured skill if one has used a broad enough battery of tests (Stefanich and Schnur, 1979).

For many, the concept of intraindividual differences has been one of the fundamental aspects of the definition of learning disabilities. The measurement of the classic learning-disabled youngster across a number of developmental domains reveals a striking pattern of hills and valleys (Gallagher, 1966). In such instances, even though the hills may represent outstanding intellectual development, the valleys can

174   *Gallagher*

create major learning problems and dramatically reduce the efficiency of that youngster in the educational setting. Tests such as the Illinois Test of Psycholinguistic Abilities (ITPA) (Kirk et al., 1968) provided a vehicle for looking at unusual patterns of development.

A major complication was that when the definition was transferred from neurological to educational, its scope broadened. Many school systems would identify learning-disabled youngsters using a general set of criteria of underachievement. Any youngster who is considered to be underachieving would be classified as "learning disabled" and placed in a learning disability program (McKinney and Feagans, 1980). This decision making seemed to be the action of practical administrators searching for a device for providing these youngsters with some special assistance. Nevertheless, such broadening of the learning disability category has had the unfortunate effect of making it even more heterogeneous than it was in the first place because it includes many youngsters whose performance in no way suggest neurological problems, but rather indicate combinations of limited opportunity, inadequate early education, and poor motivation.

SPECIAL EDUCATION PROGRAMMING
FOR LEARNING-DISABLED/GIFTED CHILDREN

When the public schools make special educational adaptations of the program for an exceptional child, there are really only three major dimensions in which such changes can take place: 1) the learning setting; 2) the curriculum content; and 3) the mastery of skills needed for future learning. In the remedial programs for the learning-disabled/gifted student, the content and learning environment are less important features than the skills because the lack of certain skills impede the forward movement of the gifted dimensions of the individual. Similarly, the content of the lessons are less important than the skills instruction.

Although there is an impressive set of theories covering both the diagnosis and treatment of learning disabilities, there is general acceptance of the procedures on how the learning-disabled child should be handled. It is generally agreed that there should be a battery of diagnostic instruments to search out the specific deficits of the individual child, a case study and case history to explore the background and past development of the problem, and perhaps some informal tests of academic performance to identify process difficulties of the child. Following that diagnosis, then, the treatment would depend upon the nature of the problem, which would be revealed by the diagnostic

Adaptation of Programming   175

study, and often by the theoretical orientation of the learning disability therapists themselves.

Several major schools of therapeutic thought may focus on motor problems (Cratty, 1969), perceptual motor skills (Frostig and Horne, 1964), language and psycholinguistic properties (Kirk et al., 1968), or on many variations of these approaches. The great diversity of problems under the classification of learning disabled has spawned a similar diversity in therapies. The eclectic professional probably would draw liberally upon all of these theoretical and practical materials, depending upon the individual case. The treatment of choice quite obviously is tutorial in style or, at best, small group activities, which would allow the teacher to shape the remedial program to suit the individual characteristics of the child. It is possible, however, also to treat the learning-disabled student within the framework of a gifted program, as revealed by Whitmore (1980).

Whitmore presented a case study of a learning-disabled/gifted child that illustrated the ability of educational programming to impact on such youngsters and also indicated the intensity of treatment that was required to achieve that goal. At age 7, Robert was placed in an underachieving/gifted program when test scores revealed he had a Stanford-Binet score of 163 while performing average or below grade level on measures of school achievement. His grade 2 teacher evaluated his daily work as unsatisfactory; Robert seemed to freeze when faced with failure. The series of tests and diagnostic procedures that Robert was administered indicated a perceptually handicapped child who had some mild visual problems. Figure 9.1 shows the pattern of his abilities at age 7.

As is typical with such youngsters, Robert tried to develop some defense reactions to protect his own self-image from the failure that he could perceive. During the first months of participation in a special class for underachieving gifted children, it was evident that Robert was suffering from very low self-esteem and a self-concept embedded with perceived failure. His behavior in class became disruptive. He wandered around the room seeking attention through verbal activity.

The key objective of the school program was to help Robert develop more self-esteem and to focus his self-concept on his potential for success and outstanding abilities rather than his lack of performance in specific areas. The instructional emphasis was to capitalize on his abilities in problem solving, verbalization, and interpersonal relationships. Through this process, a sense of self-worth slowly developed, but Robert needed frequent affirmation of his ability in order to succeed academically. As he began to revise his self-image for pos-

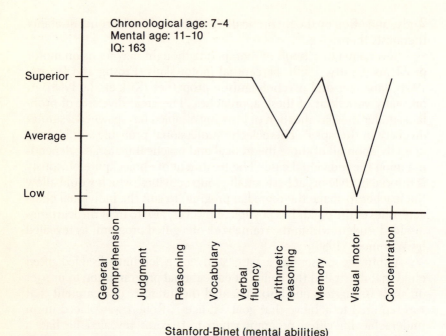

Figure 9.1. Strength and weaknesses in Robert, grade 2 (from Joanne Rand Whitmore, Giftedness, Conflict, and Underachievement. Copyright © 1980 by Allyn and Bacon, Inc. Reprinted with permission.)

sible success, any hint of failure was extremely threatening and he became very self-critical, sometimes crying in frustration.

Over time, Robert responded very well to the program. After leaving it, he became a high-achieving student in the district's elementary program for the gifted. He actively participated in high school sports, student government, and theater productions. The message from this case study is that careful diagnosis and planning to meet the special needs of the individual learning-disabled/gifted child can result in meaningful gains and improvement.

Gifted Learning Environments

The types of learning environments that are provided for the special education of the gifted vary from community to community and from age group to age group. Some of the more common adjustments are:

1. *Mainstreaming* The gifted child remains in the regular classroom but has the instructional program enriched through such things as additional assignments and independent study.

2. *Resource room* The gifted student leaves the regular program for an hour a day or thereabouts, and receives differential instruction by a specially trained teacher.
3. *Special class* The gifted students remain in a special group and receive a differential education program designed by specially trained teachers.
4. *Special school* A few special schools focus on a particular content area that encourage participation of gifted students. Mathematics, science, and art are some possible program focal points in many of these schools.
5. *Mentor program* Gifted students may leave the school under this plan and on a regular basis, meet with a specialist in their area of interest for specialized instruction. The mentor typically is not a school employee but a specialist in a field of interest (such as music, computers, scientific research, and economics).

In each of these settings, it is possible to insert the specialized clinical instruction—the hallmark of instruction for learning-disabled

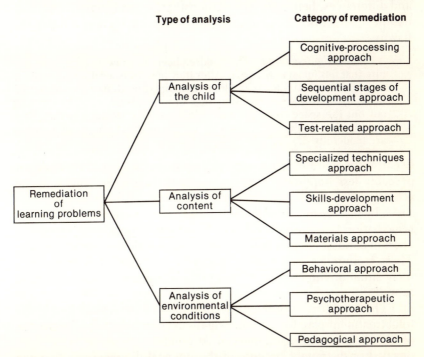

Figure 9.2. Classification of remedial approaches (Reprinted by permission from: Lerner, J. 1981. Learning Disabilities: Theories, Diagnosis, and Strategies, 3rd Ed. Houghton Mifflin Co., Boston.)

178   *Gallagher*

students. Figure 9.2 presents a summary of remedial approaches (Lerner, 1981) to learning disabilities. It focuses on the child, the remedial content, and the environmental factors related to learning. The child analysis deals with an individual diagnosis of strengths and weaknesses, and the identification of specific developmental stages to be traversed in the remedial effort. The content approach focuses upon the content to be learned and its organization, as opposed to the learner. A variety of criterion reference systems and associated materials and techniques provide the base for this approach. The environmental conditions approach tries to remove external barriers to learning. If the child is hyperactive or emotionally disturbed, then the remedial effort should help remove these barriers. Obviously, elements of all of these approaches will be utilized in most individual cases.

The literature suggests many devices for improving motor skills or visual perception. For example, Gair (1977) used the vehicle of art in specialized instruction for children with learning problems. He assumed that general perceptual or attentional problems needed to be met and developed exercises to improve the perception of similarities and differences, figure-ground relationships, critical analysis and evaluation of art work, etc. One example of such instruction will give the flavor:

> A *game of figure-ground*   The children begin by drawing a busy city picture that fills up an entire page. After they have finished drawing as many things as they can think of to fill up their city, they draw a second picture made up of little space monsters that all look related. . . . The children cut out the space monsters and hide them all over the city they have drawn. . . . Children stand back and try to discover where the monsters are hidden (p. 32).

Because there are so many activities provided by Gair, their design is probably less important than the match between the child and the activity.

The discrepancy model is not by any means the only one used in remediation practice in the 1980s. Lovitt (1975) presented a model of operant conditioning techniques for children with learning disabilities. These techniques have proven successful in many behavior management situations and can be applied to the learning-disabled/gifted child as well.

The need for counseling parents is an area often neglected in the total treatment plan for the learning-disabled/gifted child. The parents of gifted and learning-disabled/gifted children are more likely to be puzzled or distraught because of the unusual discrepancies that can be observed. These discrepancies can be easily interpreted as laziness or stubbornness and defiance. Thompson (1975, p. 360) gave some principles to aid parental understanding which, if filled in with practical examples from the specific case, can be helpful in encouraging a more healthy parental perspective.

- Children tend to repeat behaviors which have yielded satisfaction.
- Attention spans tend to lengthen when tasks are short and successful.
- Constant reminding of children increases their dependency upon being reminded.
- It is easier to bring about compliance and cooperation when requests are tied to desirable events immediately to follow.
- Learning is facilitated in atmospheres of pleasantness, joy, and humor.

Another common parental problem is the concern about implications that the child suffered from brain injury or minimal brain damage. The concept of brain injury as a possible etiology has been gradually replaced by the concept of unusual brain organization. There is no necessary implication in the second condition of traumatic injury or neural destruction but merely a different patterning of the complex neurological systems. The recent discoveries regarding the differential responsibilities of the left brain and the right brain would lend some credence to such an idea, at least in some of these children. Thus, it is unnecessary for the parents to shoulder additional anxieties and sometimes guilt about the neurological integrity of their child.

Who Shall Instruct?

Who should carry out the specialized instruction for the learning-disabled/gifted child? Should the child be taught by the specialist who understands the nature of programming for gifted children, or the specialist who understands remedial programming for special skills? One thing is certain: the learning-disabled/gifted child does not need to serve as a battleground upon which competing professions and professionals can work out their "turf" problems.

There has been an increasing use of the individualized education plan (IEP) for all exceptional children. This plan is supposed to detail the specific problems of the individual exceptional child and specify appropriate educational objectives and methods for remediating the problem. Because individual diagnosis seems to be the key to proper special education for these children, the process of producing IEPs should motivate the school to focus upon proper identification and treatment procedures. The emergence of the IEP and related group meetings that must occur around a single exceptional child probably

180   *Gallagher*

provides one vehicle for a staff decision as to the allocation of professional responsibilities.

It is likely that an understanding of the child's problem will result in a capable job by either profession, and the decision as to how it should be done in any particular circumstance should depend on other local factors. Case reports demonstrate that capable professionals from either discipline can be productive and helpful.

Evidence has shown that clinical teaching methods, in fact, are beneficial. Kavale (1981) conducted a metaanalysis of remedial programs based on the ITPA. Metaanalysis is a term given to a systematic review and synthesis of a body of research through methods developed by Glass (1976). Kavale (1981) concluded that the accumulation of literature demonstrated that it was possible to improve meaningfully the skills of learning-disabled students through special attention to individual strengths and weaknesses. Because this study covered children with all levels and kinds of abilities, it seems to provide an even more encouraging prospect for those students who are gifted and thus have more personal and intellectual resources to draw upon under such special instruction.

Educators are on the verge of a new experience in finding and helping learning disabled/gifted students. In the 1980s, the concept is new, and much of the treatment ideas are barely tested. Nevertheless, the signs are favorable, and the possibility of making a meaningful improvement in the child is most promising.

REFERENCES

Bryan, T., and Bryan, J. 1980. Learning disorders. In: H. Rie and E. Rie (eds.), Handbook of Minimal Brain Dysfunctions, 456–482. John Wiley and Sons, Inc., New York.

Cratty, B. 1969. Perceptual-Motor Behavior and Educational Processes. Charles C Thomas Publisher, Springfield, IL.

Cruickshank, W., Bentzen, F., Ratzeburg, F., and Tannhauser, M. 1961. A Teaching Method for Brain-Injured and Hyperactive Children. Syracuse University Press, Syracuse, NY.

Elkind, J. 1973. The gifted child with learning disabilities. Gifted Child Q. 17:45–47.

Frostig, M., and Horne, D. 1964. The Frostig Program for the Development of Visual Perception. Follett Publishing Co., Chicago.

Gair, S. 1977. Form and function: Teaching problem learners through art. Teach. Except. Child. 9:30–32.

Gallagher, J. 1966. Children with developmental imbalances: A psychoeducational definition. In: W.M. Cruickshank (ed.), The Teacher of Brain-Injured Children, pp. 23–43. Syracuse University Press, Syracuse, NY.

Glass, G. 1976. Primary, secondary and metaanalyses of research. Educ. Res. 5:3–8.

Kavale, K. 1981. Functions of the Illinois Test of Psycholinguistic Abilities (ITPA): Are they trainable? Except. Child. 45:496–513.

Kirk, S.A. 1966. The Diagnosis and Remediation of Psycholinguistic Disabilities. University of Illinois Press, Urbana.

Kirk, S., McCarthy, J., and Kirk, W. 1968. Illinois Test of Psycholinguistic Abilities. University of Illinois Press, Urbana.

Lerner, J. 1981. Learning Disabilities: Theories, Diagnosis, and Strategies, 3rd Ed. Houghton Mifflin Co., Boston.

Lovitt, T. 1975. Operant conditioning techniques for children with learning disabilities. In: S. Kirk and J. McCarthy (eds.), Learning Disabilities: Selected ACLD Papers, pp. 248–254. Houghton Mifflin Co., Boston.

Maker, J. 1977. Providing Programs for the Gifted Handicapped. Council for Exceptional Children, Reston, VA.

Marland, S. 1972. Education of the Gifted and Talented, Report to the Congress of the United States by the U.S. Commissioner of Education. United States Government Printing Office, Washington, D.C.

McKinney, J.D., and Feagans, L. 1980. Learning Disabilities in the Classroom. Frank Porter Graham Child Development Center, University of North Carolina, Chapel Hill, NC.

Pressey, S.L. 1955. Concerning the nature and nurture of genius. Science, 68:123–129.

Stefanich, G., and Schnur, J. 1979. Identifying the handicapped-gifted child. Sci. Child. 17:18–19.

Strauss, A.A., and Kephart, N.C. 1955. Psychopathology and Education of the Brain Injured Child: Vol. II, Progress in Clinic and Theory. Grune and Stratton, New York.

Thompson, A. 1975. Working with parents of children with learning disabilities. In: S. Kirk and J. McCarthy (eds.), Learning Disabilities: Selected ACLD Papers, pp. 360–364. Houghton Mifflin Co., Boston.

Whitmore, J. 1980. Giftedness, Conflict and Underachievement. Allyn and Bacon, Inc., Boston.

Chapter 10

Adaptive Methods and Techniques for Learning-Disabled/Gifted Children

Lynn H. Fox, Dianne Tobin, and Gilbert B. Schiffman

Three instructional approaches typically are recommended for learning-disabled students: 1) developmental instruction in areas where learning problems do not interfere with understanding the material; 2) remediation in those areas in which the child is having a problem; and 3) adaptive techniques for the problem areas. Too often, programs for learning-disabled students focus solely on the remediation of the problem; yet, there is no doubt that some handicapping conditions can be circumvented by using simple equipment along with some modifications of instructional strategies. This chapter explores the application of the concept of adaptive techniques. Such techniques enable gifted students who have learning disabilities to participate in programs designed for either gifted students or academically able students who have no problems.

Consider the following analogy: a physically handicapped person may have a brilliant mind, but the lack of physical control of his or her body limits the power to interact with others in the world of business, industry, the sciences, or humanities. Spending long hours trying to correct the physical problem may be fruitless; but with the development of the personal computer, this person can be given access to "interface" equipment, which will circumvent the problem. The equipment might be a simple rod activated by the nod of a chin so that typing on a terminal is possible. Suddenly, complex intellectual operations can be executed on paper vis à vis a printer attached to the computer or communications transmitted by telephone. This person is no longer isolated from interaction.

184   *Fox, Tobin, and Schiffman*

Learning-disabled children have fewer visible problems to overcome than the physically handicapped, but they, too, can benefit from the use of appropriate adaptive techniques to help circumvent their problems. If the ultimate goal of education is to produce adults who can lead productive lives, instructional programs for children in school should reflect this goal.

On a day-to-day level, students have two primary responsibilities when they are in school: 1) acquiring knowledge and skills; and 2) demonstrating what they have acquired. Depending on the nature of the learning disability, children may have trouble with either or both. A dysfunction may manifest itself in the inability to read, write, spell, or do some aspects of mathematics. In most schools, *acquisition of knowledge* is primarily through reading, even in mathematical areas, whereas the *demonstration of this knowledge* is usually through writing. The problem may be not that the child cannot acquire knowledge and/or demonstrate its acquisition, but that the child cannot do so within the framework of some specific activities designed by the school. If concepts are presented in an auditory mode, these children may be able to learn and manipulate ideas at a high level more readily than if the same concepts were presented visually. The way in which the child can best demonstrate learning may be auditory rather than written.

READING

One of the major issues that must be addressed in the area of reading is the goal of learning to read. Several purposes may be considered:

1. At the literacy level, reading is necessary in order to survive in the modern world.
2. Reading is an efficient and effective way to learn and understand information in order to act upon it ultimately. A person can be introduced to an idea, value, or concept once he or she can read about it.
3. Reading in itself is an enjoyable activity—a way to spend leisure time, a form of relaxation, a chance to dream dreams and to go mentally to places where it is not possible to go physically.
4. Reading is a way through which a deeper sense of language is instilled—not only the decoding of the language, but its beauty, ambiguity, and nuances. An appreciation for the poetic flow of language can be gained through reading.

Adaptive Methods and Techniques   185

If a learning-disabled/gifted child is not functionally literate it is probably reasonable to set a goal of literacy attainment; the most obvious approaches are remedial techniques. This goal, however, should not become so dominant that when planning for the child, other purposes of reading are overlooked.

If the purpose of a reading assignment is to acquire information that is needed for studying a science or social studies topic, some consideration should be given to alternative ways of acquiring the same information. If the child is capable of understanding the facts and concepts that are presented orally rather than through independent reading, the use of alternatives is necessary. For example, talking books (for the blind), films, videotapes, or tape recordings which cover the topic may be available. If not, perhaps a highly able reader could be tape-recorded reading aloud. Or, a parent, teacher, or teacher's aide could read the material to children or summarize it for them.

With the increased use of media, some people eventually may acquire considerable skill and knowledge completely from the auditory mode. For example, the busy physician now can learn about new medical discoveries, treatments, etc. by listening to taped lectures while driving to and from home. Newspapers are fighting the competition of radio and television news programs. It is quicker for people, including those who read well, to learn from a news flash what is current rather than to read it in a newspaper even when a special edition is available. Teaching children to use adaptive techniques so that they are able to function better in a class for gifted children ultimately may help them to function better as adults as well.

If the purpose of reading instruction is to develop the beauty and practical flow of language, the child who has difficulty understanding and decoding the printed word may get so bogged down trying to decode the printed word that the beauty is lost. How much better it would be to allow the child to see a Shakespearean play or hear it on the tape recorder so that the true beauty of the flow of the language becomes evident.

If the reading is taught so that eventually it will become enjoyable for leisure activity in the future, individual preferences must be recognized. Not everyone is expected to like athletics as a leisure activity. Perhaps there should be the recognition that some people will not enjoy reading so that time is not spent worrying about it. People who find reading difficult may never read for enjoyment, and perhaps educators should accept this situation.

A potential danger with gifted children who are also learning-disabled readers is that too much attention directed towards reme-

186　Fox, Tobin, and Schiffman

diating the problem will deny them access to opportunities to develop their critical and creative thinking skills. Often, programs that are designed to emphasize evaluative thinking and abstract content at a higher level are restricted for gifted children who score two or three grade levels above their grade placement or achievement tests. Thus, a bright child may have good reasoning powers and well-developed oral vocabularies; but if the same child reads or writes poorly, he or she may be kept from attending career symposia, participating in an enrichment class in mathematics or science, or taking an elective course in playwriting. That child might well have benefited from exposure to role models in a career class, or a unit on statistics, astronomy, or oceanography, even if he or she had taped lectures rather than taken notes. Perhaps the child's sense of creative plot and counterplot would far excel that of others in the writing class, but the script would need to be dictated rather than printed.

Of course, some programs designed for gifted students place a great deal of emphasis upon the acceleration of learning and placement through independent reading and learning outside of class. It may be difficult for the learning-disabled student to function in these programs because of time constraints. For example, in fast-paced mathematics classes (Fox, 1974; George, 1981) or the diagnostic testing-prescriptive instruction tutor model for mathematics, developed by Stanley (1980), students may learn 1 to 3 or more years of mathematics in intensive summer classes or in once-a-week meetings during the school year. Mathematically gifted but learning-disabled readers might still be able to learn advanced mathematics at a faster rate or at an earlier age than grade peers. They may need a tutor-mentor, audiotape, or computer-assisted alternative to a traditional textbook.

A reading disability should not preclude a child's placement in more involved science or social studies programs unless independent reading is the only way in which the child can have access to necessary information or concepts. Many programs for the gifted emphasize creative problem solving or future studies. Such programs often do not require a great deal of reading but may require a fair amount of writing. Again, the issue is whether or not the writing of ideas is critical, or if taped or oral presentations could be equally acceptable in light of the program goals.

In areas related to reading, adaptive techniques can be a great help to learning-disabled/gifted children. These techniques allow them to function in gifted classes that teach thinking skills which are unrelated to reading but which usually require reading in order for the child to grasp the content of the course or demonstrate the acquisition of the content and concepts. A gifted child should not be excluded from these programs, even if some special consideration needs to be given to alternate learning styles.

Reading programs for gifted children often include participation in a literature program, such as the Great Books or Newberry Award Winners programs. Gifted children with reading disabilities may be excluded from such programs, even though they may be just as able to participate in the discussions and can appreciate the beauty and depth of the stories. Should the children be excluded because they have more difficulty reading? Could they instead listen to the stories on tape, or be given more time to read them?

Allowing children to read classic comic or summary versions of famous books instead of the original full text is highly controversial. In a review of a computer software package that uses an abbreviated version of literature, Lubar expresses the view that these types of materials should not be permitted:

> The value of literature comes not from the plots, which are often ancient and borrowed, but from the way the words are put together. . . . Each work is a classic because of the style and art of the writer. These tapes (computer software tapes) are pale images of the classics. If they interest a student enough to get him to read the originals, fine, but that doesn't seem likely (Lubar, 1981, p. 85).

Educators should be careful, however, about allowing their dislike of so-called "watered-down crutches" to outweigh students' individual needs. These needs must be taken into account before judgments can be made about the appropriateness and relevancy of materials used by students.

WRITING

Writing is another area where adaptive techniques should be considered for helping a child cope better in classes in which the primary learning is not related to writing per se. Schoolchildren use writing both to demonstrate the skills and knowledge that they have learned and to help them learn the material itself, such as when the child has to take lecture notes. Poor motor coordination or inability to express oneself in writing can lead to enormous frustration when a child has to listen to and write down what is being said. Children who have writing disabilities can function in gifted classes in social studies and science. If, for example, instead of having to write notes, they can be allowed to bring a tape recorder to class, copy a set of notes from

188   Fox, Tobin, and Schiffman

another student, or even allow another student to take notes for them by using carbon paper.

In the area of demonstrating knowledge and skills, dysgraphic children, especially those who are gifted, face the most frustration. Often, they are able to verbalize their answers better than they can write them, but most teachers expect written essays or assignments. Children who verbalize better than they write could record their answers on tape, type them and/or have them typed, and then submit them. One young man was faced with having to write an essay. He agonized for days, staring at the paper. Finally, he was asked, "What do you want to say?" Not knowing that a tape recorder was on, he began to talk. His essay was typed and after minor revisions, was quite acceptable. Many successful adults compose their written work better with the aid of a tape recorder rather than a pencil and paper.

Another case study illustrates the ways in which adaptive procedures can help writing-disabled/gifted children. Consider the case of Thomas—a boy with a tremendous handwriting problem, who became severely depressed when in grade 10, he could not cope with the demands of his social studies class. The teacher lectured and expected the students to take copious notes. Thomas' attempts at note-taking were painfully slow, leaving him exhausted and confused about the "meaning" of the lecture. Nor was Thomas able to satisfy the teacher's demands for essay answers on examinations. His self-esteem plummeted. His parents believed that he was contemplating suicide and referred him for a psychological examination. An interdisciplinary team found Thomas to be well above average in intellectual ability, but he did have a severe problem with motor coordination. The team recommended a number of approaches for helping Thomas with his motor problem, but they also emphasized that he easily could learn the content of the social studies course by tape-recording lectures in class. The teacher at first refused but was finally persuaded to allow another classmate to use a carbon paper booklet for recording notes, and the carbon was given to Thomas. With respect to essay examinations, the teacher agreed to allow a counselor to administer oral examinations to Thomas and to tape-record his responses. Thus, Thomas was allowed to learn the course material and continued to participate in the social studies class.

Thomas hopes to attend college, and if he learns to type and use a tape recorder in class in lieu of note-taking, he will probably be able to function adequately. In fact, computer programs will be available to proofread text, comment on the stylistic features of text, and provide certain reference information about the English language. One such

Adaptive Methods and Techniques   189

program, from Bell Laboratories, is able to detect split infinitives, spelling and punctuation errors, sentences that are too long, wordy phrases, and passive sentences (MacDonald et al., 1982). Word processors, too, will also be common in the future as an enormous help to children with writing disabilities.

MATHEMATICS

In the area of mathematics, remedial techniques should be introduced early to see if the disability can be corrected. As Block (1980) pointed out, it is wise to wait before introducing adaptive techniques in case some students are slow to acquire skills but will, given time. Understanding number facts, for example, might be helpful for estimating and making judgments as to whether an answer is possible. By grades 5 or 6, however, a student who still has trouble remembering number facts may not benefit from continued remediation. In most schools, 2 years are spent teaching long division. This includes all units devoted to it in grades 2–9. Moursund (1981) advised that, "although it may not be wise to abandon the teaching of long division altogether, it may be sensible to know when to give up" (p. 3).

A case in point is John, whose memory problem became evident fairly early in his educational experience when he failed to learn simple arithmetic facts, such as multiplication tables. Indeed, after 3 years in an intensive remediation program with long hours of drill on the basics, John still was unable to recall simple facts, such as "3 times 9." John was often disruptive in class to the point that he had to be sent to a small room by himself to complete his arithmetic worksheets. His school was concerned that John could not begin to learn more abstract mathematical concepts until he mastered these basics. Testing results confirmed John's serious memory deficit but also showed him to be superior in general reasoning. It was learned that John behaved disruptively on purpose so that he would be allowed to do his arithmetic by a finger-counting system that he had developed. He feared ridicule if seen by teachers and peers. When he was offered a ruler or counter, at first he refused to use them because he thought it would be viewed as cheating. When given instruction in the use of a simple handheld pocket-style calculator, John demonstrated his capacity to solve complex arithmetic reasoning problems and to grasp some abstract principles of algebraic equations and relationships. It took less time to instruct him in the use of a calculator than it did to convince his school that he should be allowed to use it in classes in order to study more advanced mathematical material, such as algebra.

190   Fox, Tobin, and Schiffman

The conventional wisdom that mastering the basics is the fundamental goal of an instructional program must be questioned. Will John fail in life if he is dependent upon a calculator for simple arithmetic computation? This will not happen if perhaps he can be taught the skills of estimation as a check on his calculator and can conceptually deal with more abstract or complex relationships. In fact, most adults in business or industry rely on their calculators or computers.

Adaptive techniques for learning mathematics should include advances such as computers and calculators. A growing technology will require students who are skilled in the use of these aids more than children who can perform long division by hand. Moursund (1981) understood that some skills are retained in curriculum because it is easier to teach what has worked in the past than to change. He stated:

> As a teacher, I am disturbed and somewhat frightened by the fact that skills that took me years to learn and even more years to learn to teach are not very important anymore. It is certainly easier to continue to teach what has been learned in the past . . . making small changes . . . to teach it better (p. 3).

Some mathematics teachers are reluctant to change instructional emphasis. Although this may not seriously harm children who learn easily, learning-disabled children may be affected seriously. If, in addition, they have the ability to understand complex operations and abstract principles but are not allowed to learn them because they have not learned number facts, a serious injustice has been done.

ADAPTATION FOR LIFE

At some point in the child's education, it may be decided that further remediation of the problem is no longer possible and that all educational efforts must be concentrated on adaptive techniques. Richards (1981) pointed out that by the time children are in junior high school, their reading behaviors are already set; and if they are not comfortable readers by then, reading is not an efficient way for them to get information because they spend so much time overfocusing on the skill. He suggested that we do a disservice to students by not suggesting dictionaries for poor spellers. He argued that it is critical for students to understand that reading is a technical skill not necessarily related to intelligence. He recommended a cadre of nonreading specialists who would help teachers and pupils learn to use tape recorders, dictating machines, and dictionaries designed for poor spellers. These specialists also would help to make efficient use of typists and secretarial help. It is critical that these learning-disabled/gifted children not see themselves as having a disease that must be cured, but rather (to carry the medical analogy further) a condition like diabetes, in which certain adaptive behaviors allow complete functioning regardless of the problem.

When to give up on remedial techniques is a more difficult problem to solve and may be different for each child. However, if repeated remediation meets with failure, it probably should not be continued. For example, repeated instruction in spelling may result in a child being able to memorize spelling words for a test, but never being able to spell those same words in a composition several weeks later. Continued concentrated efforts on spelling rather than in areas in which the child may be able to learn developmentally may not be in the child's best interests. If instead, the child's teachers are alerted to spelling problems, they can require that the child be allowed to use a dictionary to correct spelling mistakes so as not to be penalized for spelling errors.

A case described by Rack (1981) illustrates a person for whom adaptive techniques proved effective. Although conflicts with his father complicated matters, his consistent reversals, word attack, and blending problems as well as poor handwriting left little doubt that he was learning disabled. The official diagnosis was developmental dyslexia. His mother, however, read to him often, and he developed a real appreciation for literary classics. When by age 12 he was reading at only a grade 2 level, his mother referred him for private help. By working with comic book versions of literary classics and using his own dictated stories in a language experience format, he could read at a grade 5 level by the age of 19. He discovered, however, that he had a real talent for writing plays. Using a tape recorder, a technique learned during his private instructional sessions, he eventually could dictate plays of sufficient quality that amateur theatre groups were willing to use and produce them. Although he still cannot read or write well, he has learned to appreciate the literary world and to compensate for his disabilities to the point that he ultimately may be a professional playwright.

CONCLUSION

Clearly, educators must not give up all attempts to teach learning-disabled children how to read, write, spell, or do computation. However, the severity of the learning disability as well as the strengths of the individual child must be taken into account when planning a program. When a child is so severely disabled that functioning in a regular classroom is difficult but psychological tests and informal evaluations

192 *Fox, Tobin, and Schiffman*

lead professionals to believe the child is gifted, a special class may have to be instituted. In these specialized classes, remedial and adaptive techniques to help the youngsters overcome their disabilities can be combined with instruction in content areas that will tap the higher-level thinking skills of which these children are capable. Examples of such programs appear in Chapters 8, 12, 13, and 15 of this book.

Many learning-disabled/gifted youngsters, however, do not have such severe learning problems that they need a special program. For the majority of learning-disabled/gifted youngsters, an advocate who would help teachers provide adaptations in the child's instructional program may be all that is necessary to allow the child to function well in a regular classroom situation. Whether or not learned adaptive techniques allow a child to function in a program for the gifted depends on the extent of the disability and its relationship to the content of the course, the difficulty of implementing the adaptive technique, and the nature of the gifted program. It may be more difficult for learning-disabled/gifted children to accelerate their progress in school vis à vis grade-skipping or participation in some fast-paced, telescoped courses of study. Many types of programs, however, especially those emphasizing enrichment, independent study projects, and/or creative problem solving, could allow the learning-disabled/gifted child to participate with only a few adaptive adjustments.

Whatever program is suggested, the interests and needs of the children, rather than preconceived notions of the one way to do things, must be paramount. Only then can learning-disabled/gifted children receive the education they deserve so that they can fulfill the promise of their giftedness when they are adults.

REFERENCES

Block, G.H. 1980. Dyscalculia and the minicalculator: The ALP program. Acad. Ther. 16:175–181.

Fox, L.H. 1974. A mathematics program for fostering precocious achievement. In: J.C. Stanley, D.P. Keating, and L.H. Fox (eds.), Mathematical Talent: Discovery, Description and Development. The Johns Hopkins University Press, Baltimore.

George, W.C. 1981. The third D: Development of talent (fast math classes). In: N. Colangelo and R.T. Zaffrann (eds.), New Voices in Counseling the Gifted. Kendall/Hunt Publishing Co., Dubuque, IA.

Lubar, D. 1981. Educational software. In: J.N. Nazzaro (ed.), Computer Connections for Gifted Children and Youth, pp. 83–89. Council for Exceptional Children, Reston, VA. (Also in Creative Computing, 1980, 9:64–72.)

MacDonald, N.H., Frase, L.T., Gingrich, P.S., and Keenau, S.A. 1982. The writer's workbench: Computer aids for text analysis. IEEE Transact. Commun. 30:105–110.

Moursund, D. 1981. Beware of saber toothed tigers. Comput. Teach. 8:3.

Rack, L. 1981. Developmental dyslexia and literacy creativity in the area of deficit. J. Learn. Disabil. 14:262–263.

Richards, J. 1981. It's all right if kids can't read. J. Learn. Disabil. 14:62–67.

Stanley, J.C. 1980. On educating the gifted. Educ. Res. 9:8–12.

Chapter 11

Computer Technology for Learning-Disabled/Gifted Students

Dianne Tobin and Gilbert B. Schiffman

Johnny was a young man attending a special summer class for children identified as learning-disabled/gifted students. He always disliked reading and was reluctant to participate in activities that were designed to teach him to read better. One component of the special summer class was an introduction to the microcomputer and some elementary programming concepts. After the first day of the microcomputer module, Johnny asked to take the manual home. The next day he arrived in class very excited. "I read the manual last night and wrote a program for the computer," he exclaimed. "Can I try it and see if it works?" Johnny had discovered an important concept—that reading was a way to learn something that he wanted to know. He had labored his way through the manual in order to be able to know how to program a computer.

Johnny is only one example of a learning-disabled/gifted child helped by an introduction to the world of microcomputers. The potential of these machines helping many more children is enormous. By definition, learning-disabled/gifted students are children who are capable of high levels of thinking and yet have deficits in specific areas, usually reading or writing. These deficits prevent them from achieving as much in school as their gifted peers who have no learning problems. This chapter explores some of the specific ways that the microcomputer can be used to help learning-disabled/gifted students realize their potential.

THE STATE OF THE ART AND THE PROBLEM

Large computers have been in the marketplace for several decades, but their size and cost have made them impractical purchases for all but the most well-endowed school systems. Time-sharing was one

195

method by which schools could make the large machines accessible at a somewhat reasonable cost, but this was difficult to install and institutionalize. In addition, a mystique developed around the use of computers. This led to a feeling by all (except the already computer-competent) that using computers was for the highly specialized and trained expert, not the average person and certainly not the average child. Although some inroads into computer-assisted instruction were made during the era of bigger computers, it was not until the development of microcomputers that the potential for a revolutionary change in school and society had begun to be recognized. Personal computers are ready to use the minute they are turned on. They are relatively inexpensive and do not seem as overwhelming as the larger computers. As a result, personal computers invaded the nation's marketplace during the 1970s as technology finally developed an inexpensive, realistic alternative to large computers and time-sharing devices.

Meanwhile, childrens' games were becoming more and more electronically oriented. The microcomputer chip made the development of handheld electronic sports and arcade-type games possible, and children were encouraging their parents to purchase these items. These games are really computers that are programmed for specific activities. In addition to providing leisure-time fun for children, the games have served to introduce even young children to computers and to reduce the anxiety and awe previously associated with the larger computers. Children, therefore, became quite comfortable and, in fact, eager to use microcomputers when they began to be marketed in stores and started to appear in homes and schools.

Developments in education are usually several years and sometimes decades behind the communities in which they function. Technological changes in society usually are not reflected in schools until pressure from society forces those changes on the schools. For years, school systems prohibited the classroom use of calculators until their widespread use in the community made hand calculations of complicated formulas obsolete. As business and home markets for microcomputers became a booming business, the educational community began to explore the possibilities of using microcomputers as well.

The introduction of the microcomputer into school systems was received with mixed reactions. Some researchers conducted studies related to microcomputers. One such study on hyperactive children showed no differences between paper-and-pencil drill and computer drill in proportions of correct problems, average time to do problems, or average time between problems. However, the children were willing to spend more time working problems on their microcomputers and, therefore, actually practiced on almost twice as many problems (Kleiman et al., 1981). It is not clear why the additional time on task did not produce better learning, nor was there any effort to determine whether, after the novelty of the microcomputer wore off, the students would continue to sit still for long periods of time. In another study with gifted children, it was found that although students did not learn mathematics any better with microcomputer drill and practice than with pencil-and-paper drill and practice, the students who did drill and practice on the microcomputer scored significantly higher on a test of computer literacy, even though they had received no specific instruction in computer literacy (Steele et al., 1982).

Data are not yet available, however, to prove that microcomputer instruction is more effective than paper-and-pencil activities, and some educators are reluctant to encourage microcomputers in schools. They cite that there is not enough hard research to prove that microcomputers enhance learning, or that they are more effective than traditional instructional strategies. Other educators focus their criticism on the lack of good educational programs (software) to run on the computers. Much of what has been marketed has been hastily prepared in order to get programs published quickly. The results are often educationally unsound, boring, or too difficult to run without an advanced degree in computer science. A third and perhaps most frequent criticism by those reluctant to embrace computers in schools is embodied by a teacher who told the NEA *Reporter*:

> Every 10 years or so there's something new in educational technology that's treated as a panacea. A few years back it was instructional television and machine learning; now it's microcomputers. Once the newness of the gadget wears off, we return to the basic need for teacher-student interaction (Watkins and Webb, 1981).

In the complex dynamics of school, a combination of distrust of innovation, the inertia inherent in bureaucracies, and the fear of many educators of technology in general contributes to the attitude of the teacher.

Yet, despite the reluctance of some educators to allow microcomputers into their schools, more school systems gradually seem to be accepting the idea. Although all children can benefit from the microcomputer as a tool in the schools, learning-disabled/gifted youngsters will be particularly helped. As educators become aware of the tremendous capabilities of personal computers, they can begin to harness the already existing technology to help in the remediation of the problems of learning-disabled/gifted children in listening, speaking, reading, writing, or mathematics. In addition, the logical and sequential

198   *Tobin and Schiffman*

thinking, of which these children are capable, is easily learned and demonstrated through the use of personal computers.

THE MICROCOMPUTER AS A MANAGEMENT TOOL

One of the most effective uses of computer systems is to manage information. This management capability is especially useful for organizing the educational facilitation of children with special learning needs and individual programs to be tracked. A major time-consuming task for those involved in educating exceptional children is writing an individualized educational plan (IEP), mandated by PL 94-142. Because of the individual nature of the required diagnosis and plan, a wide range of educational services may be required; goals, objectives, and strategies must be developed for each service and each child. In addition, parents may expect to receive written documentation detailing the testing, diagnosis, and plan for their children. Students are expected to be carefully monitored as they move from initial referral through appropriate placement. Usually, federal and state regulations control the process, specifying the dates by which school systems must report information. In addition, teachers are expected to group students, even learning-disabled/gifted ones, for instruction based on their learning strengths and weaknesses as outlined on an IEP. These administrative needs, which are related to individualizing instruction, can be a nightmare for the teacher or specialist who assumes responsibility for implementation of IEPs. In fact, it may be one of the reasons special education teachers seem to burn out so quickly.

Introducing a microcomputer to help manage IEPs can relieve teachers of many of these administrative burdens and allow them to spend more time working with their students. The microcomputer has the potential to administer the necessary tests, score them, and report the results as an IEP for a child. Hasselbring and Crossland (1982) developed a microcomputer version of the Test of Written Spelling (TWS) and compared it to the original written version administered and scored by teachers, the teacher time required to score and administer the test, and the accuracy of the scoring. Even with the extra time needed by the teacher to explain to the students how to run the computerized program, the microcomputer version required significantly less of the teacher's time than the traditional method of administration and scoring. In addition, because of the problem of interpreting handwriting, the computer's scoring was more accurate than teacher-scored tests.

Other diagnostic tools may soon be adapted for the microcomputer and then pretesting should require a minimum of the teacher's time. Only the tests that need judgments, like an individual intelligence test, will have to be administered personally.

The computer is already being used by some school systems to teach and manage individual educational plan (IEP) programs. Microcomputer programs can scan students' diagnostic tests, evaluate strengths and weaknesses, and print an IEP in a form suitable for presenting to a parent or a professional review committee. A small county school system in Maryland uses one software system for a microcomputer that generates reports based on the required Maryland State competencies in reading, language, speech, and functional living skills. A hierarchy of skills, including goals, corresponding objectives, criteria to achieve mastery, methods to teach the objectives, and references for further information, have been entered into the microcomputer. The computer could report the students' status to the teacher, which objectives had been tested, for which objectives the student was or should have been receiving instruction, and which students succeeded in completing certain objectives (Schiffman, Tobin, and Cassidy-Bronson, 1982).

Other management programs have also been reported in the literature (Anderson and Glowinski, 1982; Adams et al., 1980; Brown, 1982; Hayden et al., 1982). Although these kinds of management programs are not widespread in the 1980s and still need adjustment for the needs of different school systems, their potential for individualizing for small populations such as learning-disabled/gifted students is enormous.

THE MICROCOMPUTER AS AN INSTRUCTIONAL TOOL

Because of their need for an individualized program, learning-disabled/gifted children should benefit from specific instructional packages designed for microcomputers. Many school systems are actively encouraging special educators to become involved in the development and use of computer technology for the instruction of exceptional children. However, the problem of finding appropriate software is a difficult one. Software is uneven in quality and sometimes produced by very small companies which do not market their programs well. Access to programs is dependent on geographical location and whether a person is on the right mailing list. Preview copies of discs generally are not available the way examination copies of books are. If instructional materials are hastily purchased and inappropriate, especially for exceptional students, the value of computer technology is negated, and the proper remediation and facilitation program is hampered. Without the quality software, students may find themselves doing meaningless drills, inappropriate games, and/or fragmented, isolated activities which have no relation to the regular curriculum.

At their best, microcomputer programs can offer learning-disabled/gifted youngsters individualized instruction in both their strengths and weaknesses with immediate and frequent reinforcement. These programs should include diagnostic and prescriptive techniques to place the learner appropriately in a comprehensive curriculum which is organized into a hierarchy of skills. In this way, learner outcomes are approached in terms of performance objectives, and progress is measured by mastery of those objectives (Caldwell and Rizza, 1979).

Even at an imperfect state of development, microcomputer instruction in the schools can offer some unique advantages to learning-disabled/gifted students. Learning-disabled/gifted students are often ashamed that they are not able to learn certain skills as quickly as their less able peers. They devise all kinds of behaviors to avoid appearing stupid. Because the microcomputer is inanimate and private, some of the stress associated with making a mistake is eliminated. Because the microcomputer can be programmed to be nonjudgmental, a learner would not be chastised for giving a wrong answer. In addition, children cannot "fake out" the computer with a lengthy but inappropriate answer. They are, therefore, forced to stay on task and continue learning the material as presented.

Rather than having the student wait until the teacher can grade the work, reinforcement for individual student responses can be immediate. The computer can be programmed to prevent the child from continuing until he or she produces the correct answer. If the child does not know an answer or gives an incorrect answer, some programs go back to a teaching mode so that the child can be retaught the skill involved in the problem that could not be solved.

Children with learning disabilities are sometimes unsure of themselves. Computers can provide continuous and positive feedback and praise, thus giving students a higher sense of self-esteem. Raising a student's confidence level can be a tremendous contribution to the ability to learn.

The computer can adapt its pace to the pace of the child's learning. Thus, when the child can comprehend quickly, the student can proceed at a fast pace. Conversely, the computer also has infinite patience and will wait as long as necessary for the child to arrive at the correct answer. It has no hidden timetable and is not in a hurry to go on to the next problem.

The computer can become a private tutor for the child. Microcomputers' interactive capabilities are commonly referred to as "user friendly." The microcomputer can use a child's name or other information to personalize its instruction. Children have been known to talk to the computer as if it could understand.

Learning-disabled students often have a greater need for drill and practice than developmental learners. The unique graphics and sound capabilities of most microcomputers on the market in the 1980s make it possible for drill and practice routines to be made dynamic and exciting. This can help to motivate students to continue through the practice they need. In the study cited earlier in this chapter (Kleiman et al., 1981), students were willing to spend more time on drill and practice on the microcomputer than on paper-and-pencil tasks.

These capabilities of the computer, (the ability to make drill and practice exciting, the ability to give immediate reinforcement in a nonthreatening way, user friendliness, the ability to adjust the pace of learning to the needs of the learners, nondistractibility, and insistence that students stay on task) make it favorable for all learners but particularly learning-disabled students.

The technology of the 1980s, although not perfected, probably will be available soon to make use of multisensory approaches to learning. This will be very beneficial for learning-disabled youngsters. Touch-sensitive screens and voice-input devices are still in the developmental stages, but projects are underway in the 1980s to use multisensory techniques for teaching learning-disabled children. The Johns Hopkins University Applied Physics Laboratory sponsored a nationwide competition on Personal Computing to Aid the Handicapped, which attracted entries by 900 professionals, amateurs, and students. Of the projects entered, 19 related to the learning-disabled students. Most of the winning entries were affordable and had already been piloted with children. One regional winner developed a simulated word-tracing program. This program used a voice synthesizer and light pen to allow a word to be said, and then the child would trace the word after it appeared on the screen. Another program related to telling time, using a voice synthesizer to speak the time to the child and paddle controls for the child to set the hands of the clock (Schiffman, Tobin, and Buchanan, 1982). Stimulating multisensory approaches to learning are especially suitable for learning-disabled youngsters. Programs which combine the microcomputer's capabilities with videotape and videodisc recorders are being developed and will make personal com-

202   *Tobin and Schiffman*

puters even more interactive and therefore more valuable for teaching disabled students (Bennett, 1982).

Certain aspects of computer learning make it especially suitable for the giftedness that is exhibited by this subpopulation of learning-disabled students. Instructional programs which emphasize problem solving, simulation, and discovery learning can help the learning-disabled/gifted child reach the higher-level thinking skills of which they are capable.

Simulation refers to the computer's ability to model a real situation or process. Computer programs can allow the user to make decisions at various points in a process, see the consequences of those decisions, and then repeat the problem solving until the process is completed or the problem is solved. Commercial software publishers have been using the principle of simulation to write adventure games in which the user goes through a series of trials to reach a goal. At each step in the program, decisions that are made have consequences which will allow users to either come one step closer to the goal or abort their efforts to reach the goal. The end point in adventure games usually means riches beyond belief or conquest of the world or universe. It can take weeks to master the process of understanding the best path to the end point, but once it is achieved, the game player can usually tell all the pitfalls of the decision points and why certain decisions have to be made in certain situations.

Although these kinds of programs are not specifically written for the education market, the possibilities for their use with learning-disabled/gifted children are great, especially if the processes and/or situations can be curriculum-related and lead to thinking through real, rather than hypothetical, problems. Processes relating to atomic energy, laws of mathematics, and/or historical events and their ramifications can all be adapted for the computer use by simulating adventure game formats. If the problem-solving strategies that are harnessed in finding the treasure of the wizard of a hypothetical, magic land could be related to understanding real problems, learning could be exciting.

Another advantage of the simulation abilities of the computer is that situations can be modeled so that students can experience first-hand that which is experienced secondhand through other media. Voyages through space or the human body can be simulated by the computer as easily as a trip through a haunted house. Students learn information by manipulating objects and/or facts and thus discover new ideas by themselves. In addition to learning information, they learn how to learn. It is difficult, time-consuming, and sometimes

Computer Technology   203

impossible to set up discovery situations in a regular classroom. Constant teacher involvement might be required. However, once written, a computer program can be used many times, and discovery-learning can become commonplace.

This principle of discovery-learning is behind the LOGO programs currently marketed for several types of microcomputers throughout the country (Papert, 1980; M. Watt, 1982). By moving a triangular-shaped object, usually called a turtle, students can discover geometric principles and learn structured programming. Although LOGO has much potential for use in the classroom, other software utilizing discovery-learning needs to be developed and perfected as well.

A more practical use of the microcomputer as an instructional aid is as a word processor. Writing on a word processor can be extremely helpful for learning-disabled/gifted students who have writing problems because mistakes are easy to correct without retyping large chunks of material. In addition, clean copies of revised editions can be available instantly so that the tedious job of editing becomes easy. Also, programs which automatically identify misspelled words can be used to help those children whose spelling skills are deficient. Word processors would be particularly good when combined with language-experience techniques and for those children who prefer to tape-record, transcribe, and then edit stories. (D. Watt, 1982). Word processors can motivate children who have difficulty writing and would allow learning-disabled/gifted students with rich vocabularies and high-level thinking abilities to play with ideas on the computer until they find the right way to express their thinking.

AN EXPERIMENTAL PROGRAM

Microcomputer instruction was one aspect of special summer classes for learning-disabled/gifted students held at The Johns Hopkins University (see Chapter 8 in this volume). Six Apple computers were available for use, and groups were rotated through the computer laboratory for 45-minute intervals each day.

The room was supervised by a 17-year-old high school senior who was knowledgeable about the Apple and was experienced in both BASIC and FORTRAN programming languages. He taught the students and teachers how to use the computer and some elementary programming commands in BASIC. In addition, he was familiar with the available library of software programs and helped teachers select suitable software for their children. There were three components to the computer

204   *Tobin and Schiffman*

module: 1) teacher training; 2) children and teachers working together; and 3) children and parents working together.

In order to reduce potential anxiety, teachers were trained to be users of the machine. They received a brief literacy course and instruction in programming the Apple. They were encouraged to use and evaluate software packages that were available in the computer laboratory so that they would be better consumers of software when they returned to their schools.

The teachers also spent time at the computers with their students. The computer aide also gave the children some instruction about computers. The children received additional help from their teachers, who had received instruction earlier in the program. After the introductory experience, the nature of the computer activities depended on the student's age, interests, and type of disability. Some children learned BASIC programming. Others worked on teacher-made or commercially available software.

During the first summer of the program, students were paired with other students at a computer while the teachers observed. This proved unsatisfactory because the students often were at different ability levels and had different interests. In subsequent summers, each child was paired with a teacher. This allowed the children to pursue their own interests and the teachers to utilize and/or reinforce previous learning in the microcomputer sessions.

The children were excited about their experiences in the computer room, and communicated that excitement to their parents. They asked their teachers if they could invite their parents to observe what they were doing. Normally, the children were excused from their instructional sessions at 11:30 a.m., at which time the teachers would meet as a group to discuss problems and successes. Those students who chose to stay longer were allowed to invite their parents as their guests in the computer room to work with them for about 1 hour. Because there were more students wanting to participate than available computers, a schedule had to be devised so that everyone could have equal time. This component was not planned initially, but it proved to be valuable because it involved the parents in their children's learning and also provided additional instructional time for the students. Although formal evaluation of the computer activities was not conducted, the following conclusions were made:

1. The students like working with the computers. Those who returned to the program for a second summer cited as their reason the fact that they could work with computers.

2. The computer was a strong motivator for individual children. Teachers found some children willing to work on vocabulary associated with computer terminology. Others were anxious to do drill and practice on needed skills when they could be done on the computer.
3. Teachers and students became comfortable with the computer, and many continued training after the summer session was over. Several teachers signed up for computer programming courses. Others returned to their home schools and convinced their principals to release a computer from the mathematics rooms (where they are usually housed) to the special education rooms so that they could work with their students in school.

CONCLUSION

It is too early to judge whether or not the microcomputer will create a revolution in education, but its introduction into classrooms will definitely create changes in instructional and administrative activities. Its use with special populations who need individualized programs, like learning-disabled/gifted students, can be very effective. However, its true potential can only be reached if special educators become involved with computer technology so that they can cooperate and communicate with computer scientists and programmers. Anxiety and negativism must be replaced by knowledge and positive attitudes so school systems can prepare children for the 21st century.

REFERENCES

Adams, J., Richards, J.H., and Brau-Langer, B. 1980. Data storage and retrieval system for use in a learning disabilities diagnostic clinic, J. Learn. Disabil. 13:13–15.

Anderson, D.O., and Glowinski, D.J. 1982. Effective use of a computer managed instruction program. J. Learn. Disabil. 15:555–556.

Bennett, R.E. 1982. Applications of microcomputer technology to special education. Except. Child. 49:106–112.

Brown, N.P. 1982. Cameo: Computer-assisted management of educational objectives. Except. Child. 49:163–172.

Caldwell, R.M., and Rizza, P.J. 1979. A computer based system of reading instruction for adult non-readers AEDS J. 12:155–162.

Hasselbring, T.S., and Crossland, C.L. 1982. Application of microcomputer technology to spelling assessment of learning disabled students. Learn. Disabil. Q. 5:80–81.

Hayden, D., Vance B., and Irvin, M.S. 1982. Establishing a special education management—SEMS. J. Learn. Disabil. 15:428–429.

Tobin and Schiffman

Kleiman, G., Humphrey, M., and Lindsay, P.H. 1981. Microcomputers and hyperactive children. Creat. Comput. 7.

Papert, S. 1980. Mindstorms, Children, Computers and Powerful Ideas. Basic Books, Inc., New York.

Schiffman, G., Tobin, D., and Buchanan, B. 1982. Microcomputer instruction for the learning disabled. J. Learn. Disabil. 15:557–559.

Schiffman, G., Tobin, D., and Cassidy-Bronson, S. 1982. Personal computers for the learning disabled. J. Learn. Disabil. 15:422–425.

Steele, K.J., Battista, M.T., and Krockover, G.H. 1982. The effect of microcomputer assisted instruction upon the computer literacy of high ability students. Gifted Child Q. 26:162–164.

Watkins, M., and Webb, C. 1981. Computer assisted instruction with learning disabled students. Educ. Comput. Mag. 4:24–27.

Watt, D. 1982. Word processors and writing. Popul. Comput. 6.

Watt, M. 1982. What is LOGO? Creat. Comput. 8:112–129.

Chapter 12

A Model Program for Elementary-Age Learning-Disabled/Gifted Youngsters

Lois J. Baldwin and Denise A. Gargiulo

Shawn is a 9-year-old boy who experiences tremendous difficulty in reading and writing. His poor phonetic discrimination and word substitutions cause a halted reading rate and poor comprehension. Writing is also burdensome for this youngster as evidenced by letter reversals and the aesthetic quality of his handwriting.

Shawn's classroom behavior reflects his efforts to avoid his learning problems. He protests that the work is too difficult, and he scribbles over or destroys his assignments and workbooks. Shawn labors over specific tasks or wanders around the room (going to the bathroom, getting a drink) in order to avoid finishing his work. He picks fights or falls off his chair to divert attention from reading group activities. His completed assignments often are handed in with purposefully illegible handwriting in order to mask his inadequacies. These behaviors are all signs of fear to fail and/or to succeed. Shawn feels that with success, he might be presented with new challenges that could lead to his failure.

In juxtaposition, although possessing a short attention span, Shawn listens and responds attentively to science-related issues and topics. He is very sensitive and perceptive when a discussion concerning social and ethical issues occurs within the classroom and is an active participant during discussions about current events and daily news. Throughout any of these discussions, however, Shawn exhibits an extreme need for the teacher's approval. He seeks this attention through OverVerbalization and constant interruptions. Shawn's intellectual potential is clouded by his maladaptive behavior. Fear of failure and/or success, consistent procrastination (destroying schoolwork, la-

208   *Baldwin and Gargiulo*

boring over tasks, inappropriate behavior), and a need for constant approval are some traits which characterize Shawn, a learning-disabled/gifted child.

Shawn has the paradoxical characteristics of giftedness as well as learning problems. His learning problems and maladaptive behaviors are impeding him from functioning productively within the regular classroom. Children like Shawn are vulnerable to patterns of academic and social failure; they need an educational environment that will reverse this trend and will help to develop their intellectual potential. This chapter discusses a self-contained classroom program for elementary-age learning-disabled/gifted children who, like Shawn, exhibit severe academic, social, and emotional problems attributable to their disabilities.

The program is one of the many diversified special education programs provided by the Board of Cooperative Educational Services (BOCES) of Southern Westchester County, New York. Twenty-nine local school districts are component members of BOCES and, therefore, can request the services and programs that are available for their handicapped and nonhandicapped students. All services that are provided must be cooperative with other school districts and approved by the state department of education. The gifted special education program continues to grow as more districts throughout the county request placement for their children who are potentially gifted but who have special learning needs. In the gifted special education program, there are approximately 50 children in grades K–12. The classes, which consist of two elementary (K–3 and 4–5), two middle school (6–8), and two high school (9–12) levels, are housed in three different school districts. The elementary program specifically discussed within this chapter is housed in the Pocantico Hills School, a small suburban school in North Tarrytown. Much of the success of the program is attributable to the cooperation and support of the Pocantico staff and administration.

IDENTIFICATION

To ensure the greatest success in identifying the children for this program, a multicriteria and multicomponent identification process is used. The screening process is initiated when a child is brought to the attention of the school's child evaluation team or the Committee on the Handicapped (COH) by a classroom teacher, parent, other interested professionals, or at the child's own request. The COH examines the referral and decides on a course of diagnostic testing. This diagnostic testing includes an individualized intelligence test, as well as achievement and perceptual tests. It includes behavioral characteristic checklists or forms filled out by the teacher and parent. Anecdotal records of the child's behavior are also carefully reviewed. When the COH feels that the child might be appropriate for the BOCES program that serves learning-disabled/gifted children, they will request that the BOCES evaluation team review the child's diagnostic test data and records. A determination is then made as to whether this program can meet the needs of the child in question.

The Wechsler Intelligence Scale for Children-Revised (WISC-R) is one of the most important screening tools. Unlike most other programs for gifted students which establish specific cutoff criteria scores for admission, this program includes a look at the total test protocol. This identifies the child's specific strengths and weaknesses in terms of scatter on the WISC-R subtest scores. When Schiff et al. (1981) analyzed WISC-R subtest scores of learning-disabled children with superior intelligence, they found that the subscale scatter was substantially greater for the learning-disabled/gifted student than for the learning-disabled child with normal intelligence. The scaled scores for the superior intelligence group were particularly high in four Verbal Subscale areas: Information, Similarities, Vocabulary, and Comprehension. The scores on Arithmetic, Digit Span, and Coding, however, were much lower, indicating discrepancies in ability.

Another way of evaluating the student is to observe the cognitive processes that the child utilizes while taking the intelligence test. Gallagher (1975) stated:

> The one factor that youngsters labeled 'gifted' have in common is the ability to absorb abstract concepts, to organize them more effectively, and to apply them more appropriately than does the average youngster (p. 19).

An alert psychologist who is specifically trained in testing gifted as well as learning-disabled children looks for indications of the child's higher-level thought processes during the test situation.

Group achievement tests are another method of measuring potentiality for giftedness. The set of tasks, norms, and high reliability of standardized tests make it possible to measure a child's potentiality. However, because of learning problems, many learning-disabled/gifted children do not score well on group achievement tests and/or will score only at grade level, thus making identification more difficult. For example, Shawn's visual motor difficulties prevent him from simultaneously finding the right answer and darkening the correct corre-

210   *Baldwin and Gargiulo*

sponding circle. On the test, any area of measurement that requires reading is also depressed because of his reading problems. Therefore, adaptations in the administration of the group achievement tests are sometimes necessary. Eliminating time limits, orally administering sections of the test and/or allowing the child to write on the test booklet may help to reduce interference caused by the learning deficit. Depending upon the child's learning disabilities, the evaluator may also prefer to administer an individual diagnostic test for a more accurate profile of the child's abilities and disabilities. Maker (1977) noted that:

> A learning disability must be more severe in one with high intellectual capacity in order to cause academic retardation comparable to that of his less gifted peers, since his higher level cognitive processes will help him to compensate for the disability (p. 66).

Therefore, careful review of student profiles is necessary with this special population.

Many schools use checklists that are filled out by teachers, such as the "Scale for Rating Behavioral Characteristics of Superior Students" by Renzulli and Hartman (1981) to identify their gifted populations. Structured checklists were devised to guide teachers in looking for specific characteristics because it was found that teachers were exceptionally poor at identifying gifted children (Gallagher, 1975; Pegnato and Birch, 1959; Renzulli et al., 1981). Checklists that are properly filled out can be valuable sources of information because teachers can provide data and information about the child that otherwise would not be available to other members of the evaluation team. In the case of the learning-disabled/gifted population, the checklist should also include unique characteristics that are not typically associated with gifted children (see Chapter 1).

There are a wide variety of parent checklists or forms which have been devised for more personal, in-depth profiles of the gifted child. Robinson et al. (1979) found that parents who reported specific examples of their child's behaviors rather than simply filling out yes/no questionnaires proved a more valuable tool in trying to identify very young gifted children. Parents of the gifted child with learning problems often see their child in settings in which the intellectual capabilities are more predominant than the deficits. Therefore, a parent form was designed to encourage the parents to provide comprehensive, anecdotal information about their child.

Once all the information and data on a child has been collected, the COH determines the proper program placement. The COH is responsible for placing the child in the most appropriate, least restric-

Model Program   211

tive educational setting. In some cases, this may mean that the child will participate in a resource room or have adaptations made to allow for participation in a regular and/or gifted classroom; in other cases, the most appropriate, least restrictive environment will be the self-contained classroom described in this chapter.

GOALS

There are three goals of this program: 1) to provide meaningful learning experiences which meet the individual needs of the children and assist them in developing their potential; 2) to provide opportunities for children to learn and to develop confidence in themselves as learners and human beings, because even those with mild handicapping conditions have experienced severe failure in school (Whitmore, 1980); and 3) to prepare the children for eventually moving back to regular and/or gifted classes which, hopefully, will be made possible by their experiences in the self-contained classroom. Each of these goals and the strategies to accomplish them are described in the following paragraphs.

Goal 1: To Remediate Student's Academic Weaknesses and To Develop Cognitive Abilities

An individual educational plan (IEP) is developed for each child. Parents are involved in this as much as possible. The IEP provides an excellent opportunity to identify the child's strengths and weaknesses; to design an instructional program that will complement the child's learning style, pace, needs, and interests; and to encourage parents and teachers to share the responsibility in order to understand and to help the child achieve his or her academic, social, and emotional potential.

Although it is necessary to work on academic deficits, the child's cognitive strengths are emphasized. It is important not to consistently associate one particular strength with one particular weakness. For example, if a teacher continually uses Shawn's science lessons as a way to teach his basic reading skills, he eventually will try to avoid both subjects. The child should understand that the teacher cares about providing opportunities for the development of interests—not just remediation. Shawn is a good example of a child who perceives himself to be a total failure in reading and language arts. His usual retort when asked to read would be, "If you want it read, read it yourself" and then he would retreat into his sweatshirt as a turtle does into his shell. The teacher developed a science unit around electricity and

212   *Baldwin and Gargiulo*

electronics, both of which were areas of interest to Shawn. He had previously avoided all of his teacher's attempts to get him interested or involved in independent activities. During this unit, however, he came in with directions on how to make an electromagnetic motor. Shawn and the teacher established a schedule and a process by which Shawn could accomplish his goal. His project was a success in several ways:

1. The curriculum and the independent study allowed Shawn to use a variety of problem-solving and analytical-thinking skills. The task had been broken into sequential steps so that he could analyze and reevaluate his progress and success at each stage.
2. The industrial arts teacher who had agreed to act as a mentor and a resource person was very pleased with Shawn's knowledge. His mentor's attitude helped to increase the child's self-image.
3. Most important, Shawn realized the need for basic skill work in order to become more independent and able to research further his area of interest.

Goal 2: To Increase Student's Self-Worth and Social Skills

Because of their conflicting exceptionalities, many learning-disabled/ gifted children feel isolated in the regular classroom. They have a need to discuss areas of intellectual interests with peers, but they often find that their efforts to establish such conversation are thwarted. At the same time, their developmental lags often result in inadequate socialization skills and, therefore, inappropriate interactions with peers. Osman (1979) indicated some of their social difficulties:

> Many of the same deficits that effect a youngster's academic skills have implications for his social adjustment. A common trait among children with learning problems is difficulty in paying attention to what is important. They tend to become mixed up and confused in a crowded or overstimulating environment. They cannot tune out what is unimportant and tune in that which is important. This may cause them to lose the essence of a conversation or not respond appropriately. Sometimes they cannot shift gears as readily as other children. They may still be thinking about the pass they fumbled although the gang has long since started another activity. And some youngsters' impulsivity and lack of judgment may cause them to lash out at imagined slights, turning them into poor sports (p. 62).

In order to enhance the child's self-esteem and to reverse the debilitating effects of poor social interactions, this program seeks to maximize the child's opportunities for positive experiences. The teacher creates a nonthreatening classroom environment, which fosters feelings of trust and security and establishes the value system which prevails in the classroom. By praising or acknowledging the child's strengths and accomplishments and teaching the child to deal appropriately with emotions and feelings of failure, the teacher communicates a message that each individual has self-worth. It is critical for the child to learn to set realistic self-expectations both academically and socially. The teacher structures class discussions so that students are allowed to explore their own feelings and mutual frustrations. This encourages the children to begin reaching out to others in a safe, secure environment.

An increase of self-esteem and feelings of positive self-worth usually result in increased academic achievement. Studies have shown that there is a significant positive relationship between self-concept and achievement (Charles, 1976; Shaw and Alyes, 1963). In the case of learning-disabled/gifted children, the pleasure that children receive from their accomplishments in the carefully planned curriculum and structured environment often increases their self-esteem and ability to achieve. Various types of activities and materials that foster positive self-concepts are listed in Table 12.1.

An example of a specific situation in which a problem-solving technique was used is as follows. The children in Shawn's class were beginning to establish more positive social relationships with each other. In the process, friendships developed between several children.

Table 12.1. Activities and resource materials for fostering positive self-concepts

Activity	Resource material
1. Classroom meetings	a) *Schools without Failure*, Glasser (1975) b) *Classroom Ideas for Encouraging Thinking and Feeling*, Williams (1971)
2. Value clarification exercises	a) *Values Clarification*, Simon et al. (1972) b) *Affective Education Guidebook*, Eberle and Hall
3. Problem-solving activities	a) *Creative Action Book*, Parnes et al. (1976) b) *Mind Benders: Deductive Thinking Skills*, Harnadek (1978)
4. Creativity activities	a) *Synectics*, Gordon (1961) b) *Ideabooks*, Torrance and Myers (1970)
5. Behavior modification programs	a) *The Aggressive Child*, Redl and Wineman (1957) b) *Contracts*, Kohfeldt (1974)

214   *Baldwin and Gargiulo*

However, these friendships also led to rivalry and jealousy among other members of the class. This resulted in name-calling and making derogatory comments about each other, which interfered with the children's academic achievement and the smooth running of the classroom.

The teacher initiated a class meeting to discuss their problem using the creative problem-solving technique from the *Creative Action Book* by Parnes et al. (1976), which included five steps: fact finding, problem finding, idea finding, solution finding, and acceptance finding. They agreed upon a course of action and successfully implemented their plan.

Goal 3: To Prepare Students To Go Back into Mainstream

When the child is placed into the self-contained class, the placement is looked upon as being temporary. The goal of the program is to mainstream the children into regular classrooms as soon as possible. The process and steps necessary to make this goal a reality are relatively sequential. There are four steps.

Step 1 The first step is primarily reflective of fulfilling Goals 1 and 2. At this stage, the students must participate successfully within the self-contained class. The children's self-concepts must improve to a point where they are able to socialize properly and to respond to their teacher and peers. Once this behavior is exhibited within the self-contained class, the teacher can move to the second step.

For example, Lisa, a younger child in Shawn's class became frightened in any new situation. She refused to participate in the small adaptive physical education class, taught by a teacher she liked. As a result, her classroom and physical education teachers incorporated a number of strategies which gradually allowed Lisa to overcome her fear. First, Lisa was given the privilege of being the physical education helper for the kindergarten class once a week. Her only responsibility during that time was to take out and put away the balls and equipment. During that half-hour period, Lisa was able to watch younger children play, thus becoming familiar with the games and equipment. She was also required to go to her physical education class at the regularly scheduled time, but as always, there was no pressure for her to participate. Second, an aide helped her to make a bean bag, which was used for a 15-minute game of catch as a "reward" once her work was completed. During the game, Lisa began to develop greater confidence in herself and her ability to participate in physical movement activities. She now participates in the adaptive physical education class and physical games during recess.

Model Program 215

Step 2 The student is mainstreamed for special classes such as music, gym, art, and other electives. Even though many of the children are academically disabled, often they have abilities and strengths in other areas. It is vitally important when integrating this special population of children into special subject classes that support personnel are cooperative, compassionate, well-trained, and willing to work. For example, knowing Shawn has a reading problem, the music teacher can help him to participate successfully with the grade 4 music class by allowing him to use his auditory strength to memorize the words to songs.

Step 3 The student is mainstreamed into specific academic classes and/or the gifted resource program. If the student is successful in step 2 and is working on grade level in certain subject areas, utilizing adequate study skills and proper socialization skills, the teacher may decide to mainstream him for specific academic classes and/or into the gifted resource program. Because of the child's superior cognitive abilities, it may be more appropriate to mainstream him or her into the gifted program even before placement in a regular classroom. A major factor to consider before mainstreaming the child is the schedule. It is necessary to establish consistent time periods and routines in order to help create a smoother transition from the self-contained class to other classes. Too many initial class changes and/or inconsistent routines may confuse the child and thus, contribute to failure.

Step 4 The student will be mainstreamed into a full-time combination of regular and gifted classes as appropriate. Prior to considering a full-time regular classroom placement, the child should be participating in the mainstream for approximately 50% of the day. A more positive self-concept, achievement in academic areas, appropriate study habits, and proper socialization skills are signs that the child is ready for the change. Once the professionals recommend a change in placement, the COH will act upon the recommendation to establish the most appropriate academic program for the child.

CURRICULUM AND INSTRUCTION

In establishing the curriculum for learning-disabled/gifted children, the dual characteristics of each exceptionality must be met through various methods, materials, and the classroom setting. There are contrasting elements between the recommended teaching approaches utilized for gifted children and for learning-disabled children. Table 12.2 shows the differences on four dimensions—the approach (philosophy), setting, methods, and materials. The curriculum for learning-disabled/ gifted children lies on a continuum between diagnostic/prescriptive

216 Baldwin and Gargiulo

Table 12.2. Elements of contrasting curricula

	Gifted children	Learning-disabled children
Approaches	Holistic, open-ended approach; child able to learn inductively, intuitively	Prescriptive teaching; narrow focus and specific (task analysis)
Setting	Classroom containing little or no desks; mostly tables and centers	Classroom containing desks, cubicles; time-out area and minimum of tables
	Lounge area incorporated into daily lessons; unlimited use	Lounge area for reading or relaxing; restricted use with rules and regulations
	Accelerated and enriched content; independent study and research	Learning centers; explicit in directions; simplified to meet needs of child
	Classroom environment stimulating with bright colors, bulletin boards, etc.	Classroom environment has less stimuli; orderly with less "clutter"
Methods	Self-selected and flexible grouping	Small group instruction; one-to-one instruction with teachers
	Unstructured periods of time for independent study and exploration of classroom materials	Structured independent work with constant supervision and positive, immediate reinforcement
	Flexible time constraints to allow the child to explore inquiries and set priorities	Time limits on lessons, 15–30 minutes depending on group or individual abilities
	Advanced material available to promote inquiry and higher-level thinking skills	Adaptation of materials and techniques such as multisensory and programmed materials to meet child's remedial needs
Materials	Materials allow for the development of higher-level thinking skills (emphasis on application and evaluation according to Bloom, 1956)	Materials ordered in cognitive hierarchical steps (emphasis on knowledge and comprehension according to Bloom, 1956)
	Materials provide opportunity for acceleration of content and self-evaluation; advanced placement offered	Criterion-mastery levels required for student to proceed to more challenging material
	Interest centers along with mentor programs and self-advanced skill work provide self-motivation	Materials have built-in reinforcement systems such as tokens and points to provide motivation

teaching and a more holistic, open-ended approach. These children do not have the capability to learn solely through intuition or induction. They walk a tightrope between needing a structured curriculum and one that provides enrichment and freedom. Through the diagnostic/prescriptive approach, the teacher identifies the child's needs and provides him with appropriate skill work. A structured environment initially must be maintained to supply the order, security, and consistency necessary for remediating these students' deficits and fulfilling their emotional needs. In conjunction with the remediation, the curriculum must make provisions for enrichment and differentiation in order to tap those intellective strengths and potential talents that have remained dormant.

The physical environment of the classroom relates an important message to the child. It tells the child if learning is going to be fun, open, and explorative or if it will be closed and restricted. Because of their repeated failure pattern in school, learning-disabled/gifted students have very low self-concepts and at first will find it hard to socialize amiably. The classroom should be provided with study carrels, desks, and tables so that the children have their own space in which to work. However, along with desks and carrels, various learning centers within the room will promote independent study and allow the child to synthesize information from various disciplines. The learning centers can also create a cooperative learning environment among class members so that youngsters might work together on particular independent study projects. A lounge area which is carpeted and supplied with pillows and chairs provides these children with a place where they can release tensions and have a quiet moment during the day. This area may also be used as a free activity center equipped with educational games, comics, books, records, and filmstrips. The physical setup of a classroom should provide the children with opportunities and materials to reach their full potential.

When the children first enter the learning-disabled/gifted self-contained class, their behavior often reflects their view of themselves as failures and freaks. This anger may be turned inward, as evidenced by self-deprecating comments, or outward in verbal and sometimes physical attacks on peers or the environment. Poor study habits and learning deficits contribute to a lack of achievement. Professionals may feel that underneath the anger, confusions, and learning problems lies the potential for outstanding intellectual achievements; but, a well-trained, competent teacher must use and adapt a wide variety of methods and materials in order to "eke out" even occasional glimpses of the child's abilities.

218   *Baldwin and Gargiulo*

A portion of the curriculum must deal with the affective and emotional development of the children. A method that can be used to facilitate the child's personal and/or social growth is the classroom meeting. Classroom meetings should take place whenever a problem arises in or out of the classroom. The meetings should be held at a round table or another similar arrangement that is conducive for discussions. Clear-cut rules that allow each child to share ideas and feelings without being criticized or interrupted must be established. Initially, the teacher needs to help the children to develop more problem-solving techniques and he or she should select topics to be discussed. However, as the children become more comfortable with the process, many of the classroom meetings will be initiated at their request. In this way, they begin to develop more appropriate methods for dealing with their emotions and social interactions. The teacher must develop techniques and classroom schedules that allow the child to work independently but within a structured setting. One effective technique is frequent conferencing with the child. This allows the teacher and student to discuss his or her progress, difficulties, and daily schedule. It also fosters a sense of responsibility and independence for the learning-disabled/gifted student. As a result of conferencing with Shawn, it was decided that he would work 20 minutes in a study carrel on skill activities, 15 minutes with the Language Master and 15 minutes at the science interest center.

Since many learning-disabled/gifted children have met years of frustration and failure using traditional techniques with workbooks and textbooks, innovative and creative ways must be utilized in presenting factual and concrete knowledge. For example, students who dislike textbook readers may fare better when their reading program is based on their choice of appropriate fiction or nonfiction literature. Shawn was required to write short summaries of each chapter he read in his novel and to participate in specific language skill lessons.

A creative way to promote independent study is the use of learning centers, which foster a more positive self-concept. These centers should reflect the children's higher-level interests (for example, space, computers, biological science) and at the same time adjust for the children's ability levels. The directions of each center should be posted clearly and simply. The child should be able to follow them step by step without constantly calling upon the teacher's assistance. A careful and thorough introduction of the center is required in order for this to happen.

Gifted children enjoy the challenge of taking educational risks. However, because of their history of school failure and dependence on rote learning, the learning-disabled/gifted population will not allow their strengths to shine forth by taking such risks. One method of extracting the children's higher-level cognitive abilities is through deductive and inductive thinking activities. The teacher may use Harnadek's *Mind Benders: Deductive Thinking Skills*, (1978) which uses charts and word problems to help develop the child's critical thinking abilities in an ordered and sequential fashion. Presenting the children with analogies is another excellent method of developing these skills.

It is important to differentiate the curriculum for gifted learners through such methods as acceleration and enrichment. Enrichment activities should not be "fun and games"; but rather they should be an expansion and more in-depth study of the various content areas. A carefully designed combined social studies/science curriculum can help the children to develop a greater understanding of the world and their place in it. The curriculum also can introduce them to a wide variety of disciplines, such as government, cultures, archeology, psychology, sociology and anthropology. For example, elementary-age children are fascinated by moving objects that are "their size," such as toy cars, boats, planes and trains. These are objects that they can move and manipulate. A curriculum that is based on these objects can lead to a wide variety of group and individual projects for the whole class. A social science curriculum based on a model railroad was developed for Shawn's class. The children used a model railroad that they helped to develop. This led to a broadening of their understanding of the complex relationship between man, his community and forms of transportation.

From the initial unit on transportation, the students became involved in studying government, politics, and various laws as they worked together to determine what agencies, services, buildings, industry, zoning, and forms of transportation were going to be needed for their miniature community. They learned a lot about human behavior, particularly their own and the interdependence and role all of these aspects play in their lives and futures. As the children established the model environment and social system, they studied the world around them and they began to analyze, synthesize, and evaluate the elements that make up society and their natural and man-made world. They became fascinated with how the various forms of transportation affected exploration and the distances traveled. That led to investigations about future travel, solar systems and inventions. Geography, map reading, measurement, and time were developing naturally as the unit progressed. The study of electricity, pollution, ecology, and concepts of physics, such as the Bernoulli Effect, internal combustion,

220   Baldwin and Gargiulo

gravity, friction and centrifugal force, were all natural outgrowths of the unit. Because of the children's interest and the various science experiments that resulted, many of the children took an area to develop as an independent project. The projects that resulted included an electromagnetic motor and a shortwave radio.

The initial unit of transportation led to an exciting year that helped learning-disabled/gifted children acquire important concepts and knowledge about themselves and the world. The point to be learned from this unit is that a hands on activity of interest to the children can expand the curriculum content beyond the concrete-knowledge level to the higher levels of thinking, such as analysis, synthesis, and evaluation. Thus, curriculum can be used to foster inductive reasoning skills. A linkage was made between one toy train and the concept of man's dependence upon his environment and his role in the preservation of our natural resources.

CONCLUSION

This program is an example of how traditional methods used with learning-disabled children and those used with gifted children can be combined to provide an optimal setting for the learning-disabled/gifted child. A crucial element of this program is the right balance between independent and structured activities. The ultimate goal of the program is to prepare students to be fully mainstreamed. In order for this to be accomplished, attention must be paid to the affective needs of the children as well as their particular patterns of cognitive strengths and weaknesses.

REFERENCES

Bloom, B. 1956. Taxonomy of Educational Objectives: The Classification of Educational Goals: Handbook I: Cognitive Domain. David McKay Co., Inc., New York.

Charles, C.M. 1976. Individualizing Instruction. The C.V. Mosby Co., St. Louis.

Eberle, B., and Hall, R.E. Affective Education Guidebook. D.O.K. Publishers, Inc., Buffalo, NY.

Gallagher, J.J. 1975. Teaching the Gifted Child. Allyn and Bacon, Inc., Boston.

Glasser, W. 1969. Schools Without Failure. Harper and Row Publishers, Inc., New York.

Gordon, W. 1961. Synectics. Harper and Row Publishers, Inc., New York.

Harnadek, A. 1978. Mind Benders: Deductive Thinking Skills. Midwest Publications Co., Inc., Troy, MI.

Kohfeldt, J. 1974. Contracts. Innovative Educational Support Systems, Wayne, NJ.

Model Program 221

Maker, J.C. 1977. Providing Programs for the Gifted Handicapped. The Council for Exceptional Children, Reston, VA.

Osman, B.B. 1979. Learning Disabilities: A Family Affair. Consumers Union, Mount Vernon, NY.

Parnes, S.J., Noller, R.B., and Biondi, A.M. 1976. Creative Action Book. Charles Scribner's Sons, New York.

Pegnato, C.W., and Birch, J.W. 1959. Locating gifted children in junior high schools: A comparison of methods. Except. Child. 25:300–304.

Redl, F., and Wineman, D. 1957. The Aggressive Child. The Free Press, New York.

Renzulli, J.S., and Hartman, R.K. 1981. Scale for rating behavioral characteristics of superior students. In: W. Barbe and J. Renzulli (eds.), Psychology and Education of the Gifted. Irvington Publishers, Inc., New York.

Renzulli, J., Hatrman, R., and Callahan, C. 1981. Teacher identification of superior students. In: W. Barbe and J. Renzulli, (eds.), Psychology and Education of the Gifted. Irvington Publishers, Inc., New York.

Robinson, H.B., Roedell, W.C., and Jackson, N.E. 1979. Early identification and intervention. In: Passow, H.A. (ed.), The Gifted and the Talented: Their Education and Development, The Seventy-Eighth Yearbook of the National Society for the Study of Education. The University of Chicago Press, Chicago.

Schiff, M.M., Kaufman, A.S., and Kaufman, N.L. 1981. Scatter analysis of WISC-R profiles for learning disabled children with superior intelligence. J. Learn. Disabil. 14:400–404.

Shaw, M., and Alyes, G. 1963. The self-concept of bright academic underachievers. Person. Guid. J. 42:401–403.

Simon, S., Howe, L., and Kirschenbaum, H. 1972. Values Clarification. Hart Publishing Co., Inc., New York.

Torrance, E.P., and Meyers, R.E. 1970. Creative Learning and Teaching. Dodd, Mead, and Co., New York.

Whitmore, J.R. 1980. Giftedness, Conflict and Underachievement. Allyn and Bacon, Inc., Boston.

Williams, F.E. 1971. Classroom Ideas for Encouraging Thinking and Feeling. D.O.K. Publishers, Buffalo, New York.

Chapter 13

A Pilot Program For Elementary-Age Learning-Disabled/Gifted Students

Anne J. Udall and C. June Maker

The combination of learning disabilities and giftedness in a child is not a new phenomenon—only a new and growing concern. In the past, the gifted child was stereotyped as a high-achieving, highly motivated, socially adjusted individual, the learning-disabled child was considered to be of average intelligence, failing in most subjects, and socially maladjusted. However, stereotypes are changing, and individuals who do not fit the traditional molds are now being considered for special services. The tremendous growth of interest in the learning-disabled/gifted child reflects this fundamental change in attitudes, and there are an increasing number of references to this population (i.e. Daniels, 1983; Elkind, 1973; Maker, 1977, 1981; Wolf and Gygi, 1981).

Although speculation and interest have grown in the 1980s, there still are only a few actual programs serving these children. This chapter describes one such program—a pilot classroom for elementary-age learning-disabled/gifted students. It is an ongoing, dynamic, evolving program that changes with each new insight. Theoretical and philosophical issues are discussed in depth elsewhere in this book. Thus, the material presented here is pragmatic, applicable to those who are or hope to be working with this challenging and unique group. This chapter describes the design and implementation of one such program, including curriculum, teaching methods, strengths and weaknesses, and future directions.

SETTING THE STAGE

The program's setting is a large school district in the southwestern part of the United States. Tucson Unified School District (TUSD) is the largest school district in Tucson, with a total school population of

224　*Udall and Maker*

50,000 students. Within its boundaries are 68 elementary schools, 16 junior high schools, and nine high schools. The district is divided into four regions, each with its own assistant superintendent and administrative office.

Each region administers the special education (usually referred to as adaptive education in TUSD) services for its schools. There are adaptive education representatives and psychologists who work with the special education teachers within their separate regions. Approximately 5,000 identified learning-disabled students are in the district's resource, extended resource, and self-contained programs. These programs are served under the mandates of PL 94-142, The Education for All Handicapped Act.

The Gifted And Talented Education (GATE) Program in TUSD is new, but growing. Presently there are 1,200 elementary-age students, who can select either a self-contained or resource program. GATE is not considered part of the special education services, and the program is administered separately. Similar referral and identification procedures are followed, but there are few state or district guidelines.

There is little overlap between special education and GATE services. Some children in GATE receive special education services; some children in special education participate in GATE. Yet, the numbers are few. The existence of two separate offices and different administrative procedures encourage the traditional distance between gifted and special education. Before the beginning of the learning-disabled/gifted program, there was little mutual understanding of concerns or problems.

The director of adaptive education (Mary Meridith) became interested in the idea of a learning-disabled/gifted classroom in the summer of 1981. The teacher who later taught the class (Anne Udall) approached the district with the idea. Further impetus was gained with the beginning of a teacher-training program in gifted education at the University of Arizona. The coordinator of the program (June Maker) had an interest in such a classroom and was willing to lend her expertise in the area of gifted handicapped to develop the program. Given this support, the director was willing to take the risk.

A part-time position entitled Teacher and Evaluator for Learning Disabled/Gifted was established that fall. The person hired for the position had a master's degree in learning disabilities and giftedness and teaching experience with both groups. The main responsibilities of the job were the following: to identify learning-disabled/gifted children districtwide; to establish a pilot classroom for learning-disabled/gifted elementary children; and on an itinerant basis, to assist any teachers who had learning-disabled/gifted children in their classrooms. This chapter describes the first two responsibilities.

The First Phase: Setting Goals

The program's first phase involved several important goals: 1) a definition of the target population had to be established; 2) the existence of the program and itinerant services had to be publicized; and 3) referrals had to be solicited.

The establishment of a definition was difficult for several reasons. Although there is a growing body of theories about the characteristics, definition, and identification of the learning-disabled/gifted child, there is a lack of empirical data to support the major hypotheses in this area. The following questions are still unanswered: Should the two most common definitions in the fields of giftedness and learning disabilities be combined? Is there a unique body of characteristics which requires a unique definition, distinct from existing ones? What data should be collected to determine if a child is learning-disabled/gifted? Should there be intelligence test cutoff scores? Until such questions are answered, an empirical definition remains elusive.

A working definition was selected, combining the district's definition of learning disabled with a broad definition of intellectual giftedness. This does not mean there are not learning-disabled children who are gifted in areas other than intellectual; but the program chose to concentrate on this area. After data were collected on the selected population, refinement of this definition could occur. The definition of the learning-disabled/gifted child used for this program is as follows.

A learning-disabled/gifted child is one who exhibits all of the following characteristics:

1. Does not achieve commensurate with his or her age and ability levels in one or more of the areas listed under item number 2 when provided with learning experiences appropriate for the child's age and ability levels
2. Has a severe discrepancy between achievement and intellectual ability in one or more of the following areas:
   a. Oral expression
   b. Listening comprehension
   c. Written expression
   d. Basic reading skill
   e. Reading comprehension
   f. Mathematics calculation
   g. Mathematics reasoning

226   *Udall and Maker*

3. Must evidence a deficit in one or more of the psychological processes. A process deficit is based on the students' unique pattern
of abilities and disabilities and the discrepancies therein in the
essential learning processes of perception, integration, and expression. Deficits are identified on the basis of a student's resultant
score(s) or test(s) that assess basic psychological processes and academic readiness skills
4. Does not have a specific learning disability if the severe discrepancy between ability and achievement is primarily the result of
the following:
a. A visual, hearing, or motor handicap
b. Mental retardation
c. Emotional disturbance
d. Environmental, cultural, or economic disadvantage
5. Shows indications of intellectual giftedness as demonstrated by test
scores and/or observable behavior that is not reflected in academic
performance

In short, for children to qualify for the program they must be learning
disabled by district standards and also show signs of intellectual giftedness.

Once a definition was established, teachers and other individuals
were contacted about the program's existence. Much of the early contact involved public relations and dissemination of information. It was
common to encounter dubious looks, incredulous faces, and sometimes outright laughter when the program was described. Quite simply,
people believed that gifted children are "smart" and learning-disabled
children are "dumb"; it was inconceivable that the two might be one.

News about the program was often spread informally in teachers'
lounges or chance meetings with principals. Although information was
circulated through numerous channels throughout the year, getting
the information out to those who needed it was a slow process. In a
district this large, teachers had to wait for the "filter effect." For example, numerous phone calls during the last 3 weeks of school concerned with the inevitable question, "Why haven't I heard about the
program before?"

Some people did not need any explanation. These were mostly
teachers who had worked with learning-disabled/gifted children for
many years but did not have a label for them. One of the notes received
sums up the feelings of many teachers:

Dear Ms. Udall:
This is the first year in 6 or 7 years when I have *no* child whom I feel
needs a dual program such as you propose. My frustration has been sec-

ond only to that of these children of bygone years and I wish you God-speed in developing such a service.
Best Wishes!

At the same time that information was being disseminated, the more formal process of collecting referrals began. The initial goal was to gather as many referrals as possible through as many channels as possible. The learning-disabled/gifted child is not easily identifiable, and it is important to investigate many different sources.

The learning-disabled/gifted teacher collected referrals from a variety of sources:

1. All district teachers of learning-disabled and gifted children were sent checklists describing both the program and possible characteristics of the learning-disabled/gifted child (see Figure 13.1). Teachers were asked to submit the names of any children who might meet the description. Twenty GATE teachers were contacted, and 23 referrals were gathered using this method; 20 referrals were received from 134 teachers of the learning-disabled children.

2. All 40 district psychologists and adaptive education representatives were sent a similar checklist along with a request for referrals. This netted 11 names.

3. The records of learning-disabled children currently placed in one region of the district were searched. Test scores, developmental history, and teacher/parent observations were scanned. Three hundred and thirteen records were searched and 28 names collected.

4. The 792 records of children referred for the gifted program but not accepted were searched. Similar information was reviewed. Eighty names were selected for further consideration.

5. Notices were printed in all district newsletters. Individuals wishing to refer a child were requested to notify the teacher/evaluator. Six people contacted the program with potential referrals.

6. Finally, local gifted and learning disabilities parent-group members were asked to submit the names of their children. Four children were referred.

Any thorough referral and identification process should also include a search for children in regular classrooms. Many learning-disabled/gifted children are hidden there. Their learning disability is severe enough to keep them from qualifying for the gifted program, and their giftedness is strong enough to keep them functioning at grade level so that they do not qualify for a learning disability program. Be-

TO: Teachers of LD and Gifted Students

FROM: Anne Udall, LD/Gifted Evaluator and Teacher

I am establishing a program for gifted children with learning problems, and I need your help in locating potential children. Contrary to often held beliefs, it is possible for a child to be both gifted and learning disabled. Do you have (or know of) any children who are (or potentially) gifted who may also have a learning disability? To help you in your identification, I have included a list of potential characteristics these children may exhibit. To be included in the program, a child does not have to be *identified* learning disabled or gifted, so please spread the word. If you know of any children, please detach the bottom portion of this letter, and return it to me. I really appreciate any help you can give me in locating children. If I can answer any questions about the program or specific children in your classes, please contact me at the GATE office, Corbett Elementary, 791-6385.

Possible characteristics

Strengths in:
_____ Verbal language (i.e., vocabulary, ability to express one's self)
_____ Problem-solving skills
_____ Leadership
_____ Shows original thought or ideas in art, music, or other
        nonacademic areas
_____ Creativity and/or divergent solving ability
_____ Quick recall of factual information verbally
_____ Has avid outside interests

Weaknesses in:
_____ Attention and motivation
_____ Self-concept
_____ Academic areas (spelling, math, reading)
_____ Handwriting
_____ Sticking with a task
_____ Memory
_____ Auditory, motor, or visual perception
_____ Realistic self-perception

Other characteristics:
_____ Discrepancies between tested potential and school
        performance
_____ Discrepancies between sub-sections on standardized tests
        (i.e., WISC, WRAT, Stanford-Binet)
_____ An attempt to hide or "mask" the disability
_____ An awareness of being "different"
_____ A high level or frustration

Teacher's name _____ School _____
Student's name(s) _____
Why do you think this child might be LD/Gifted
(clues, characteristics, etc.)?

Figure 13.1.   Pilot program checklist

Pilot Program 229

cause of time restraints, no regular classroom teachers were contacted; however, there are plans for referrals to be solicited in the future.

The Second Phase: Identification

The second phase was to collect as much information as possible about the referred children. When it became obvious that the number of referrals was large and growing, a decision was made to initially concentrate on children in one region for placement in the pilot program. This made the numbers more manageable and assured the beginning of the program in the first year.

The following information about each child in the referral pool was collected:

1. Test scores, including an intelligence test, achievement tests, and processing tests. (The Wechsler Intelligence Scale for Children-Revised (WISC-R), the Detroit Tests of Learning Aptitude, the Woodcock-Johnson Psychoeducational Battery, the Peabody Individual Achievement Test, and the Otis-Lennon School Abilities Test are the commonly used tests in the school district)
2. Interviews with the teachers of the children, including both regular and special services teachers
3. Classroom observations, preferably in all settings
4. Interview with the child
5. Miscellaneous information, including cumulative records, developmental history, and records of previous conferences

A placement committee was established to determine the population of the pilot classroom. Although this was technically not an identification committee, the children who were selected had to meet the chosen definition criteria. The committee consisted of the coordinator of the University of Arizona teacher-training program, a psychologist, an adaptive education representative, the learning-disabled/gifted teacher, and the GATE program specialist.

In total, 30 children were reviewed by the committee. The committee reviewed each folder and the observation/interview summaries. Then, a group discussion was held. Several general questions were used as guidelines in the decision-making process. Which children would benefit most from the program? Which showed the most potential giftedness in the face of the most severe disability? Did the child clearly demonstrate both learning disability and giftedness? No minimal intelligence test score was required; the severity of the disability was compared with the indications of giftedness.

Decisions were not easy. This was untraveled terrain. It was hard to weigh the potential benefits, who was the most "gifted," or who had

230   *Udall and Maker*

the most severe disability. The desire to be objective was hampered by the relative lack of objective guidelines about the identification of learning-disabled/gifted children. The collected information which had at first seemed sufficient suddenly was inadequate. The meetings were a curious blend of objective-weighing and gut feelings. Fifteen children were initially selected.

Most of the children who were accepted into the program were initially referred by adaptive education personnel, either teachers or representatives. Of the 15 children who were eventually accepted, 14 were originally referred by teachers of learning-disabled/gifted children, psychologists, or adaptive education representatives. One child was identified through the record search of learning disabilities folders. It is interesting to speculate about the effectiveness and efficiency regarding teacher identification of the learning-disabled/gifted child. In this program, teacher referral was, by far, the most efficient and effective method. In contrast to the research available in gifted education (Gear, 1976), perhaps teacher identification of these children is a reliable method.

No girls were referred by teachers or adaptive education personnel. The record search of the adaptive education folders revealed only four names. Based on the collected information the four referred girls did not qualify for the program.

After the committee's decisions were made, a meeting was held for parents. Teachers were invited to attend. Some knew about the program; others did not. It was a group meeting, held one evening in early March. For the first time, parents were able to meet others who, like themselves, had children who alternately baffled, frustrated, and inspired them. They shared stories and difficulties. A dawning sense of "I'm not the only one" was evident as the meeting progressed.

The program was described in detail. Questions were answered. The most poignant, memorable question came toward the end: "If my child is so smart, how come he can't spell?" Permission to place the children on a trial basis was obtained. Most parents were eager and excited. One parent, concerned that her son's performance might suffer in the regular classroom, was willing to try. All the parents signed placement forms.

The Classes Begin

The first pilot classroom with nine students began in late March and the second with six students began 1 month later. Each group met with the learning-disabled/gifted teacher for 1 full day per week. A part-time volunteer aide assisted in the class most of the day. The

Pilot Program   231

program was housed in an elementary school, where the self-contained GATE classes were also held. This meant that school transportation for the learning-disabled/gifted child could easily be provided, because the transportation system for the GATE program was well-established and covered the entire district. Furthermore, this placement allowed an opportunity for the learning-disabled/gifted students to interact with other gifted children, informally and during special GATE events. During the rest of the week students attended their home schools.

There were five students in grade 5, seven students in grade 4, and four students in grade 3. Grade 6 students were eliminated from consideration because of the late start of the program and the subsequent inability to provide services the following year. Twelve of the children were Anglo, one was a Chicano, one was a Yacqui Indian and one was an Eskimo. One child came from an upper middle-class family, seven came from middle-class backgrounds, six from working-class families, and two from poor families. Over one-half came from single-parent homes.

This was a unique group. It is difficult to describe a single composite profile of the students. Objective data provide part of the story. The WISC-R scores varied considerably. The majority had higher Performance scores, but a few had higher Verbal scores. Most had a significant discrepancy between the Verbal and Performance scores, with a wide subscale scatter.

A compilation of nine WISC-R profiles revealed some interesting facts. The mean Performance score was 118.7; the mean Verbal score was 114. The mean Full-Scale WISC-R was 118.4. The ranges were high; Performance scores ranged 106–136; Verbal scores ranged 95–137; and Full-Scale scores ranged 102–141. Lowest subscale scores were in Digit Span (4), Information (8), Block Design (7), and Coding (5). The highest scores were Arithmetic (19), Comprehension (19), Vocabulary (18), Block Design (18), and Picture Arrangement (17). Discrepancies between Verbal and Performance scores ranged between 1 and 31 points, with a mean of 18. In summary, there doesn't seem to be a "typical" WISC-R profile of the children in this program.

All the students could read, but functioned 1–3 years below grade level. The weakest academic areas included handwriting, spelling, and mathematics. Some students were performing close to grade level in some subjects, but needed a tremendous amount of time to complete assignments.

It is difficult to capture on paper the complexities of the group, their strengths and weaknesses, and the characteristics which made them distinct—neither gifted nor learning disabled, but somehow both. It

232   *Udall and Maker*

is impossible to write of one child as a "typical" example because the interaction of giftedness with the learning disability produces characteristics which are often puzzling and specific to the individual child.

The majority loved to talk, share ideas, and ask questions. Many children possessed large amounts of information about hobbies or areas of interest. The nonverbal children liked performance tasks. Most of the students loved to draw. They shared a sophisticated sense of humor. Several children had excellent coordination and loved athletics. These same children were socially very skilled in relating to adults and interacted well with their regular classroom peers. Creative and imaginative thinking was obvious.

Listening and concentration skills were poor or nonexistent. During class meetings, students were always interrupting, ignoring, and talking simultaneously. The children's attention spans were short for any academic work, increasing only when the topic caught their interest.

Although some of these children related well with adults and their regular classroom peers, the group often had difficulty relating to each other in the pilot classroom. Behaviors would feed other behaviors, setting off a chain reaction. Class time was often spent discussing recess fights and interpersonal conflicts during activities. It is possible that all of these children together accentuated the socially unacceptable behaviors of the group; it is also possible that the simple act of putting them together in the same room revealed behaviors that might not be seen in the regular classroom.

A series of short, memorable vignettes can illustrate the diversity, the strengths, and the deficits of this group:

> It is Dick's turn to roll the dice. He 'golfs' with the dice one turn, spins it off the table next. Every turn he devises a new or different way to roll the dice. He cannot perform this task like any of his classmates. In most of what he does, he steps to the beat of a different drummer.
>
> Paul spends hours concentrating on the building of a model airplane, asking for help only when he needs it. The other children are fascinated by his project and cluster around him.
>
> The group is working quietly on individual assignments. Sam gets up, starts talking to someone else, within minutes the group is in an uproar, work forgotten, and chaos abounds.
>
> Derek brings his favorite book, *1001 Interesting and Amazing Facts* to class. There is not a single fact he does not know. The kids quiz him to find a flaw.
>
> Larry spends hours at home preparing a demonstration of a model rocket for the class. He explains patiently to the group how the mechanism works.

Derek turns from an adult fifth grader to a tantrum-throwing child when he does not understand an instruction. He will cry, scream, and stomp his feet when he can't do something.

Ed goes immediately to the visitors who enter the classroom. He introduces himself and converses with them for a long time. Once, noting an outfit Dr. Maker was wearing, he commented: "I didn't know professors wore leopard vests and knickers."

In summary, the pilot class was not typical of a regular class. The diversity of these learning-disabled/gifted children proved challenging. Each child possessed a unique blend of deficits and strengths. This was, as one visitor put it, a very "strange" group of children. They were also fun, frustrating, and enlightening.

CURRICULUM

Three beliefs provided the guidelines for curriculum design. They were as follows:

1. Learning-disabled/gifted children exhibit unique characteristics, produced by the dynamic interaction of giftedness and learning disability; consequently, special teaching methods are necessary.
2. The major emphasis in the classroom should be on the strengths of the population, not the weaknesses. All the students in the pilot classroom had received learning disability resource help, concentrating on their deficits for most of their lives. This class would focus on their giftedness.
3. The students should be active participants in the classroom. Learning to be self-directed, responsible members of the group should be a central goal.

There were three components of the curriculum: a work-hour component; a counseling component; and an enrichment component.

The Work Hour

During the work hour, children worked on assignments from their regular or learning disability classroom. The original idea developed because of a fear that the children would fall even more behind in the regular curriculum if absent for a day. The work hour gave children an opportunity to maintain their classroom performances.

Although the rationale behind the work hour was sound, the actual implementation of this component was less than perfect. Children were responsible for bringing work weekly from their home schools.

234   *Udall and Maker*

Given the nature of this population, it is not surprising that assignments were often forgotten. Furthermore, students brought a variety of lessons and materials and were being taught through different techniques. The teacher and aide had difficulty working with the diverse needs of the group.

The Counseling Component

The counseling component was designed to encourage self-concept development, and improve affective skills. The fears, self-doubts, sense of inadequacy, and constant school failure of these children created strong emotional needs and feelings. This was the first time that they had met others like themselves. The counseling activities provided them with an opportunity to discuss the problems of being learning disabled and gifted. Several methods were used. A class meeting was held every morning. Values Clarification exercises (Simon et al., 1978), role playing, discussion skills, and the Un Game were used alternately during this time. (At the end of this chapter is a list of resources used for all activities described in this section.) The Un Game proved to be extremely popular, although a few of the students never did adjust to the fact that they could not win. For example, one student commented "What do you mean, we keep going around the board?" When the class encountered interpersonal problems, most often during recess, the dynamics of the interaction would be discussed. Simple questions would be used to facilitate talking, such as "What happened?" "What could have been different?" and "What could we do in the future to prevent this misunderstanding?"

The central focus of the program was enrichment. Several teaching/learning models popular in education of the gifted served as a framework for curriculum design. These were Taylor's Multiple Talents Model (Stevenson et al., 1971; Taylor, 1968a, 1968b); Parnes' Creative Problem-Solving Model (Parnes, 1977), and Taba's discussion model (Institute for Staff Development, 1971a, 1971b). These models were selected for several reasons: 1) they encourage the strengths of the children; 2) they were adaptable to both a high performance and high verbal group; and 3) they encouraged higher-level thinking skills. Using these models as a guide, it was possible to design a classroom curriculum based on strengths, the teaching of self-directedness, and the special needs of learning-disabled/gifted children.

Science was the major subject area studied and art the secondary focus because neither subject necessarily requires reading or writing. Both emphasize thinking and a systematic approach. They were also motivating areas of study for the group. Students selected science themes that interested them and units were designed around each topic. During the first year, two themes were studied—electricity and flight. In designing the units, the teacher attempted to incorporate the Taba, Parnes, and Taylor models into activities. Consequently, brainstorming and problem solving were encouraged as well as the six talent areas of Taylor's—decision making, evaluation, forecasting, communication, creativity, and planning.

The Science Curriculum Improvement Study (SCIS) and Science—A Process Approach, were used as guidelines for the electricity unit with adaptations for learning-disabled/gifted children. For example, background information was presented to the students orally and visually. Students worked with 1½ volt dry cells, wires, and conductors. They started with simple experiments (learning about closed and open circuits) and moved to more complex ones (building magnets and a tiny motor). Prediction and planning were important parts of the unit. Students were asked to design and hypothesize findings before executing the various experiments. They were asked at the end of the unit to demonstrate mastery through self-selected means. One student elected to build a final project, another designed a skit, another chose to take a teacher-designed test, and another built a model.

At the beginning of the second unit, flight, the students were asked to choose a final project. The rationale was to encourage more self-directedness so that children would learn to systematically carry through an idea or interest. Interest in flight was facilitated through an introductory discussion, exposure to books from the library, and a film. Initially, students were required to research their project in the library. Projects included building the interior of a spaceship, replicating the moon's surface, demonstrating a toy rocket, and building a replica of Sputnik.

A TYPICAL DAY

A brief glimpse into a typical day offers more insight into the actual workings of the program. The students arrive and the class meeting is held. The events of the past week are discussed and the children share jokes for the joke board. ("How do you keep a turkey in suspense?" "I don't know." "I'll tell you tomorrow") Un Game was played for a half hour. Then, the vocabulary words are shared (students acted out the words, "bellicose" and "acidulous").

By 9:00 a.m. the students are ready to plan the day. They decide the structure of the day—when work hour will occur, when they will

236   *Udall and Maker*

go outside for recess, and what other planned activities will occur. A vote is taken and an agreement is reached.

The daily schedule determines the series of events. Students may choose the work hour, first exhibiting a "let's get it over with" attitude. They then work individually with the aide or teacher for 45 minutes. Sam may constantly venture away from his desk, wanting to know what all the other students are doing. Perhaps two of the students have forgotten their work so they type or work on Science Research Associates' *Thinklab.*

The children choose to play soccer during recess. Ken and Larry direct the game. The teacher and aide settle two "major" fights over boundaries and goals. Dick refuses to do the requested exercise at the end of recess. Consequently, he and the teacher spend 20 minutes after recess negotiating alternatives. Both agree that they were involved in a power struggle and need to reach a compromise in order to preserve their dignity.

The electricity unit starts on this day. The class brainstorms several lists—what they already know about electricity, what they want

Name _____ Date _____

		Poor				*Excellent*
1.	Cooperation with other students	1	2	3	4	5
2.	Listened to other students	1	2	3	4	5
3.	Respect shown for the rights and property of others	1	2	3	4	5
4.	Accepted responsibility for own actions	1	2	3	4	5
5.	Effort put forth during "work hour"	1	2	3	4	5
6.	Effort put forth during class activities	1	2	3	4	5
7.	Use of class time	1	2	3	4	5
8.	Contribution to group tasks or discussion	1	2	3	4	5
9.	Overall conduct	1	2	3	4	5
10.	Overall involvement in class activities	1	2	3	4	5

Additional comments:

Figure 13.2.   Pilot program self-evaluation form

to learn, and how they might learn the things they want to know. A woman from the local power company comes and shows a film about the dangers of electricity.

After lunch, the teacher reads from one of the *Choose Your Own Adventure Series*. The children take turns making a decision. Students justify their decision to the rest of their classmates before the reading is continued. In the final 30 minutes, students draw with the aide and complete their self-evaluation forms. (See Figure 13.2). Both the teacher and student complete the form separately and then meet to discuss their individual perceptions. A goal for the following week is set. For example, Sam may decide that next week he really wants to work on his interrupting behavior during class meetings. After the children leave, the teacher sends a summary of the day to the students' other teachers.

SPECIFIC TEACHING METHODS

The challenge for teachers of learning-disabled/gifted children is enormous. There are no materials designed specifically for this group. A teacher must contend with short attention spans, impulsive behavior, and little reading or writing skills. These students have not been taught to be self-directed. The teacher must be able to motivate and challenge them without creating paralyzing frustration. The learning-disabled/ gifted child needs to experience success, but not without constructive criticism.

Teaching methods utilized in the program were based on the unique needs of the group. Some are not used in the regular classroom, whereas others are. A teacher must use methods that will encourage the strengths of the children while teaching them to compensate for their weaknesses. It makes little sense to ignore a child's gifts, concentrating instead on deficits. A child can achieve success in the world through the maximization of his or her talents and strengths.

What were some of the teaching methods used? Students were encouraged to use a means of expression other than writing. The frustration and agony of having to write often limits the emergence of creativity and talent. Tape recordings were used frequently. The teacher would transcribe the material. Drawing and other art media, role playing, drama, or oral expression were also alternative means of expression. For example, based on what they had learned about aerodynamics, children designed a spaceship and then explained their design to the class. The work of each child was critiqued by other classmates, who pointed out strengths and weaknesses.

238   *Udall and Maker*

Vocabulary development was stressed. Words from the units that were studied or general vocabulary were taught every week. However, unlike in the regular classroom, pronunciation and meaning of words received the only emphasis. Spelling was not considered important. Children were encouraged to type. During work hour and for assignments, students would often choose to use the typewriter available in the room. They were also taught how to use a calculator.

Students were involved in planning the day. They were also encouraged to become more self-directed in their learning. Problem-solving strategies and cognitive behavior modification techniques were integrated into the program (see summary of typical techniques in Maker, 1981). Material was presented both verbally and visually, taking into consideration the varying processing preferences of the students. Small chunks of information were presented.

Evaluation techniques were used. Students learned to self-evaluate and to evaluate others. For example, students evaluated each other after an activity, citing strengths and weaknesses. The teacher and student met frequently to discuss progress and improvements. Using self-evaluation, disputes were settled often.

Many other teaching methods are available to the teacher of the learning-disabled/gifted. When designing specific teaching methods for their students, the following questions can be used as guidelines for selecting the best strategy. What are the deficits of the children? How can the information or material be presented in an interesting but comprehensible way? How can the strengths of the children be utilized and emphasized? What are the children's interests and how can they be used to increase motivation and self-directedness?

Finally, a teacher should be cautious not to set unrealistic expectations for the learning-disabled/gifted child. It is important that the teacher not fall into the trap of believing that because children are gifted, they will be able to perform like other gifted children. It is not that simple. Motor skills, processing deficits, and emotional behavior have a profound effect on a child's performance. There must be a tremendous amount of patience and perseverance. Gains will often be small but they will accumulate over time.

EVALUATION OF THE PROGRAM

Although no systematic formal evaluation using pre- and post-measures was conducted because of the short duration of the program, informal assessment and observation led to the following conclusions:

Pilot Program   239

1. Students' self-concepts became noticeably more positive. As one parent said: "For the first time in his life, my son thinks he is worth something. Someone is finally accepting him for what he is."
2. The students had opportunities to develop their talents and gifts because the program emphasized strengths and not weaknesses. For most of their prior school experience, these children had worked only on their deficits.
3. Special educators and GATE educators began to talk to each other. Stereotypes of learning-disabled and gifted children were being eliminated.
4. The program was implemented and continued without federal funds or special funds of any kind; therefore, it *is* possible to start a program of this type without additional financial support.
5. Appropriate services can be provided to children who, for years, had been ignored by a system that said they might be either gifted or learning disabled but not both.
6. The student-teacher ratio needs to be smaller. Learning-disabled/gifted children require a tremendous amount of individual attention and focus. The nine children in the first group proved to be too overwhelming.
7. The problems related to the management of the students' assignments from their regular classes needs to be addressed better. The work hour needs to be restructured so that students gain more from the time.
8. Although the 1-day-a-week format is a concentrated span of time, it was limiting in terms of overall contact.
9. An evaluation system for the program, which assesses ongoing and overall program progress, needs to be implemented. This should include pre- or post-testing of student progress in selected areas, evaluation of the program by students and parents, and informal assessment of student progress during the year.

FUTURE DIRECTIONS AND CONCLUSION

The first year gave the planners new ideas and direction based on both the successes and failures of the program. A new design is being considered. The elementary school where the pilot program was housed would become the home school for the children in the learning-disabled/gifted program. The children would attend this school 5 days a week and would be seen by the learning-disabled/gifted teacher 1 to 3 hours a day, 4 days a week. For the rest of the time, the students

240   *Udall and Maker*

would be in the regular classroom. Finally, the learning-disabled/gifted teacher would provide both gifted services, as described above, and traditional remedial services.

There are several reasons for considering this new design. It would allow the learning-disabled/gifted teacher to see the children more often. Regular classroom teachers would be provided with the constant support, and the number of teachers per child would be reduced from three to two because the services of a learning disabilities resource teacher would no longer be needed.

The curriculum would change with the new format. Using strengths to improve weaknesses would become a primary component. The Structure of Intellect (Meeker, 1969) is being considered as one potential method. The talents of the children would be stressed along with help on their deficits. A computer is being requested for use in the program.

The classroom would become more research-based. Pre- and post-testing will be collected, and progress monitored continually. Implicit in any pilot program is an obligation to gather as much information as possible to expand our knowledge further. A strong evaluation component will be included and the learning-disabled/gifted teacher position will become a full-time job. There is an obvious need for these services, as evidenced by the number of referrals and the success of the program.

In conclusion, the learning-disabled/gifted child requires special services. This chapter has described one way to meet the needs of this unique and challenging group. The pilot program was based on the strengths of the children in contrast to the focus of much of their school lives. In the short time of the program's existence, much has been learned. There are few guidelines to follow. This is still unexplored territory. Programs must continue to be developed for the learning-disabled/gifted children who have been overlooked for years.

SELECTED RESOURCES

Abruscato, J., and Hassard, J. 1976. Loving and Beyond: Science Teaching for the Humanistic Classroom. Goodyear Publishing Co., Santa Monica, CA.

American Association for the Advancement of Science. 1964. Science—A Process Approach, all volumes. Author, Washington D.C.

Bromberg, M., and Liebb, J. 1979. Words with a Flair. Barrins Educational Series, Inc., Woodbury, NY.

Burnes, M. 1976. The Book of Think. Little, Brown and Co., Boston.

Pilot Program 241

Eberle, B. 1974. Classroom Cues: A Flip Book for Cultivating Multiple Talent. D.O.K. Publishers, Inc., Buffalo, NY.

Eberle, B., and Stanish, B. 1980. CPS for Kids: A Resource for Teaching Creative Problem Solving to Children. D.O.K. Publishers, Buffalo, NY.

Grimmer, G.B. 1973. It's Me . . . You'll See. D.O.K. Publishers, Inc., Buffalo, NY.

Harnadek, A. 1977. Patterns: Basic Thinking Skills. Midwest Publications, Pacific Grove, CA.

Harrison, Jr., A., and Musial, D. 1978. Other Ways, Other Means: Altered Awareness Activities for Receptive Learning. Goodyear Publishing Co., Santa Monica, CA.

Maker, C.J. 1982. Curriculum Development for the Gifted. Aspen Systems Corp., Rockville, MD.

Meeker, M.N. 1961. The Structure of Intellect: Its Interpretation and Uses. The Charles E. Merrill Publishing Co., Columbus, OH.

Montgomery, R.A. 1982. Space and Beyond, Choose Your Own Adventure Series. Bantam Books, Inc., New York.

Parnes, S.J. 1977. Guiding Creative Action. Gifted Child Q. 21:460–476.

Packard, E. 1982. Inside UFO 54-40, Choose Your Own Adventure Series. Bantam Books, Inc., New York.

Price, R., and Stern, L. 1977. Mad Libs. Price, Stern, Sloan Publishers, Inc., Los Angeles.

Roll-a-role (board game) 1976. Un Game, Co., Anaheim, CA.

The Un Game (board game) 1975. Un Game Co., Anaheim, CA.

Weker, K.J. 1974. Thinklab. Science Research Associates, Chicago.

REFERENCES

Daniels, P.R. 1983. Teaching the Gifted/Learning Disabled Child. Aspen Systems Corp., Rockville, MD.

Elkind, J. 1973. The gifted child with learning disabilities. Gifted Child Q. 17:45–67.

Gear, G.H. 1976. Accuracy of teacher judgment in identifying intellectually gifted children. Gifted Child Q. 20:478–490.

Institute for Staff Development (eds.). 1971(a). Hilda Taba Teaching Strategies Program: Unit 1. Author, Miami, FL.

Institute for Staff Development (eds.). 1971(b). Hilda Taba Teaching Strategies Program: Unit 2. Author, Miami, FL.

Maker, C.J. 1977. Providing Programs for the Gifted Handicapped. The Council for Exceptional Children, Reston, VA.

Maker, C.J. 1981. Problem Solving: A general approach to remediation. In: D.D. Smith, Teaching the Learning Disabled Child. Prentice-Hall, Inc., Englewood Cliffs, NJ.

Simon, S.B., Howe, L.W., and Kirschenbaum, H. 1978. Values Clarification: A Handbook of Practical Strategies for Teachers and Students. Hart Publishing Co., Inc., New York.

Stevenson, G., Seghini, J.B., Timothy, K. et al. 1971. Project Implode: Igniting Creative Potential. Bella Vista Institute for Behavioral Research in Creativity, Salt Lake City.

Taylor, C.W. 1968(a). The multiple talent approach. Instructor. April.

Taylor, C.W. 1968(b). Be talent developers as well as knowledge dispensers. Today's Educ. December.

Wolf, J., and Gygi, J. 1981. Learning disabled and gifted: Success or failure? J. Educ. Gifted. 10:198–206.

Chapter 14

Working with Parents of Learning-Disabled/Gifted Children

Patricia M. Bricklin

Parenting patterns and home environments are critical factors in the development of society's great achievers. The University of Chicago Development of Talent Project (1982) studied 100 internationally famous musicians, mathematicians, and athletes and found that responsive parents and the home atmosphere created by their special interests were key factors in producing these exceptional achievers. The most exciting outcome of this study was the realization that the capacity for excellence is not as rare as had been thought; but what a child needs for the excellence to emerge is a combination of innate talent, an urge to succeed, persistence, and a home environment that uncovers these qualities and nurtures them.

Professionals working with learning-disabled/gifted children and their parents must be keenly aware of the importance of parents to their children's progress and ultimate realization of their potential. There are many routes to good parenting. Parenting is based on day-to-day interaction, companionship, and shared experience, the quality of which determines the quality of the parenting. There are several types of awareness for parents of the child who is both gifted and learning disabled:

1. The parents may be aware of their child's giftedness but not the learning disability. They might increase parental pressure for achievement in very negative ways.
2. The parents may be aware of the learning disability but not the giftedness. They are likely to focus on the child's handicap to the exclusion of his or her giftedness.
3. The parents may be aware of both aspects of their child's functioning. They may become confused and anxious about what it

243

244   *Bricklin*

all means and may also become frustrated in their efforts to help the child. This type of parent may alternate between "pushing" the child and a "hands off," "what's the use?" approach. This confusion influences their relationship with the child.

All of these types of awareness naturally will influence the day-to-day interactions with the child and will create unintentional barriers to good parenting.

It is clear that the learning-disabled/gifted child requires education which takes into account both giftedness and talent on the one hand and the handicap on the other. It also is extremely important for parents to be full partners in the habilitation process (Marion, 1981). For the professional who seeks the positive involvement of parents in this process, awareness of a number of important issues is critical.

The first set of issues surrounds family integration, health, and achievement. The professional must be aware of the characteristics of a strong family, of a healthy person, and of what is involved in the readiness to parent. The professional must know what is involved in family diagnosis, family indicators of good prognosis, and most important, family influence on achievement, self-concept, and receptivity to learning. Through sensitivity to these issues, the professional, regardless of organizational setting (school, clinic, etc.), will be able to act on behalf of the children to assist and support parents in their efforts.

In addition, the professional needs to be aware of the factors which increase or inhibit positive parent/professional communication and the characteristics that are important to have in order to work successfully with parents. Finally, the professional also must be aware of effective intervention models that can be useful at the time of diagnosis, program planning, and during habilitation of the learning-disabled/gifted child. In order to be effective, these models must have educative, training, and counseling components.

FAMILY STRENGTH AND EFFECTIVE PARENTING

The family is the primary group in which a child learns how to learn. For a given child, the effectiveness, of this "learning how to learn" process depends, at least in part, on the extent to which a given family possesses the following characteristics of a strong family (Bricklin and Bricklin, 1970, pp. vii-viii):

Working with Parents   245

1. Clear structure and organization exist. This is required because the family is a mini-society. The structure may be quite unique, democratic or autocratic; traditional or innovative. Its nature is not nearly as important as the fact that an organizational model does exist and that it is clear to the child.
2. For the most part, the parents support each other. Open disagreement, should it occur, is better understood and handled by a child than if one parent subtly tears down the other.
3. Although realizing that everyone is different, family members are truly interdependent and share some common goals.
4. No one lives at anyone else's expense.
5. There is relatively clear communication. Family members generally do not say one thing and mean another. What is said tends to match nonverbal behavior.
6. People are not trapped in negative roles . . . "Poor Mom," "the smart one," "the dumb one," "clumsy," etc.
7. Clear models exist. What parents do, say, and believe should be clear, not blurred or hazy.
8. There is a system for engendering rules and implementing decisions.

Within the structure of a strong family, it is possible to develop the following assets of a psychologically healthy person: 1) a sense of the goodness of life—that it is worthwhile to live; 2) a sense of personal goodness—that "I am good, at home with myself, my body," etc.; 3) a sense of independence; 4) the ability to be productive; and 5) the ability to find a place in society where "I can put into practice all of what I am and most of what I hope to be." The degree to which parents can provide the structure of a strong family and develop in their children the assets of a healthy person depends in many respects on their readiness to parent.

The readiness to parent involves achieving the ability to nurture and become dispensible. The process of giving and weaning is simultaneous and develops from the earliest parent/child interactions. This process depends on a parent's achievement of the following:

1. The capacity to give while avoiding drained feelings
2. A sense of goodness and meaningfulness, which allows the parent to feel less vulnerable in interactions with the children and to eliminate communicating with blame
3. A sense of independence and initiative, which permits comfort with decisions and responsibilities concerning children
4. An ability to enjoy sex and the relationship with the spouse or, in the case of a single-parent family, the relationship with "important adult others"; this permits the parent to avoid competition with

246   *Bricklin*

his or her own children for attention. In other words, the readiness to parent demands a sense of one's own adequacy as a person.

FAMILY INFLUENCES ON SELF-CONCEPT AND LEARNING

It is important to review influences on achievement, self-concept, and receptivity to learning. Communication, experiences, language development, and the formation of attitudes toward school and achievement are of primary concern.

Communication

The communication system that develops within the family provides the context in which all future contact or lack of it occurs. Parents teach children to be good listeners by being good listeners themselves and by sending clear messages. Where there are distortions in the communicative process, for whatever reason, future distortions in perception or conceptualization may take place. The skill of communication, first learned within the family, is the cornerstone for all future relationships and learning.

Experiences

A rich and varied background of experience, appropriate to the age and ability of the child, is critical to learning. The family's role in providing these experiential opportunities is paramount and influences the development of accurate perceptions and concepts. The toddler confined primarily to a playpen or high chair, or the preschool child who is never allowed to go beyond the front yard, will probably not have the necessary varied experiences. However, the simple sum total of experiences is not the primary issue. Although the child should be provided with opportunities to do many things (to see, hear, touch, accompany parents to interesting places, etc.), these experiences, trips, etc. are important only to the extent that they are also *meaningful.* Parents contribute to meaningfulness through careful comment, questions, and the relating of the new experience to past experience and also by helping the child to categorize, summarize, abstract, analyze, and synthesize. The parents assist the child in organizing experience in a meaningful way. This develops integrative thinking skills, a primary learning tool.

Language Development

Through imitation and interactive feedback, language development occurs within the family unit. It is here that the child learns the pur-

Working with Parents   247

poses of language as a communication tool and as a means of influencing others.

Formation of Attitudes Toward School and Achievement

Attitudes toward school and achievement, both spoken and unspoken, are learned within the family. Assertiveness, risk-taking, and the ability to self-start and self-evaluate all begin in response to parental support, concern, and interest. Sometimes pressure ("Achieve or I won't love you") may be the unspoken message. Aspirations toward family achievement are critical.

The major issue for the school-age child is mastery—the development of critical skills. A child cannot do this unless he or she is psychologically receptive to learning. This depends to a large extent on the child's self-concept or how the child views himself or herself as a learner. The child who *overly* links the sense of self-worth with his or her ability to achieve fears failure, e.g., "I must succeed or I'm a worthless nothing"; "If I cannot be perfect, why try anything?"; or "If I try and fail, I'm nothing" (Bricklin and Bricklin, 1978). This child's view of self as a person who cannot learn comes partly from how others view the child. Every child arrives at school with an invisible price tag . . . "smart," "clever," "not good enough," etc. Subsequent experiences confirm or amend this evaluation. The critical factors, which may affect parental reaction to a child and the difficulties presented, are age of onset, severity of the symptoms, and the aspiration level of the parent. If a child has been colicky and fussy from birth or was delayed in important developmental milestones, he or she will elicit different responses from a parent than the child whose development has been superior but who, at school age, fails to develop concepts, respond to written symbol systems, or develop more complex language patterns. The aspiration level and expectations of the parent are as important as the severity of any disability.

From the perspective of the parents of a child who is both gifted and learning disabled, these factors become even more crucial. Communication, language development, experiences, and the way in which the child integrates those experiences will be influenced by the parents' differential awareness of the child's giftedness or learning disability and their own level of aspiration for the child. The child's development of self-concept and overall attitudes towards achievement, risk-taking, assertiveness, and independence will also be positively or negatively affected.

When parental focus is on the giftedness, this developmental interaction may result in unrealistic expectations for the child with pres-

248   Bricklin

sures not geared to his or her capability. Information overload, where the child literally "shuts down," will result. On the other hand, when the emphasis is on the handicap, parents may develop an overprotective stance with a tendency to rescue the child from any perceived stress or difficulty. In order to truly support and help the child, the parents must ultimately abandon these positions and focus on the child who is actually there with all of the characteristics of both giftedness and learning disability—curiosity, perfectionism, supersensitivity, unique learning style, negative response to criticism, poor coordination, struggle to read and write, etc.

This is no easy task. In order for it to happen, the parents must first give up the child of their dreams, that fantasied child who was smart, well-behaved, and achieving with no complications. This task of giving up the "dream child" for the child as he or she actually exists is a task for all parents. For the parent of a child with unique gifts and a handicap as well, it becomes even more difficult. The process of "mourning" the dream child often becomes the major task of counseling parents of learning-disabled/gifted children.

FAMILY DIAGNOSIS AND PROGNOSTIC INDICATORS

The professional who works with the families of learning-disabled/ gifted children should search for how the family communicates, what it implicitly values, and the manner and means by which it differentially reinforces or punishes certain outcomes. For example, is "perfection" the ultimate family value or "personal best?" What are the differential responses to a child's painting, original poem, math paper, etc.? Where do "mistakes" fit in the family picture?

Within the family constellation, the professional should search for who can do what and how much for the child. How does the child perceive the support, concern, and interest of each parent or sibling? Is there perceived indifference or rejection by adults or is there the perception of excessive pressure? The proper sequence of giving help is an important diagnostic decision. Parental understanding may be a necessary prerequisite to program planning. Reduction of parental anxiety may be critical so that program implementation will not be sabotaged.

A family that possesses the characteristics of a strong family and the readiness to parent is already in an excellent position to provide the child with the help needed. It is an excellent prognostic sign when the parents can agree that the child does in fact need help and also can agree to do what is necessary to make things better. When the

Working with Parents   249

child already has a good interpersonal relationship with at least one parent, there is a solid base on which to build. A parent's ability to accept the child with all positive and negative characteristics is critical. To be a parent is never an easy task. When a parent must struggle to understand a child's unique abilities and handicaps, and cope with hurt, frustration, and anger, parenting sometimes seems an insurmountable task. In other words, just where the parents are in the process of mourning the dream child is an important prognostic indicator.

PARENT/PROFESSIONAL COMMUNICATION

Legislative acts in the 1970s have mandated parent participation in educational planning for their child. Parents have been given access rights to educational records. However, the longstanding attitudes of professionals and parents still get in the way of clear communication. Becoming aware of these attitudes is the first step in eliminating their potential negative influence. Many professionals have mixed feelings toward parents and their role in a child's habilitation. "Professional educators must change their perception of parent participation in educational planning. The importance of teamwork . . . cannot be overemphasized. When school and home do not cooperate, communication breaks down, and children suffer" (Hardman et al., 1981).

Although seeming to give credibility to parent participation, there is still a tendency to blame parents for their children's behavior or failure to learn and to question the parents' capacity for change. These beliefs often are based on professionals' unresolved feelings towards their own parents, sometimes as a projection on the childrens' parents of professionals' own self-anger at not helping the child more, or as the legacy of the environmental school which saw the parent-child relationship as a one-way street of causality rather than an interactive phenomenon. The tendency to blame parents and deny their capacity for change can be a self-fulfilling prophecy in any parent/professional communication.

Professionals may fail to realize that they have entered the situation after a long history in which the parents may have felt angry, impotent, and humiliated at not having been able to solve their child's problem. Parents may have lived through years of confusion, blame, and advice and may have tried many things inconsistently. The reverse may also be true. To the parent, the problems, such as a failure to learn to read, a sudden drop in grades, or a behavior change may seem to be brand new. Previous history may have seemed without incident.

250   *Bricklin*

Both of these possibilities exist in the case of parents of the learning-disabled/gifted child. The resultant confusion, disturbed feelings, and unasked questions make it difficult for the parent to pay attention to information being presented by the professional. If unacknowledged, this factor can be the source of frustration and anger to both professional and parent. Communication is crisis-oriented. Each is talking at the other. It is monologue disguised as dialogue (Webster, 1976). Acknowledging just where parents are in their understanding of their child is the first step in good parent/professional communication. The professional can accomplish this by being willing to listen to the parent and by not being too quick to give advice or strategies. Particularly in the case of the learning-disabled/gifted child, the parents may be the only ones who can supply sufficient data to permit the eventual recognition of both the child's giftedness and learning disability.

CHARACTERISTICS OF THE EFFECTIVE PROFESSIONAL

All professionals who work with parents of learning-disabled/gifted children, whether at the level of diagnosis, educational program planning, or behavioral counseling, provide counseling. Educators or . . .

> . . . clinicians who would do any kind of counseling must be capable of identifying with others. They must be able to respond accurately to parental messages sent through verbal expression with all of its intricacies, through behavioral clues, through body language, and even through silence (Webster, 1976).

Effective professionals' goals are infinitely modest. They are aware that change can happen only one step at a time. Also, they are aware that people learn and absorb information differently and so they have a variety of strategies, utilizing different sensory modalities as well as sequential versus holistic "gestalt" approaches. They are keenly aware of the point at which the parent is currently at an impasse in coping with a child and can provide a variety of nonadversary ways of phrasing communication. They develop a keen awareness of what change will mean to a parent, for example, giving up the idea that the child has no disability or recognizing the giftedness. They help people to complete what they are already doing prior to requesting something new. In the case of the parents of the learning-disabled/gifted children, this involves teaching them how to get past the deep hurt and to mourn the dream child.

Working with Parents 251

PARENT INTERVENTION MODELS

An in-depth study conducted with parents who were members of the Association of Children with Learning Disabilities indicated that parents want professionals to:

1. Be straightforward with parents; use language that they comprehend and omit professional jargon
2. Include both parents, when possible, in conferences that involve the child
3. Give parents reading material that is relevant to their child's problem and helps them understand their child better
4. Share with parents all reports written about their child
5. Engage in interdisciplinary communication with other professionals who are working with the child
6. Give parents concrete and relevant advice on handling management and learning problems (Dembinski and Mauser, 1977, pp. 582–583).

When describing people who made a difference to gifted children, it is reported that:

All of these special people . . .

1. Communicated that the child, his beliefs, his feelings, and his behaviors were important.
2. Facilitated identification, expression and acceptance of the child's feelings.
3. Made it clear that they cherished the whole child—not just his abilities or achievements.
4. Expressed that they valued his unique qualities.
5. Allowed or encouraged him to pursue his special interests.
6. Set aside some focused time to share with the child.
7. Gave encouragement and support for attempts, not just for successes.
8. Emphasized the value of productive cooperation and were, themselves, models that sharing worked (Webb et al., 1982, p. 36).

When working with parents of learning-disabled/gifted children, both the needs of the parent as noted and the needs of the child for support and encouragement from the parents need to be considered. Whether at the time of diagnosis, program planning, or habilitation, any intervention with parents should focus on the following:

1. An understanding of both giftedness and learning disability, the interaction of the two, and how this interaction relates to normal child development
2. The importance of educational intervention, which addresses both the giftedness and the disability, the dangers of inappropriate placement, and labeling and its effects

252   *Bricklin*

3. The parents as full and skilled partners in the habilitation process
4. Parental feelings and attitudes dealing with the paradox, and where the parents are in the mourning process

A high level of commitment to the supportive participation of parents results in more significant gains for the child. Whitmore (1980) described the following three kinds of parent involvement as highly desirable in a program for gifted underachievers:

1. A parent-teacher contract, covering both parent and teacher responsibilities in the program; aside from the specific commitment of who will do what, "the psychological impact of the pledged partnership" on teacher, parent and child was considerable
2. Collaborative communication and shared problem solving through conferences and group meetings;
3. Supportive assistance in the classroom when appropriate.

Generally, parent involvement programs have followed one of three models—behavioral, psychological insight, or experiential (Clements et al., 1975). In the behavioral model, parents are taught basic terminology, principles of reinforcement, observation, and measurement. Following training procedures, the parent trainer usually serves as a consultant to the parents to help them apply what they have learned to specific behaviors that they want to change. By contrast, the psychological insight model focuses on developing a comprehension and understanding of why children behave as they do, and emphasizes analysis of the interaction-dynamics between parent and child. The experiential model focuses on providing direct learning experiences for parents through modeling exposure, role playing, directed structured activities and interactions between parent and child.

Effective work with parents of learning-disabled/gifted children should involve educative, training, and counseling components. Research evidence supports the inference that group or individual work with parents is most successful when it deals with three functions rather than concentrating on one exclusively. These functions are: 1) educating parents concerning what may be expected; 2) dealing with parent and child feelings surrounding the difficulty; and 3) developing strategies for communication and coping with the child, based on awareness and sensitivity.

AN INTEGRATED PARENT INTERVENTION MODEL

A detailed parent intervention model, which includes the Whitmore components and draws on behavioral, insight, and experiential meth-

Working with Parents 253

odology, follows. This model evolved from the author's many years of experience in leading parent counseling groups and working with children and their families in a variety of settings. The model is based on numerous series of actual parent sessions held at Parkway Day School, Philadelphia, and in independent practice with parents of learning-disabled/gifted children.

Such an intervention program may be organized as individual family sessions, group sessions, or a combination of both. It is usually better when there is opportunity for some group sessions because sharing experiences is important in helping to eliminate the alienation and isolation that are experienced by some parents of learning-disabled/ gifted children. The sessions may be led by one professional or different professionals for each component. They may be planned as one continuous sequence or can occur in separate discrete units. The major objectives of the sessions are to develop in parents an awareness of and sensitivity to the following:

1. Normal child development
2. Characteristics and identification of giftedness
3. The nature of learning disabilities
4. The problems of particular children, their similarities and differences
5. The emotional and academic phases of habilitation
6. How to assess progress
7. Their own anger, hurt and fear and ways to accept and deal with them
8. The feelings of their children and the behaviors which such feelings are apt to generate
9. The need for and strategies to implement effective limit setting through nonblaming communication and gentle confrontation

Meetings need to be held on a regular basis. The tone should be supportive and educational in nature, focusing on the objectives as outlined above. The educative phase involves more activity on the part of the group leader and includes some reading, tapes, and film presentations. The Association for Children and Adults with Learning Disabilities, the Council for Exceptional Children, the American Association for Gifted Children, and the National Association for Gifted Children are resources for materials. Webb et al. (1982) is another excellent source for suggested readings about the gifted child as well as suggested content for a series of sessions ranging from motivation, discipline, and stress management to tradition-breaking and depression. *Perceptions*, a publication for parents of learning-disabled children, is also a good information source. When utilizing these materials it is important to realize that parents of learning-disabled/gifted children in some ways will feel alienated from materials dealing exclusively with gifted children or exclusively with learning-disabled children. It will be necessary to assist parents in identifying with the relevant issues of both groups and, at the same time, support them in creating their own identity and advocacy.

In the sessions, similarities and differences among children should be discussed. "How can he be so smart and dumb at the same time?" "What is this learning disability my child has?" "How can he be both gifted and disabled?" "How long will it take to overcome the disability?" Questions of causality should be handled honestly in terms of current professional knowledge. The question of the amount of time that will be necessary for habilitation is impossible to answer directly. However, it does make sense to talk of sequences that the children will go through as they improve. Improvement is gauged by observing their movement through these stages. How long a particular child will remain at a particular level is difficult to predict in advance (Bricklin, 1971).

Differences in learning style and the importance of capitalizing on the child's unique strengths and means of compensating should be stressed. There should also be an emphasis on the importance of finding alternate routes of providing the child with information and knowledge and ways to communicate ideas and information. This is particularly important if the child has a reading or writing disability.

As parents are guided in the development of understanding the issues involved in giftedness and learning disabilities, it is important that they do not focus exclusively on either the giftedness or the learning disabilities. It is important that parents see and feel that:

> . . . the problem and the child are not synonymous. The child must be viewed first as a child, within the perspective of normal growth and development and with the same needs as any other child along with some special needs. There is a tendency for parents, as well as professionals, to focus excessively on the child's disability and, therefore, on his difference (Ohrenstein, 1979, p. 240).

Parents must be guided ultimately to see their youngster as a child who is both gifted and has learning disabilities.

In the next phases of the intervention program, the primary focus is on dealing with feelings and developing effective ways for understanding and coping. Here, the sharing of experiences within the group can be an important support. The leader serves as facilitator and clarifier.

Working with Parents 255

In this phase, parents begin to explore and get in touch with their own emotional reactions to the child's situation and the barriers which interfere with their ability to accept the child as he or she is. The "Why did this have to happen to us?" reaction emerges. "It is not fair." "It should not be so." Sometimes the parents are uncomfortable about certain aspects of the child's giftedness, such as persistent questioning, uniquely individual responses, or considerable curiosity. These aspects may confuse, exhaust, or bother the parents. This may be difficult for them to acknowledge. The sudden shifts in the child from super maturity to extreme babyishness requires a flexibility and creativity of response which the parent is not always able to produce. Parental feelings of powerlessness, confusion, anger, hurt, and fear gradually emerge.

The next few sessions usually deal with the negative feelings, themselves. Sometimes, parents feel guilty for having these feelings. Although they may be reluctant initially to talk about them, the process of sharing these feelings and reactions with other parents who feel the same way helps to lessen their feelings of isolation and puts things into perspective.

In their discussions, parents progress through the following stages:

1. Denial—"Things are not really the way they are"
2. Resentment—"Things *should* not be this way. Why us? Things ought to be different"
3. Anger and blame directed first at others, then at themselves and even at the child

They begin to be able to look at what is true in their situation; that they indeed have a child who is both gifted and learning disabled. They are ready to mourn the "dream child."

At this stage, a technique called "inner shouting" can be very useful in helping the parents get past the deep hurt of an unchangeable event in order to ultimately accept the situation as it exists. The mourning process and the Bricklin Inner Shouting technique are explained to the parents. They are given the following explanation and instructions and urged to repeat the process several times a day for several weeks.

> The mourning process involves a series of psychological reactions a person has to fully experience in order to get over what to that person is a tragic and unchangeable event. A happening or situation that *can* be changed through active effort and/or intervention need not be mourned. It is critical, by the way, for mental health, that an individual learn to differentiate the two conditions i.e., situations which can be changed via

256   *Bricklin*

effort from those which cannot be altered. Many serious psychological consequences follow from an individual's, child or adult, unwillingness to see when nothing further can be done to effect a given situation in any meaningful way. This differentiation is important because the two different conditions, a situation which can be changed and one which cannot be changed, demand different psychological responses for maximum health. A situation which can be changed demands active, assertive, goal-directed effort. A situation which cannot be changed requires mourning. Something that happens over which the person has *no* control *has to be* mourned. Examples of the latter would be death, body mutilation, divorce, disability, etc.

The mourning reaction consists roughly of three stages, shock-denial, tears of rage, tears of loss. (Our technique, called "inner shouting," breaks this down into more categories.) For a long time after some tragic event, the person cannot believe that what happened did in fact happen. It is as if part of the person, inside, is saying: "No! No! This cannot be happening!" Following (or intermixed) with the shock-denial phase, we may identify several other necessary parts of the mourning process. There is a feeling of rage, a feeling of hurt, a feeling of fear, and what we call frustrated love and also positive love.

The Bricklin Inner Shouting technique was designed to help mourning "complete." It consists of getting in touch with the five different levels mentioned above. Here is how to do it.

Close your eyes. Visualize who you need to speak to. (If you do not know, try each parent, your spouse, children, etc.) Get eye contact with the image. Begin five separate sentences, as outlined below. The purpose is to allow yourself to fully experience your thoughts and emotions at what we call the "anger" level, the "hurt" level, the "fear" level, and the "frustration" level.

Repeat the process several times a day, for about 3 weeks. There will be no immediate, startling changes, but you will note a gradual shift in your mood—in a positive direction.

Here are the sentences to say. Finish each with whatever comes to mind. These sentences need not be said out loud. They can be sort of "shouted", said quickly and spontaneously to one self.

1. The anger level. Say the phrase, "It burns me up that . . ." and then complete this with whatever comes to mind.
2. The hurt phase. Say, "It hurts me that . . ." and end this with whatever comes to mind.
3. The fear level. "It scares me that . . ." and end with whatever comes to mind.
4. The frustrated love level. "I wanted (or want) so much for you to love me, and . . ."
5. The positive love phase. "I wanted (or want) so much to find a safe and secure way to love you and . . ."

The inner shouting technique has applications in other varieties of mourning situations and can also be used to insure "completed communications." In some, other sentence beginnings are used, e.g., "It makes me happy that . . ." (Bricklin, 1980).

Occasionally, some parents find it extremely difficult to get past the belief that things "should not be the way they are." Inner shouting clarifies which parents will need additional therapeutic help. However, subsequent to utilizing inner shouting, many parents report that they are now more comfortable and better able to handle situations with the child which formerly produced anger and frustration. Although the parents are often unable to articulate exactly what is happening, they report reactions like "Somehow it's as if a weight has been lifted." "I feel lighter, less oppressed." Or, they may say "Nothing seems to be happening" and at the same time, report incident after incident involving better interaction with the child. Mourning via inner shouting is a powerful and natural therapeutic experience utilizing both right and left hemisphere modes of processing information.

Clarifying or "defogging" communication is another such natural therapeutic process. The next phases of the sessions focus on communication skills. Parents develop listening and observational skills, through role playing and other techniques, which permit them to discover what the child is really communicating. Perhaps the child goes to great creative lengths to avoid tasks, is supersensitive to mild criticism, seeks negative attention, or constantly says "it's boring" or "too easy," even when it is not. Is the child really using words and behavior to say "I'm angry," "I'm scared I'll fail," or "Am I really worthwhile?" Variations on the Bricklin Inner Shouting technique are useful in this phase to help youngsters mourn and also to complete communications.

Parents learn how to help the child find a clearer way to say what needs to be said. Parents also may find that they, too, have been sending "mixed" messages to the child. For example, a parent may say "I really want to hear what you have to say" while walking away from the child. The parent works to clarify messages so that behavior and words are saying the same thing. They work to develop communication skills which match the learning styles of the learning-disabled/gifted child. Any given child may understand things better when they are presented in short, clear sentences. Another child may grasp a message better if it is presented visually or kinesthetically. Some children interpret messages intuitively, holistically; others process information in a step-by-step, sequential fashion. In addition to becoming more efficient in directing communication in ways that the child can use most effectively, the parent also develops "nonblaming" and nonadversary ways to communicate.

The next focus in the sessions is on implementing strategies to increase and buttress effective family functioning. Working from the

258   Bricklin

characteristics of a strong family, the parents may institute a family council or family meeting (Bricklin and Bricklin, 1971). In family meetings, house rules may be developed based on honesty, responsibility, and self-respect—traits most valued by gifted children (Colangelo, 1979). In addition to setting up a system for engendering rules and implementing decisions, family meetings provide a vehicle in which children can become clear about the family organization, the roles each member plays in relation to the others, and the true interdependence of the family unit. Within a family council framework, the family may develop:

1. The mechanisms for effective limit setting (discipline)
2. Independence in each family member
3. Better sibling relationships and parent-child relationships through improved communication
4. A clearer notion of the contributions of each family member to total family functioning, where opportunities for 'scapegoating' are reduced

Learning-disabled/gifted children generally are particularly responsive to the family meeting process. The respect with which each family member's contributions are valued, the opportunities provided for creativity and responsibility and structure take advantage of the child's giftedness and at the same time support areas of weakness. For example, within the family council structure, many learning-disabled/gifted children begin to feel psychologically comfortable with failure and mistakes, an attitude which is critically important to their progress. The fact that the very best baseball players bat somewhere in the 0.300s, means that out of every ten things attempted at the plate, there are seven "failures." This is often a compelling example utilized in helping parents to develop this "comfortableness with error" in the family meetings.

For a time, parent sessions should focus on issues arising in the family meetings. Once family council meetings are functioning smoothly and parents feel comfortable with what may be new communication skills and strategies, this phase of the parent sessions is complete. Sometimes it is useful to set up a mechanism for future contact, perhaps a scheduled meeting or phone call.

These parent sessions have focused on providing information to assist parents in better understanding their learning-disabled/gifted child, the process of therapeutic mourning to get over past hurts, the development of improved communication and parenting skills, and a family meeting mechanism in which to implement them. This combination of factors allows parents: 1) to be more effective advocates for their child in the educational system through a greater awareness of what the child needs; and 2) to create in the family the context for maximum growth in the child who is both gifted and learning disabled. This is accomplished through *acceptance* of the child with all strengths and liabilities and the parental ability and skills to *appropriately challenge the child in terms of capability*, which takes into account receptivity to learning, giftedness and the handicap.

CONCLUSION

There is a convincing body of data to support the premise that parents and families are the most important elements in a child's achievement. Families create the context in which the child develops a view of self as "learner" or "nonlearner" and provide the physical and emotional environment in which the development of skills and abilities is either facilitated or inhibited. For the learning-disabled/gifted child, a facilitating family environment is especially critical.

This chapter has focused on the background knowledge and skills necessary for professionals working with parents of learning-disabled/gifted children. Although several types of parent intervention programs were presented, the major emphasis was placed on one model, which the author believes combines the critical educative, training, and counseling components necessary for successful and effective intervention.

It is a significant and potentially costly mistake to consider parent programs only as ancillary or related services which may or may not be included in the educational planning for learning-disabled/gifted children. When parent programs are not included, the mistake may be costly from two standpoints. First, the child's giftedness is often not recognized or nurtured, and an important potential resource, the child, is essentially wasted. Second, experience has shown that providing structured opportunities for parent education and growth is a far more cost-effective way to handle *all* the educational needs of learning-disabled/gifted children.

Parents and families must be assisted and supported in every way possible so that they may be truly productive participants in the child's habilitative program as well as effective advocates for appropriate programs and services. Resources, time, and money for staff development and delivery of services to parents must be allocated as an integral component of programs for learning-disabled/gifted children. Through programs which involve education, training, and counseling, parents

260   *Bricklin*

are able 1) to create the kind of psychological climate within the home which supports a child's growth and development, and 2) to provide skillful instructional and review aid to the child. This family process of acceptance and appropriate challenge is an essential element in the habilitation of the learning-disabled/gifted child.

REFERENCES

Bricklin, B. 1980. The mourning process and Bricklin inner shouting techniques: Explanation and instructions. WCAU-FM, Philadelphia.

Bricklin, B., and Bricklin, P. 1967. Bright Child—Poor Grades: The Psychology of Underachievement. Delacorte Press, New York.

Bricklin, B., and Bricklin, P. 1970. Strong Family—Strong Child. Delacorte Press, New York.

Bricklin, B., and Bricklin, P. 1980. Improving your Child's Learning Ability. Buckingham, Buckingham, PA.

Bricklin, P. 1971. Counseling parents of children with learning disabilities. In: R.C. Bradley (ed.), Parent-Teacher Interviews. University Press, Wolfe City, TX.

Clements, J.E., and Alexander, R.N. 1975. Parent training: Bringing it all back home. Focus Except. Child. 7:1–12.

Colangelo, N., and Zaffran, R.T. (eds.) 1979. New Voices in Counseling the Gifted. Kendall/Hunt Publishing Co., Dubuque, IA.

Dembinski, R.J., and Mauser, A.J. 1977. What parents of the learning disabled really want from professionals. J. Learn. Disabil. 10:578–584.

Hardman, M.I., Egan, M.W., and Landau, E.D. 1981. What will we do in the morning? The exceptional student in the regular classroom. Wm. C. Brown Co. Publishers, Dubuque, IA.

Marion, R.L. 1981. Educators, Parents and Exceptional Children. An Aspen Publication, Rockville, MD.

Ohrenstein, D.F. 1979. Parent Counseling. In: W.C. Adamson and K.K. Adamson (eds.) A Handbook for Specific Learning Disabilities. Gardner Press, New York.

University of Chicago Development Talent Project, 1982. Parents and home environment: critical factors in development of society's great achievers. Today's Child News Magazine, April. 30:1.

Webb, J.T., Meckstroth, E.A., and Tolan, S.S. 1982. Guiding the Gifted Child: A Practical Source for Parents and Teachers. Ohio Psychology Publishing Co., Columbus.

Webster, E.J. (ed.) 1976. Professional Approaches with Parents of Handicapped Children. Charles C. Thomas Publisher, Springfield, IL.

Whitmore, J.R. 1980. Giftedness, Conflict and Underachievement. Allyn and Bacon, Inc., Boston.

Chapter 15

Teacher Training in the Clinical Method for Learning-Disabled/Gifted Children

M.E.B. Lewis and Paul R. Daniels

The clinical model for instructing learning-disabled/gifted children is based on the assumption that these children are truly disabled. The implication is that real disability can be documented by a solid clinical diagnosis, not just underachievement. It must also be recognized, however, that some very bright children who have failed for reasons other than process problems might be accepted into a clinical setting because their problems can only be dealt with in such a setting.

The children in the clinical instructional setting require more direct professional services than the children in a regular classroom setting. They need services more frequently and more quickly, and the ratio between the professionals and the children will be smaller than conventionally found. As in most educational settings, the most important professionals in a clinical setting are teachers.

The preparation of an effective teaching staff in a clinical setting is, by nature, structured and technologically removed from the traditional methods of teacher-training institutions. Teachers must immediately establish their role and position among other service-providing professionals, such as social workers and psychologists, and must consciously seek and maintain that position of equal partnership in order to contribute fully to effective programming for their students.

When teachers have experience in a regular classroom setting, it is best to capitalize on their strengths while in that environment and then teach the necessary policies and procedures for effective diagnosis, prescription, follow-through, and evaluation within the more structured clinical setting. This involves the extension of professional talents and the addition of some highly technical skills that contribute to the distinct environment known as the clinical center.

261

262   *Lewis and Daniels*

Training staff in such a clinical setting involves a reeducation of sorts for the teacher, who was probably trained to work in the traditional classroom. It is necessary for the teacher to understand completely exactly what distinguishes the clinical setting from the regular educational setting, and why some students flourish in one and flounder in the other. The very nature of the disability being studied here calls for a highly trained group to meet fully the needs of this confounding phenomenon—the potentially extraordinary and yet practically inhibited learner.

Teacher training as discussed in this chapter draws from the authors' experiences with graduate degree programs and practicums developed in the Division of Education of the Evening College and Summer Session of The Johns Hopkins University. These programs are inter- and intra-disciplinary in nature and involve supervised clinical experiences at the Kennedy School for Learning-Disabled Children. As part of the doctoral program in Human Communication and Its Disorders, initiated in 1974, a student may do all or part of their 800 to 1,000 hours of internship at the Kennedy Institute. In September, 1981, a Master degree in Science with a major in Clinical Education was initiated in the Division of Education. This program, designed for part-time students who already have a masters degree in child development or disabilities, includes courses such as Techniques in Clinical Education, Medical and Clinical Aspects of Reading and Learning Disabilities, Language Disorders in Children, and Survey of Intelligence and Personality Tests as well as extensive advanced seminars and diagnostic and clinical practicum experiences at the Kennedy Institute.

In addition, an experimental and intensive summer practicum for classroom teachers interested in learning-disabled/gifted children was initiated at the Kennedy Institute. The goal of this program was to provide the opportunity for these teachers to experience the clinical approach. Participants would include teachers of the gifted who were interested in providing for learning-disabled children and learning disabilities teachers who were interested in doing more for the gifted children in their classes. Hopefully some of these skills could be incorporated into their regular or special (learning-disabled or gifted) classroom setting.

CLINICAL SETTING

The Kennedy School for Learning-Disabled Children is a component of the John F. Kennedy Institute at The Johns Hopkins University and Medical Institutions. The Kennedy School offers a nongraded

Teacher Training   263

program for learning-disabled children of elementary school age. The program is clinical in nature, including counseling, occupational therapy, pediatrics, and speech and language services.

The individualized instructional program reflects specialized goals and objectives for each student. The pupil/teacher ratio is 5 to 1. The program is thematic, with instruction through a common theme approach to curriculum. For example, the November theme might be *sports* for all aspects of instruction (language, math, science, etc.). Instruction is through multisensory activities, language experience, structural and phonetic analysis and can involve a whole group, small group, one-to-one peer learning, and the use of personal computers.

Referrals to Kennedy can be made by parents, physicians, psychologists, social agencies, or local education agencies. Decisions about placement at Kennedy are based on an extensive battery of diagnostic tests, including a Wechsler Intelligence Scale for Children-Revised (WISC-R), a physical examination, neurological examination, educational testing, and other information as applicable. The average length of stay is expected to be 3 years.

QUALIFICATIONS FOR THE CLINICAL EDUCATOR

Learning-disabled/gifted students require special education to circumvent the disability before they can actualize their intellectual potential in their academic careers. For this reason, their teachers must have very special preparation. A highly successful teacher in an average grade 3 or 4 is not necessarily the best candidate for working with learning-disabled students nor gifted students. When both giftedness and learning disabilities are present in the individual learner, adaptability and creativity of a remarkable nature are required on the part of the teacher. Ideally, the best teacher would be one who has experience dealing with both areas.

The primary qualification for a teacher in the clinical setting is a firm understanding of what distinguishes the clinical setting from other instructional settings, and what kind of student gets referred to such a structured environment. The clinical setting, one in which classes are small and the teacher is required to act as a member of an interdisciplinary team, allows greater opportunity for the teacher and student to remediate weak areas and enhance skills in areas of strength. This recognition of the learning-disabled/gifted student as a mixture of strength and need is essential so that the student does not lose self-esteem and the teacher can address the appropriate areas in the most effective ways.

264   Lewis and Daniels

Furthermore, the clinical educator must be familiar with the administration, scoring, and interpretation of valid and reliable measures of performance because he or she will fill the often unfamiliar role of diagnostician. A vital need on the part of any clinical team member is the ability to recognize where his or her expertise ends and when to make a referral to other professionals. Although the clinical educator is expected to be flexible and able, it is vital that accuracy take precedence over ego.

Clinical teachers must learn to write concise observational summaries and reports of performance. In such a small setting, it is a luxury of sorts that opportunities for close observation of student progress are available and anecdotal notations can be made so that later exchange in the interdisciplinary meetings can be as complete as possible. Although it is possible to train teachers to conduct observations and write reports, following generalized guides, basic skills in organization and expository writing are necessary prerequisites.

Clinical teachers need to be quick learners. They must be able to read research studies critically and locate information in a speedy and well-organized manner. Finally, creativity may be an asset. In order to program effectively, clinical educators must be able to develop instructional devices, reverse or create curriculum, and perceive new ways to adapt old techniques, especially in the multisensory learning center.

THE ROLE OF THE CLINICAL
EDUCATOR IN THE INTERDISCIPLINARY SETTING

The clinical/interdisciplinary setting is a structured one, requiring regular contact among the professionals and paraprofessionals who provide services to the learning-disabled/gifted student. This team can include physicians, therapists, counselors, social workers, psychiatrists, administrators, and of course, teachers. Indeed, this unique role as equal team partner in programming and assessing student needs distinguishes between the regular classroom teacher and the clinical teacher. It is imperative that the teacher in the clinical setting maintain a posture of equal contribution with other members of the interdisciplinary team because it is the teacher, after all, who sees the child daily in the learning environment, usually performs most of the assessment, and creates the educational program.

Training for this role involves intern meetings on at least a weekly basis to review data and give teachers an opportunity to share with

Teacher Training 265

each other what they will later share with other team members. An excellent training ground is the weekly staff meeting in which cases are presented using an organized format for information, such as a case-typing sheet. (See Chapter 7 in this book.) This sheet is projected on a wall by the overhead projector, and the presenting teacher interprets the data for the group, allowing questions as the presentation proceeds. Questions, in fact, are encouraged in order to challenge the presenting teacher and make the teacher clarify information. Such a training session held weekly keeps teachers in practice and allows them to share information and suggestions for treatment in the classroom. In addition, other service-providers for the individual cases being discussed, such as a counselor or social worker, can be invited to contribute to the discussion.

Understanding the interdisciplinary setting also involves educating the teachers as to the contributions that each member of the team should be expected to make. The physician, for example, contributes opinions on diagnosis of medical or medically related aspects of the case. The psychologist contributes in the areas of intellectual functioning, emotionally related aspects of the case, and other data revealed in a psychological evaluation. The social worker is responsible for collecting data and presenting information on the social factors influencing the case, including family history and existing social factors contributing to the student's present functioning.

In addition to knowing the role of other disciplines in providing service to students, clinical educators should help professionals in other disciplines understand the function of the teacher in treating cases. It should not be assumed that other professionals know the needs and methods employed in instructing learning-disabled/gifted students. For example, a pitfall of any interdisciplinary team with a physician as a member is the tendency of the other members to defer to the judgment of the physician. In matters requiring medical judgment, naturally the judgment of a physician is valid; but physicians are not teachers and decisions about appropriate materials and methods for individual students should not be left to them. Clinical educators should share the responsibility with other team members by being well-prepared in their area of expertise and unafraid to challenge those less able to make decisions in that area. Students referred to the clinical setting have been unable to prosper academically in the regular setting, and so each member of the interdisciplinary team has something to contribute to programming for that student. Teachers need to be able to articulate to others their opinions and methods in dealing with this complex student.

Selection of Curricular Materials
for Learning-Disabled/Gifted Students

Another aspect that distinguishes regular teachers from teachers in the clinical setting is the selection of a curriculum. Regular teachers working in traditional classrooms may be given a curriculum to use, and little choice may be involved when programming is started. Clinical educators have the opportunity to create a hierarchy of skills for the student, creating the means for the achievement of those personally developed goals.

Training in this area begins with the creation of meaningful, accurate, and measurable objectives and goals. The distinction between *goals* as long-term plans, and *objectives* as short-term steps to the achievement of the goals is the initial step in training. The objective for instruction must indicate for whom the objective is being created (such as "the grade 3 social studies student" or "the grade 8 mathematics student"), the anticipated performance ("will name the capitals of the original 13 colonies" or will "draw an equilateral triangle"), the materials or conditions under which the objective will be met ("the capital will be identified orally" or "given paper, pencil and a compass"), and the acceptable criterion for success ("the student will name at least eleven of the thirteen capitals correctly" or "all angles will be equal for credit"). An unstated criterion indicates an implied 100% success, as some tasks (e.g., the execution of the triangle) are either done correctly or not.

Once objectives are created, they must be sequenced in some sort of hierarchy of difficulty so that the student and teacher can see how instruction and learning are progressing. If a student is moving ahead rapidly, it is vital that the clinical educator provide challenging lateral enrichment activities in order to stimulate the learning-disabled/gifted student and draw on strong points to engender a feeling of success.

One of the complex and challenging aspects of creating learning experiences for gifted students is maintaining their interest and attention. Bright children can progress rapidly through tasks while other students may have to spend considerably more time. It is necessary, therefore, for activities to provide challenge as well as the opportunity for success. Learning-disabled/gifted students can progress rapidly through some tasks although other tasks may be difficult for them. In most cases, they are quite aware of the areas in which there is a discrepancy between their potential to achieve and their overall achievements. It is frustrating for these children to see a younger sibling of average ability able to perform tasks with ease while they find great difficulty and, perhaps, a total lack of success in performing the same tasks. Consequently, learning-disabled/gifted students are often prey to the academic depression that results in acting out behavior in the classroom and also at home. The clinical educator must deal with such resentment. Using the services of the psychologist as consultant, or referring the case to a counselor or social worker, can help in what may eventually become severe and global problems.

Programming for learning-disabled/gifted students requires a multisensory approach. The value of this approach is twofold. First, by nature, such an approach can be designed to capitalize on the stronger channel of learning for the individual student. Those who are visual/auditory learners (rare among learning-disabled/gifted youngsters), can be channeled into "see and say" experiences, such as the well-known Orton-Gillingham method. The pure auditory learning experience, using cassette tapes of classic pieces of literature or oral directions for performing tasks in science or social studies, can be employed for the auditory learner. For the student in need of broad programming, language experience and the modified Fernald Visual-Auditory-Kinesthetic Tactile (VAKT) multisensory approaches work well. The second advantage of such programming is variety, which stimulates the children and encourages them to progress just a bit further along the line. Teachers are trained to analyze their plans for a variety of activities used.

Adequate selection of curricular methods and materials also involves appropriate and creative teaching strategies. Because placements in clinical settings involve small groups of students, the opportunity for attention to the detailed needs of each student must be provided without question. Learning in small groups with a teacher or team of teachers should be part of every lesson, but an independent block of time in each lesson should be provided for those things that the students can reinforce or learn on their own. In addition, opportunities for using students in a peer teaching/learning arrangement should be arranged. Students' egos can be easily boosted by their participation as teachers for part of a lesson.

Managing the learning environment as a multisensory place full of group and independent activities also requires adequate management of behavior on the part of the clinical teacher. Students should be made responsible for their behavior as early as possible. There is no circumstance under which the teacher should feel intimidated by or not able to control the learning-disabled/gifted student. The use of a behavior management system providing nontangible rewards for positive behaviors and little or no response for negative behaviors works

268   Lewis and Daniels

well. This type of system stimulates the student to be more mature, responsible, and independent. Teachers should be trained to set positive criteria for behavior, such as "comes to class prepared" or "completes assignments within time allotted." Reward for positive behavior and no reward (rather than penalties) for negative behavior establishes the teacher as the consistent manager of the learning environment and helps produce students who are able to manage themselves in an adult fashion.

Finally, training of the clinical educator involves the appropriate selection of commercial materials when applicable in the learning center. Because most of the learning-disabled/gifted students referred for clinical intervention into their learning problems have not managed well with the commonly used basal and kit series for learning, it is not likely that the use of such commercial materials, even in a specialized classroom, will produce good results. The best commercial materials for learning are still the newspaper and current periodicals. Their timely, up-to-date, and adaptable nature appeals to the quick mind of the gifted student while their simple presentation of material also appeals to the learning-disabled student. The able clinical educator can use any part of a newspaper for any content area. When combined with tapes and multimedia presentation, such as radio and public television, the student is stimulated and totally involved rather than bombarded with meaningless and sterile drill.

Skills taught in isolation have a transient rather than permanent effect. When students are challenged through curricula using the thematic approach, they can see learning as a more purposeful and directed series of experiences. Teachers are more easily able to create materials centering around such themes, and the interconnectiveness of the curriculum allows for continued reinforcement of skills.

Use of Appropriate Diagnostic and Prescriptive Methods

Diagnosis of a learning problem in a gifted student is the original point of reference for the clinical educator. The clinical picture generated from that assessment provides the springboard for the interdisciplinary intervention that occurs. The instructional program designed by the clinical teacher is generated from diagnostic information provided in the initial referral. An important component in training teachers in the clinical setting is training them to administer a variety of appropriate measures of performance so that in small steps, the progress of the student can be most accurately assessed and reported to all concerned—parents, agencies, and the members of the interdisciplinary team.

Teacher Training   269

At this stage, teachers in technologically adapted environments should be instructed in the use of computers for ongoing assessment of objectives. (The use of the computer for this purpose is discussed in Chapter 11 of this volume.) There should be a brief assessment device for each objective created by the teacher. Only through such devices can a pattern of progress begin to emerge. Ongoing assessment allows the teacher to intervene and alter the program where necessary so that the students do not waste time on objectives already met or fail to receive adequate reinforcement for skills not yet attained.

Diagnostic procedures should include measures of intellectual ability, such as the WISC-R, administered by a psychologist; measures of associative learning, such as the Gates Associative Learning Test; measures of reading ability, both formal, such as the Gates-Mac-Ginitie, or informal, such as an informal reading inventory; measures of mathematical ability, such as the Key Math Diagnostic Test; and other measures of aptitude and concept formation, as needed. Among the most important duties of the clinical educator in the diagnostic/prescriptive role is making timely and appropriate referrals to other members of the interdisciplinary team for their expertise in areas of diagnosis the teacher is not able to handle. Timeliness is essential because overtesting can be a danger and inappropriately spaced testing sessions can invalidate results.

Determination of Appropriate Evaluative Methods

The teacher in the clinical setting must periodically present data on the student as a summary of ability and progress toward the previously established goals and objectives. When standardized or normative data is used, the result is usually a grade-equivalent score, not a particularly useful piece of information. Grade-equivalent scores are easily misinterpreted and are nebulous in the clinical, nongraded situation. Training in both standardized and nonstandardized assessment is necessary.

Clinical educators should evaluate students in conjunction with the objectives that already have been established either as part of the student's classroom program or in the diagnostic evaluation made at the initial referral. There should be training sessions in which model reports are analyzed and teachers are taught how to write the narrative summaries. These summaries are most useful as sources of information about the progression of the learning-disabled/gifted student in their weak as well as strong areas. The narrative should begin with the initial reason for the referral of the student, his or her potential for achievement and a statement of each objective in the step-by-step

270   *Lewis and Daniels*

hierarchy, and statements of methods used to meet the objective and the outcome. From this data, a summary paragraph can project the student's program for the next brief period of evaluation. Periodic evaluations should be presented approximately every 3 months during the instructional program and should include the clinical teacher's anecdotal records.

Interacting with Families and Agencies

Students spend the greater part of each day with their family and friends, utilizing the skills that they have practiced throughout their academic and social career to date. Therefore, clinical educators also need to interact with families and outside agencies. When educators deal with the families of learning-disabled/gifted children they must remember that the families will vary as much as the students do. Some families are not aware of the scope of their child's learning potential or learning problem. The apparently contradictory nature of the condition labeled "learning-disabled/gifted" baffles some, and they turn to the clinical educator for information and support. Knowing that intellectual testing revealed a potentially high degree of achievement early in the child's school career, many families have high expectations for their children. The anger and disappointment that some of these families feel is often combined with the misinformation and misinterpreted data that they are sometimes given. These parents can seem impatient, creating demands for performance from the teacher. The clinical teacher has a responsibility to explain what is being done in the child's educational program, and how the families fit into the program.

Once a student has progressed through the clinical education program, referrals must be made by the clinical educator. The final role of the teacher is that of a follow-up specialist. The clinical teacher has the responsibility for recommending programs for students preparing to leave the clinical program in order to return to a regular program (if that is indicated). The teacher should be trained to use the state department of education and the local education agency as resources for placement. If the public systems do not seem to have programs suitable for learning-disabled/gifted children, then it is the responsibility of the clinical educator to find out what nonpublic and private programs exist to meet these needs. Whenever possible, the clinical educator should observe other programs that are designed for the gifted, for the learning-disabled, and for the learning-disabled/gifted student.

Agencies provide services to students in need of accurate placements. Hospitals, health departments, state departments of education, local education agencies, social service agencies and physicians are all sources of information for locating assistance for the student who shows high levels of potential but who has problems in organizing, processing, or retaining information. Clinical educators must become knowledgable about all of these resources and adjunct services and must keep in constant contact with representatives of each.

EXPERIMENTAL SUMMER PRACTICUM

During June and July, 1980, a practicum was developed for teachers interested in learning-disabled/gifted children. It was further revised in the summers of 1981 and 1982. Because of funding by the Spencer Foundation, all of the children who participated and many of the teachers were given scholarships. The following description refers specifically to the summer of 1982.

One learning-disabled/gifted child was assigned to each graduate student for instruction. The teachers attended class daily from 8:30 a.m. to 12:30 p.m. Between 9:00 and 11:00 a.m. they worked with the children under the supervision of the two major professors, an instructor, and a doctoral student. When the teachers were not working with the children, they attended sessions in theory and practices, planning and critique. All teachers participated in a series of minisessions on computer literacy. Individual and group evaluations were provided daily. Each teacher was held responsible for the diagnostic/prescriptive program for the assigned child and for a final report to the parents, which could be made available to the school. As part of the practicum requirements, each teacher had to prepare a teaching sequence for alleviating a given learning problem.

The children ranged from 7 to 14 years of age. There were some children with no fundamental reading skills; others had specific problems in word-learning; nearly all had organizational problems; and a majority had pronounced difficulty in comprehension. Prior to their acceptance into the program, all of the children had at least some diagnostic workup. However, the depth and quality of the diagnosis varied widely. Some children had been labeled with simple standardized tests; two others had elaborate clinical evaluations. These evaluations were used as the diagnostic hypotheses to be tested in the diagnostic/prescriptive program.

The 2 hours of instruction were formulated as a time block of four half-hour sessions. The time blocks could be modified according to

272   *Lewis and Daniels*

the particular concentration capability and interest span of the child. A built-in modification of the block was for computer literacy training for the older students. They were given 45 minutes of instruction on computer literacy while the younger children were given 30 minutes. (See Chapter 11 in this volume for a description of the computer component.)

Certain procedures were required for all students each day:

1. Learning a modified VAKT procedure for word-learning and applying it to an individual project
2. Developing a modified language experience article on an area of interest
3. Doing a follow-up activity on new and previous learnings
4. Listening to materials, either for enjoyment or information, that were read by the teacher

Besides the required activities, teachers were encouraged wherever appropriate to use directed reading activities and to encourage independent reading at home. Systematic, organized instruction was required for each child.

The areas investigated by the students ranged from human anatomy to cooking and sewing. Many of the children were interested in birds and fish, and only one child showed a preference for storytelling and writing. Two older boys, who seemed to have the most serious learning problems, chose academic subject matter for their activities in preparation for being mainstreamed in junior high school. Although each made considerable progress, it seemed that their learning problems were so severe that intensive clinical education would be absolutely required.

Two very bright boys seemed to have interests that were worlds apart—one child was fascinated by the Middle Ages, especially chivalry and the way of life; the other boy was enamored of heavy vehicles of any type. Through a mutual sharing activity, both children began to find elements of interest for themselves in the interest of the other. Soon there were regular exchanges of pictures, articles, and stories between them. They began to share their work and worked together on mutual projects. The basic "need to know," so often overlooked in these children, became operative. Their mutual growth in interests, concepts, and vocabulary in no way interfered with development of the appropriate process skills by the teacher. This example demonstrates how vital it is for bright children to have ample opportunity to associate in learning activities with other bright children.

Teachers in the program seemed to feel that the exposure to and use of various learning procedures and teaching techniques were important. However, several teachers had some difficulty in adjusting to the use of the computer. It was also obvious that some of the teachers who were excellent classroom teachers found it difficult to adjust to the clinical education procedures. The reality of the learning-disabled/gifted child often frustrated some of them. The fact that the entire school day was a diagnostic/prescriptive activity was disconcerting to some teachers, whose basic approach was rather developmental.

It became apparent that, if the child was motivated, the mastery and use of a VAKT procedure could be obtained. In many of the children, self-esteem rose dramatically when they realized that they could learn hard words and read long passages with some effort on their part. One child learned 52 words concerned with plants, including photosynthesis, during the 4-week program. The children were also pleased to be able to use the procedure with increasing independence. The fact that they created, wrote, and were able to read materials of their specific interest delighted them. For some, the computer activities were especially motivating; for others, these were not particularly effective. It was evident that learning-disabled/gifted children profited from the nonconventional, nondevelopmental instructional program.

If there is a lesson to be garnered from the practicum, it is that learning-disabled/gifted children will suffer in programs that utilize regimented instructional practices and materials. Their obvious talents and contributions will be lost unless their individuality and needs are recognized.

CONCLUSION

Graduate courses and degree programs can be developed to train teachers in diagnostic/prescriptive techniques, curriculum development, individualized case management, multisensory instructional techniques, and some counseling strategies. Ideally, these techniques require smaller teacher-pupil ratios, more teacher aides, and better psychological support services, such as those available in the very special setting at the John F. Kennedy Institute. Even if the costs of creating such programs within the public schools would not allow for all of the services described in this clinical model, many of the techniques used by teachers in a clinical setting could and should be applied in other classroom situations as well. A well-trained teacher who is knowledgeable about the needs of learning-disabled/gifted children can be the key to unlocking their potential.

Conclusion
Future Directions for Research and Practice
Lynn H. Fox, Linda Brody, and Dianne Tobin

This volume is a collection of chapters addressing conceptual and operational definitions as well as the educational needs of learning-disabled/gifted children. Theory, research, current practice, and model programs are all considered. The chapter authors were drawn from both the fields of learning disabilities and gifted education. Although they each presented their own particular viewpoint, many threads of agreement emerged throughout the various chapters with respect to identification and programming. These common themes are summarized briefly in the following two sections. Although there is clearly a need for more research, some policy implications can be suggested. Thus, this volume closes with ideas for research and for promoting changes in current practice.

IDENTIFICATION

Although the term *learning-disabled/gifted* rarely appears in the research or professional literature, the concept is by no means inconsistent with the current conceptual definition of the learning disabled as described by Senf (Chapter 2). Nor is the learning-disabled but gifted child a rare phenomenon in clinical practice, as described by Rosner and Seymour in Chapter 4. The term is only paradoxical to those in the area of gifted education who insist upon high levels of achievement in all academic areas as measured by standardized tests. Tannenbaum and Baldwin (Chapter 1) point out that few experts in the 1980s would

276   Fox, Brody, and Tobin

advocate such a narrow definition. Indeed, the view that gifted individuals may show patterns of strengths and weaknesses is not new.

In practice, however, probably only a small number of learning-disabled/gifted students are identified as either gifted or disabled. This is the result of the widespread use of common operational definitions of learning disabilities and giftedness which fly in the face of the broader conceptual definitions. For example, the concept of discrepancy between achievement and potential described by Senf and by Berk (Chapter 3) is often translated by school practice into a discrepancy of 2 years below grade placement. Fox (Chapter 6) finds that such an operational definition would exclude many gifted students who are at grade level or above in achievement measures but still well below estimated achievement based on potential. Another related problem is that children might be identified on the basis of a severe reading problem, and the fact that they are gifted in some other areas is totally ignored in a remediation approach to the learning problem. Yet because of the reading problem, the child is excluded from consideration for gifted programs in other areas. Indeed, as Fox and Brody (Chapter 5) note, most operational definitions of giftedness rely heavily on the use of standardized in-grade achievement tests and teacher nominations in the initial screening stage. This practice is likely to exclude many learning-disabled children.

There is no immediate easy solution to the problem of identification. The case-typing approach described by Rosner (Chapter 7) can be used by school systems to incorporate estimates of the discrepancy between achievements and potential without reference to grade placement as well as include suggestions of specific processing deficits or disorders. However, a full clinical evaluation is expensive, and school systems cannot afford to do this for all children. Thus, what should be the prescreening measures? Tannenbaum and Baldwin suggest that classroom teachers should complete more sophisticated behavioral checklists in a referral process. Fox suggests more research to validate the use of teacher-administered, informal assessments of listening comprehension, and instructional reading level discrepancies. Fox and Brody recommend a multimethod approach to screening and identification, including some untimed nonverbal reasoning tests, such as the Raven's Progressive Matrices. Tannenbaum and Baldwin further suggest a wider variety of enrichment programs for all children so that they have an opportunity to identify and develop their specific strengths, and that these enrichment classes should serve as a part of the screening and identification process to select students for more advanced or extensive work in the area.

PROGRAMMING

There are few existing programs for the learning-disabled/gifted child. This book has offered suggestions for the kind of programs these children need, and model programs functioning in school systems have been described by Baldwin and Gargiulo (Chapter 12), and Udall and Maker (Chapter 13).

There is general agreement that a carefully designed identification/screening procedure is the first step toward designing a good program. The program should be appropriate for the specific needs of the child. Baldwin and Gargiulo, and Udall and Maker describe identification procedures which utilized a variety of measures, in their model programs. An interdisciplinary team approach to assessment is described by Lewis and Daniels (Chapter 15) and Daniels (Chapter 8) emphasizes the need for ongoing diagnosis. These authors, as well as Gallagher (Chapter 9), recognize the need for a variety of assessment measures in order to evaluate the specific pattern of strengths and weaknesses in the learning-disabled/gifted child.

In designing a program, there is strong feeling that the learning-disabled/gifted child whose disabilities are rather severe needs to be in a special class with other learning-disabled/gifted children. Daniels suggests that multiage, multigrade grouping, which may be necessary in order to have enough students to form a class, is desirable to allow for more flexibility in the nongraded environment. The class described by Baldwin and Gargiulo draws students from several school districts. The authors generally agree that the placement of learning-disabled/gifted students with other learning-disabled/gifted students will allow them to stimulate each other intellectually, thereby contributing to the development of self-esteem.

A thematic approach to instruction is described by Udall and Maker, Baldwin and Gargiulo, Daniels, and Lewis and Daniels. It provides the framework in which skills can be remediated at the same time that the child is intellectually challenged. Topics can be based on the children's areas of interest. This will help to motivate them to want to learn. In addition, multisensory techniques of language instruction are recommended by Daniels, and Lewis and Daniels. They point out that most of these children have not succeeded with traditional visual/auditory techniques and that a different approach is needed.

Learning-disabled/gifted children who are less disabled may not need to be in a special class; they can often function successfully in the regular classroom. These children are often excluded from programs for the gifted, however, in spite of their high intellectual po-

278   *Fox, Brody, and Tobin*

tential. Gallagher discusses the appropriateness of gifted programs for learning-disabled/gifted children, and Fox, Tobin, and Schiffman (Chapter 10) recommend the use of adaptive techniques to circumvent the area(s) of disability in order to allow the child to successfully participate in a program for the gifted.

Low self-esteem is recognized as a problem with many learning-disabled/gifted youngsters. They have problems reconciling their discrepant abilities or understanding why a less able friend or sibling may learn something more easily. The importance of designing instructional programs that encourage success and of building counseling components into programs for learning-disabled/gifted children is emphasized by Daniels, Lewis and Daniels, Udall and Maker, and Baldwin and Gargiulo. Parent counseling is also recognized as needed by many of these authors, and a program for parent counseling is described by Bricklin (Chapter 14).

Microcomputers are increasingly being utilized in education for instruction as well as management by teachers. These applications for use with learning-disabled/gifted children are discussed in the chapter by Tobin and Schiffman (Chapter 11).

It is recognized that the programs advocated in these chapters may require teachers with special training. A process for training teachers in the clinical method is described by Lewis and Daniels. This method would be useful for teachers who would return to public school environments as well as for those who would stay in a clinical setting.

AREAS FOR FUTURE RESEARCH

In spite of recent efforts to conduct research on learning-disabled/gifted children, some of which are summarized in this volume, there is still much that is not known. There is a definite need for further research in both identification and facilitation.

A major effort is needed to determine what percentage of the school population is indeed learning-disabled/gifted because it seems that many such children are not being identified at present. More research is therefore needed into the characteristics of these children so they can be more easily identified. While clinicians feel confident about their ability to discover learning-disabled/gifted children, there is still a lack of standardization in their methods; individual clinical diagnosis is expensive, time-consuming, and not practical for a school system to use on a large-scale basis. Because paper-and-pencil group tests seem to be inefficient in identifying learning-disabled/gifted students, research is needed to find innovative ways to develop new meas-

Conclusion   279

ures or adapt existing quick screening procedures. In addition, use of
the microcomputer should be further explored for purposes of testing
and management to make it more efficient and effective to screen large
populations.

A few model programs for the truly disabled but gifted student
were discussed in this volume. More research is needed, however, to
compare various program models and to provide a longitudinal evaluation of the effects of participation in the programs on the students'
future performance in school and in life. Furthermore, there is a need
for systematic study of the effects of using adaptive techniques for the
mildly disabled gifted child who is included in general programs for
the gifted. With the growth of microcomputer instruction in schools,
special problems which learning-disabled/gifted children may encounter in becoming computer-literate need to be studied. Far more work
is also needed to tap the ways in which the microcomputer can best
be used to enhance learning and compensate for disabilities in the
gifted population.

PUBLIC AWARENESS AND POLICY IMPLICATIONS

Consider a situation in which a child who is perceived by the parent
as bright is described by the teacher as a behavior problem in school.
The teacher suggests that the parent take the child to a pediatrician
for evaluation for hyperactivity. In such a case, the hypothesis that
the child is gifted but learning disabled should be investigated. Such
a hypothesis may not be considered unless there is greater awareness
among professionals and the general public as to the existence of such
children.

The logical starting point for a campaign of awareness is institutions of higher education, which provide training for educators and
physicians. Lectures and readings on learning-disabled/gifted children
should be incorporated into basic courses on exceptional children
which, in turn, should be required in undergraduate and/or graduate programs in every area of general education. More in-depth
training should be required for all educators who plan to work in any
area of special education and for guidance counselors and school
psychologists.

Educators who have already completed graduate training programs may be informed through journals and meetings of professional
organizations, such as the Council for Exceptional Children, the National Education Association, the National Association for Gifted Children, the Association for Children with Learning Disabilities, and the

American Personnel and Guidance Association. In turn, they might request or develop in-service workshops or conferences at the state or local educational agency level.

As the educational community becomes more knowledgable about this special population, information can be communicated to parents individually or in groups. Perhaps eventually, there will be enough parent concern to influence school boards or state legislatures to provide funding for services to such children.

Many gifted children with severe learning disabilities are now legally entitled to special services within the framework of existing federal and state guidelines and mandates for services to learning-disabled children. They must, however, be properly identified in order to receive appropriate services, and this requires some revision of current identification and program practices in many schools. This can only evolve from the efforts of better informed educators in positions of leadership in special education.

There may be resistance to classifying some children as learning disabled if they are indeed functioning at or above grade level. Actually, many such children may not require the extensive special programming described in some of the chapters of this book. They will, however, need to be recognized and understood by those teachers of programs for the gifted as well as those in the mainstream of classes.

This book is one step toward providing the professional educational community with information about the learning-disabled/gifted population and their special needs. Hopefully, it will serve as a catalyst for research and changes in identification and programming practices.

Individualizing instruction and programs for special populations is not a new idea. However, it is not yet universally practiced. Until the educational system capitalizes upon the unique strengths of each child instead of penalizing them for their inability to conform to some standard of normal development, society is likely to suffer from the loss of talents not developed among many children.

Author Index

Abruscato, J., 240
Ackerman, P. T., 128, 129, 138
Adams, J., 199, 205
Adamson, K. K., 38, 44, 48
Adamson, W. C., 38, 44, 48
Adelman, H., 35
Albert, R. S., 103, 111, 113
Alexander, P. A., 111, 113
Alexander, R. N., 260
Algozzine, B., 59, 73, 74
Alyes, G., 213, 221
Anderson, D. O., 199, 205
Anderson, M., 106, 113
Avery, S., 81, 87, 96

Baldwin, L. J., 5, 6, 11–36, 111,
    113, 207–221, 275, 276, 277, 278
Bannatyne, A., 3, 6, 106, 113,
    132, 138
Bateman, B., 53, 57, 74
Battista, M. T., 206
Beck, E. C., 22, 34
Beery, R., 33–34
Benbow, C. P., 113
Bennett, R. E., 202, 205
Bentzen, F., 180
Berk, R. A., 5, 51–76, 120, 138, 276
Bersoff, D. N., 62, 74
Biondi, A. M., 221
Birch, T. W., 108, 115, 210, 221
Bish, C. E., 102, 114
Block, G. H., 189, 192
Bloom, A., 106, 114
Bloom, B. S., 16, 34, 220
Brau-Langer, B., 205
Bricklin, B., 260
Bricklin, P., 6, 243–260, 278
Brody, L., 1–6, 101–116, 275–280
Bromberg, M., 240
Brown, N. P., 199, 205
Bruch, C. B., 108, 114

Brumbough, F. N., 78, 96
Bryan, J., 21, 34, 39, 45, 48, 56,
    173, 180
Bryan, T., 21, 34, 39, 45, 48, 56,
    62, 173, 180
Bryant, N. D., 62, 74
Buchanan, B., 201, 206
Burnes, M., 240

Caldwell, R. M., 200, 205
Callahan, C., 35, 221
Cassidy-Bronson, S., 199, 206
Charles, C. M., 213, 220
Chalfant, J. C., 54, 57, 60–61,
    67, 74
Chauncey, H., 22, 34
Ciha, T. E., 25, 34
Clements, J. E., 252, 260
Clements, S. D., 29, 34, 53, 56,
    74, 80, 96, 106, 114
Colangelo, N., 258, 260
Coleman, M., 116
Collins, E. C., 104, 114
Comrey, A. L., 45, 49
Covington, M. V., 33, 35
Cox, C. M., 103, 111, 114
Cratty, B., 175, 180
Crockenberg, S. B., 111, 114
Crossland, C. L., 198, 205
Cruickshank, W., 2, 6, 38, 48, 56,
    62, 74, 172, 180
Cushing, H., 1

Daniels, P. R., 6, 118, 153–169,
    223, 241, 261–273, 277, 278
Dembinski, R. J., 251, 260
Dice, C., 68, 76
Dykman, R. A., 138

Eberle, B., 213, 220, 241

282 Author Index

Egan, M. W., 260
Elkind, J., 1, 6, 92, 96, 171, 180, 223, 241
Elkins, J., 73, 75

Feagans, L., 174, 181
Feldman, D., 103, 114
Feshbach, S., 25, 35
Feverstein, R., 28, 35
Fiedler, V. D., 74
Flewelling, R., 115
Fliegler, L. A., 102, 114
Forgnone, D., 75
Fox, L. H., 1–6, 101–116, 117–139, 183–193, 275–280
Frampton, M., 88, 96
Frase, L. T., 192
Frostig, M., 175, 180
Fry, E., 2, 6
Fuller, W., 35

Gair, S., 178, 180
Gall, E. D., 96
Gallagher, J. J., 3, 6, 15, 35, 54, 55, 57, 61, 74, 75, 128, 129, 138, 171–181, 209, 210, 220, 277, 278
Galton, F., 14, 35
Gargiulo, D., 6, 111, 207–221, 277, 278
Gaynor, P., 116
Gear, G. H., 110, 111, 114, 230, 241
Gearhart, B. R., 57, 62, 74
George, W. C., 186, 192
Gerken, 11, 35
Getzels, J. W., 3, 7, 19, 35, 111, 114
Gillespie, P. H., 71, 72, 74
Gingrich, P. S., 192
Glass, G., 180
Glasser, A., 30, 35
Glasser, W., 213, 220
Glowinski, D. J., 199, 205
Goertzel, M., 1, 7
Goertzel, V., 1, 7
Gordon, W., 213, 220
Grimmer, G. B., 241
Grotberg, E., 78, 96
Guilford, J. P., 107, 111, 114
Gygi, J., 223, 242

Hagen, E., 35
Hall, R. E., 213, 220
Hallahan, D. P., 39, 45, 48, 62, 65, 74, 75
Hammill, D. D., 57, 59, 61, 62, 65, 75
Harber, J. R., 68, 69, 70, 75
Hardman, M. I., 249, 260
Harnadek, A., 213, 219, 220, 241
Harris, R., 34, 81, 87, 96
Harrison, Jr., A., 241
Hartman, R. K., 25, 35, 111, 115, 210, 221
Hassard, J., 240
Hasselbring, T. S., 198, 205
Hayden, D., 199, 205
Hilton, T. L., 22, 34
Hodges, L., 70, 76
Hoffman, C., 34
Hoffman, J., 120, 138
Hollingworth, L., 77, 78, 96
Horne, D., 175, 180
Howe, L. W., 221, 241
Humphrey, M., 206

Irvin, M. S., 205
Isaacs, A., 86, 96

Jackson, N. E., 221
Jackson, P. W., 3, 7, 111, 114
Jacobs, J. C., 25, 35, 110, 114
James, H., 88, 96
Johnson, D. J., 56, 75
Johnson, S. W., 57, 75

Kauffman, J. M., 65, 75
Kaufman, A. S., 48, 106, 107, 113, 114, 120, 138, 221
Kaufman, N. L., 48, 113, 221
Karnes, M. B., 24, 35, 104
Kavale, K., 68, 69, 70, 75, 180, 181
Keating, D. P., 7, 102
Keenau, S. A., 192
Kephart, N. C., 172, 181
Kerlinger, F. N., 67, 75
Khatena, J., 78, 96
King, F. S., 57, 67, 74
Kirk, S. A., 39, 48, 52, 53, 55, 57, 60, 62, 73, 75, 172, 181

Author Index   283

Kirk, W. D., 75, 174, 175, 181
Kirschenbaum, H., 221, 241
Kleiman, G., 197, 201, 206
Kohfeldt, J., 213, 220
Krippner, S., 79, 86, 87, 96
Krockover, G. H., 206

Labuda, M., 88, 96
Landau, E. D., 260
Larsen, R., 48
Larsen, S. C., 75
Lehtinen, L., 38, 49
Leigh, J. E., 75
Lerner, J. W., 62, 76, 173, 178, 181
Lessinger, L. M., 108, 114
Lewis, J. G., 108, 115
Lewis, M. E. B., 6, 108, 115,
    261–273, 277, 278
Liebb, J., 240
Lieberman, L. M., 40, 48
Lindgren, S., 106, 115
Lindsay, P. H., 206
Lloyd, J., 72, 75
Lovitt, T., 178, 181
Luber, D., 187, 192
Lucito, L., 128, 129, 138

MacDonald, N. H., 189, 192
MacKinnon, D. W., 16, 35, 103,
    111, 114
Maker, C. J., 2, 4, 7, 171, 181, 210,
    221, 223–242, 277, 278
Mann, L., 75
Margenau, H., 66, 75
Marion, R. L., 244, 260
Marland, Jr., S. P., 3, 7, 15, 35,
    103, 114, 172, 181
Martinson, R. A., 108, 114
Mauser, A. J., 251, 260
McCarthy, J., 3, 7, 181
McCurdy, H. G., 103, 114
McGrady, H. J., 21, 34
McKinney, J. D., 174, 181
McLoughlin, 57, 60, 62
McNutt, G., 75
Mackstroth, E. A., 260
Mealor, D. J., 68, 69, 70, 76
Meeker, M. N., 107, 114, 240, 241
Meisgeir, C., 32

Mercer, C. D., 62, 71, 75, 108, 115
Michael, W. B., 112, 115
Miller, T. L., 74
Montgomery, R. A., 241
Morasky, R. L., 57, 75
Moursund, D., 189, 190, 193
Muia, J. A., 111, 113
Musial, D., 241
Myers, P., 57, 59, 62, 65, 75
Myers, R. E., 213, 221
Myklebust, H. R., 38, 48, 53, 56,
    75, 120, 121, 123, 124, 125,
    126, 132, 139

Newland, T. G., 102, 103, 115
Noller, R. B., 221
Nye, C., 68, 69, 70, 75

Oden, M. H., 77, 105, 115
Ohrenstein, D. F., 254, 260
Olson, J. L., 68, 69, 70, 76
Orton, S. T., 38, 48, 79, 97
Osman, B. B., 212, 221

Packard, E., 241
Papert, S., 203, 206
Parnes, S. J., 213, 214, 221, 234, 241
Passow, A. H., 111, 115
Patten, B., 1, 7
Patton, G., 1
Pegnato, C. W., 108, 115, 210, 221
Peters, J. E., 29, 34, 138
Pieschowski, M. M., 16, 35
Potter, M., 34
Pressey, S. L., 172, 181
Price, R., 241

Rack, L., 191, 193
Raskin, L., 106, 114
Ratzeburg, F., 180
Redl, F., 213, 221
Renzulli, J. S., 15, 16, 17, 25, 35,
    102, 103, 111, 115, 210, 221
Richards, J. H., 190, 193, 205
Richman, L., 106, 115
Rizza, P. J., 200, 205
Robinson, H. B., 14, 15, 35,
    210, 221

Roe, A., 19, 23, 35, 103, 115
Roedell, W. C., 221
Rosner, S. L., 5, 77–97, 141–149, 275–276
Ross, A. O., 2, 3, 7, 56, 76
Rourke, B., 106, 115
Rugel, R., 132, 139

Salvia, J., 60, 70
Scheffelin, M. A., 54, 57, 60, 61, 74
Schiff, M. M., 29, 35, 44, 48, 209, 221
Schiffman, G., 6, 118, 183–193, 195–206, 278
Schur, J., 173, 181
Seghini, J. B., 242
Senf, G. M., 5, 37–49, 67, 70, 76, 275, 276
Seymour, J., 5, 77–97, 275
Shaw, M., 213, 221
Simon, S. B., 213, 221, 234, 241
Siperstein, G. N., 45, 49
Stanish, B., 241
Stanley, J. C., 3, 7, 102, 104, 115, 186, 193
Steele, K. J., 197, 206
Steeves, K. J., 110, 115
Stefanich, G., 173, 181
Stern, L., 241
Sternberg, R. J., 103, 115
Stevenson, G., 234, 242
Strauss, A. A., 2, 38, 49, 172, 181
Sutherland, J. 73, 74

Tabachnick, B., 106, 115
Tannenbaum, A. J., 5, 11–36, 111, 113, 275, 276
Tannhauser, M., 180
Taylor, C. W., 234, 242
Terman, L. M., 3, 7, 14, 15, 16, 36, 77, 78, 97, 102, 107, 110, 115
Thompson, A., 179, 181
Thompson, L., 1, 7, 44
Thomson, L. J., 49
Thorndike, E. L., 102, 116
Timothy, K., 242
Tobin, D., 1–6, 183–193, 195–206, 275–280

Torgeson, J. K., 68, 76
Torgerson, W. S., 66, 76
Torrance, E. P., 3, 7, 97, 111, 112, 116, 213, 221
Thurlow, M. L., 67, 70, 71, 76
Tolan, S. S., 260

Udall, A. J., 6, 223–242, 277, 278

Vance, B., 205
Vance, H., 106, 116
Vaughan, R. W., 70, 76
Veltman, E. S., 62, 74

Wallace, G., 57, 60, 62, 76
Wallach, M. A., 16, 22, 36
Walsh, A., 21, 36
Watkins, M., 197, 206
Watt, D., 203, 206
Watt, M., 203, 206
Webb, C., 197, 206
Webb, J. T., 251, 253, 260
Webster, E. J., 250, 260
Wechsler, D., 102, 105, 106, 116, 120, 126, 132, 139
Weker, K. J., 241
Wender, P., 56, 76
Whitmore, J. R., 4, 7, 22, 36, 102, 116, 175, 181, 211, 221, 252, 260
Wiederholt, J. L., 38, 49, 62, 76
Williams, F. E., 213, 221
Wineman, D., 213, 221
Witty, P., 78, 97, 102, 116
Wolf, J., 223, 242
Wolking, W. D., 75

Young, G., 115
Ysseldyke, J. E., 59, 60, 67, 70, 71, 72, 73, 76

Zaffran, R. T., 260
Zimmerman, I., 29, 35

Subject Index

Abbreviated Binet for the
Disadvantaged (ABDA), 108
Ability—achievement discrepancy,
see Underachievement
Academic disorders, in learning-
disabled child, 59, 70
Acceleration activities, 219
Achievement, family and attitude
toward, 247–248
see also Underachievement
Achievement tests, *see* Aptitude and
achievement tests
Acquiring knowledge, 184
Adaptive methods, *see* Teaching
programs
Administration, *see* Teaching
programs
Adolescence
defenses against status as
learning-disabled/gifted,
84–88
negativity in, 93–95
Agencies, clinical teacher involved
with, 270–271
Aides, in teaching programs for
learning-disabled/gifted child,
158
Anomalous talents, as criteria for
giftedness, 13–14
Aptitude and achievement tests,
109–110
for BOCES model program,
209–210
in case-typing, 142, 146–147
giftedness identified with, 104
Raven's Progressive Matrices, 110
Scholastic Aptitude Test, 109
Aptitudes, in giftedness, 17–18
Arithmetic Subscale, of
WISC/WISC-R, 127, 128,
129, 130, 131, 136

Associative learning, in case-typing,
142, 147
Associative Learning Test, 93
Auditing procedure, for
standardized tests, 161–162
Auditory discrimination, difficulty
in, 92, 93
Auditory modes, of information
acquisition, 185

Bannatyne recategorization of
WISC, 132
Behavioral characteristics, as factor
leading to screening, 45–46
Behavioral definitions, of learning
disabilities, 56–57
Behavioral disorders, of learning-
disabled/gifted child, 43
Behavior modification program,
self-esteem fostered with, 213
Bender Gestalt test, 90
in case-typing, 148
Biological definition, or learning
disability, 56
Block Design Subscale, of
WISC/WISC-R, 85, 90, 128,
129, 130, 131, 136, 137
BOCES model program, 208–220
curriculum, 215–220
goals, 211–215
identification of children for,
208–211
individual educational plan in,
211–212
mainstreaming as goal of, 214–215
placement, 210–211
self-esteem fostered by, 212–215
social skills enhanced by, 212–215
Brain dysfunction
learning disabilities as, 56,
172–173, 179

286   *Subject Index*

Brain dysfunction—*continued*
 minimal brain damage, 52, 56,
  80, 172
Bricklin Inner Shouting techniques,
 in parent intervention
 program, 255–257

Careers, predicting success in,
 22–23
Case history
 in case-typing, 141, 142, 143–144
 in learning-disabled/gifted child,
  85
Case reports, of reading problems,
 133, 134
Case study approach
 examples of, 95
 identifying the learning-
  disabled/gifted child with, 81
Case-typing, 119, 141–149
 achievement tests in, 142,
  146–147
 associative learning in, 142, 147
 case history in, 141, 142, 143–144
 for clinical teacher, 265
 developmental skills in, 142, 148
 identification and, 276
 intelligence and, 142, 144–145
 language and conceptual
  development in, 142, 148
 learning-disabled identified
  with, 120
 Memory Span battery in, 147
 personal adjustment in, 142, 148
 readiness in, 142, 147
 reading in, 142, 148
 word recognition and spelling in,
  142, 145–146
Chance factors, in giftedness, 18–19
Checklists, for screening, 111
 for BOCES model program, 210
Children with Specific Learning
  Disabilities Act of 1969
  (PL 91-230), learning
  disabilities defined in, 54, 57,
  62, 63, 64, 71, 72
Classes, *see* Teaching programs
Classroom meetings, 234
 for emotional development, 218
 self-esteem fostered with, 213

Classroom placement, *see*
 Placement
Clinic
 learning-disabled/gifted child
  and, 42
 learning-disabled/gifted child and,
  41–43
Clinical identification
 case history for, 85
 case study approach to, 81–82
  examples of, 88–95
 feedback interview for, 85
 informal reading inventory for,
  85–86
 intellectual functioning
  assessment and, 85
 response of child to learning-
  disabled/gifted status, 84–88
Clinical teacher, 261–273
 agencies involved with, 270–271
 case-typing for, 265
 clinical setting, 262–263
 curricular materials chosen by,
  266–268
 diagnostic and prescriptive
  methods of, 268–269
 evaluation by, 269–270
 families involved with, 270
 interdisciplinary team working
  with, 264–265
 multisensory approach used by,
  267
 practicum for, 271–273
 qualifications for, 263–264
 role of, 264–271
Clinicians, reading problems
  identified by 126–134
Coding Subscale, for WISC/
  WISC-R, 128, 129, 130, 131,
  136, 137
Communication
 in family, 246
 in parent intervention
  program, 257
Comprehension Subscale, of
  WISC/WISC-R, 127, 128,
  129, 130, 131, 135, 136
Computers, 167, 195–205
 for assessment by clinical
  teacher, 269

Subject Index   287

capabilities, 200–201
for clinical setting, 272
discovery-learning with, 203
effectiveness of, 196–197
experimental program using,
    203–205
for individualized education plan,
    198–199
as instructional tool, 199–203
LOGO, 203
as management tool, 198–199
for mathematics, 190
for multisensory approaches to
    learning, 201–202
for screening, 279
short-term memory problem dealt
    with by, 164
for stimulations, 202–203
state of art of, 195–198
as word processor, 203
writing disabilities helped with,
    188–189
Concentration problems, teaching
    programs dealing with,
    163–164
Concept development, in case-
    typing, 142, 148
Conference on Exploration into the
    Problems of the Perceptually
    Handicapped Child, 52
Conferencing, for emotional
    development, 218
Confidentiality, in counseling
    sessions, 168
Content units, in teaching learning-
    disabled/gifted, 165, 178
Counseling
    for parents of the learning-
        disabled child, 178–179
    intervention programs for,
        251–259
    in pilot program, 234
    teacher of learning-disabled/gifted
        students understanding
        techniques, 156
    teaching programs offering,
        167–169
Creativity
    self-esteem fostered with activities
        in, 213

tests of
    learning-disabled/gifted child
        and, 112
    for screening, 30, 111–112
Culturally disadvantaged children,
    intelligence tests for, 107–108
Curriculum
    of BOCES model program,
        215–218
    critical thinking in, 218–219
    for gifted children, 216
    for learning-disabled children, 216
    of pilot program, 233–235
    for teachers in clinical setting,
        266–268

Defense mechanisms, of learning-
    disabled/gifted child, 84–88
Definition, of learning-
    disabled/gifted child, 2–4,
    104–105, 225–226
    see also Gifted; Learning-disabled
Demonstrating knowledge, 184
Detroit Tests of Learning Aptitude,
    Memory Span battery of, 147
Developmental dyslexia, 79–80
Developmental sequences
    in case-typing, 142, 148
    teacher of learning-disabled/gifted
        students understanding, 156
Developmental Test of Visual
    Perception, 60
Diagnosis, 141
    by clinical teacher, 268
    multisensory learning approach
        for, 164
    ongoing, 161
    in teaching programs for learning-
        disabled, 174–175
    in teaching programs for learning-
        disabled/gifted child, 159–161
    see also Case-typing
Diagnostic teaching, prior to
    placement, 160
Differentiation, 33–34
Digit Span Subscale, of
    WISC/WISC-R, 127, 128,
    129, 130, 131, 133, 136, 137

288   *Subject Index*

Discovery-learning, computer for, 203

Discrepancy, *see* Underachievement

Discrepancy formula, *see* Expectancy formula

Discrepancy model, in teaching children with learning disabilities, 178

Divergent thinking, measures of, 30
  see also Creativity

Dysgraphia, adaptive methods for teaching children with, 187–189

Education for All Handicapped Children Act of 1975 (PL 94-142)
  failure, 40
  individualized educational plans in, 179, 198–199, 211–212
  learning-disabled defined in, 8, 39–40, 54, 55, 57, 58, 62, 63, 65, 66, 71, 73
  least restrictive environment, 154–155
  related services of, 47–48
  researchers and, 41

Education of the Handicapped Amendments (PL 93-380), 57

Ego, in learning-disabled/gifted child, 87
  see also Self-esteem

Elementary and Secondary Amendments, 57

Emotional and social development
  BOCES model program fostering, 212–214
  curriculum for, 218
  of gifted, 14–20
  intellectual development and, 78–79
  of learning-disabled/gifted child, 21, 86

Enrichment, 219
  differentiation via, 33–34
  identification via, 23–24, 32
  learning-disabled/gifted children in class for, 32–33
  in pilot program, 234

Environmental conditions approach, in teaching learning-disabled, 178

Environmental factors, in giftedness, 18

Evaluation, in teaching programs for learning-disabled/gifted child, 161–162

Exclusion clause, in definition of learning disabled, 57, 60–62, 65, 69, 70, 71

Expectancy formula, 120–121
  learning-disabled/gifted identified with, 120–121, 123, 124, 125, 126
  for reading problems, 133

Experiences, within family, 246

Family
  clinical teacher involved with, 270
  strength of, 244–245
  strengthening, 257–258
  see also Parents

Family meeting, for strengthening family, 258

Federal definition, of gifted, 3–4, 15–17, 104, 172
  see also Learning-disabled

Federal Register, see Procedures for Evaluating Specific Learning Disabilities

Feedback interview, for learning-disabled/gifted child, 85

Fernald Visual-Auditory-Kinesthetic Tactile (VAKT) procedure, 163, 267

Figure-ground game, in teaching learning-disabled, 178

Full-Scale, of WISC/WISC-R, 119, 122, 125, 126, 127, 129, 132, 135, 137

Future research, areas for, 278–279

GATE, *see* Gifted and Talented Education Program

Gates Associative Learning Test, 142, 147, 269

General ability, in gifted, 17
General assessment history for,
    screening, 47
Genetic Studies of Genius, 14
Gifted
    in adults as distinct from
        children, 17
    career success prediction, 22–23
    chance factors in, 18–19
    curriculum for, 216
    definition, 3–4, 15–16, 77–79, 172
        conceptual, 101–103
        creativity for, 103
        criteria for, 12–14
        federal, 3–4, 15–17, 104, 172
        information processing theory
            and, 103
        legal and operational, 103–104
        Marland Report, 172
        as a potential, 19–20
        socioeconomic factors and, 78
        sociopsychological, 103
        states,' 103–104
        Terman and, 14, 15, 77–78, 105
    enrichment program for, 219
    environmental factors in, 18
    general ability in, 17
    identifying, 104, 119, *see also*
        screening, *below*
        enrichment for, 23–24
        Johns Hopkins empirical study
            for, 118, 121–126
        problems in, 22–24
    information use skills of, 103
    intelligence test scores equaled
        with, 14–15
    learning environment for,
        176–177
    mainstreaming, 176
    mentor program for, 177
    metacomponents of, 103
    nonintellective factors in, 17
    performance components of, 103
    personal problems in, 46
    resource room for, 177
    screening for, 105, 159, *see also*
        Aptitude and achievement
        tests; identifying, *above*;
        Intelligence tests
        checklists, 111

creativity tests, 111–112
for learning disabilities, 46
teacher recommendations, 104,
    110–111
social-psychological perspective
    14–20
special aptitudes in, 17–18
special class for, 177
special school for, 177
state guidelines, 79
stereotype of the, 2
underachievement in, 102
Gifted and Talented Education
        Program (GATE), 223–240
    counseling in, 234
    curriculum, 233–235, 240
    description of children in,
        228–231
    evaluation, 238–239
    future of, 239–240
    goals of, 225–229
    identification of children for,
        229–230
    referrals to, 227–229
    teaching methods of, 237–238
    WISC-R profiles of, 231
Groupings, in teaching learning-
        disabled/gifted, 165–166
Group tests, of intelligence, 108

Hyperactivity, 91

Identification, 20–22, 41–43,
        275–276
    for BOCES model program,
        208–211
    clinician judgment for, 126–134
    differentiation, 33–34
    expectancy formula for, 120–121,
        123, 124, 125, 126
    individual differences and, 42, 43
    Johns Hopkins research with, 118
    of learning disabled, 120–121
    for pilot program, 229–230
    selection, 31–33
    see also Aptitude and
        achievement tests; Clinical
        identification; Gifted;
        Informal reading inventory;
        Intelligence tests; Screening

290   *Subject Index*

Illinois Test of Psycholinguistic
    Abilities (ITPA), 46, 60, 174
Independence
    in curriculum, 218
    teaching programs fostering,
        166–167
Indexing, recall problems dealt with
    by, 164
Individual differences
    identification, 42
    learning disability and, 173–174
Individualized education plan (IEP),
    179, 198–199, 211–212
Informal reading inventory (IRI),
    92, 137
    in case-typing, 142, 146
    in clinical setting, 269
    gifted identified with, 121–122
    learning-disabled/gifted identified
        with, 85, 124, 125, 126
    learning-disabled identified with,
        92
    Word Recognition Inventory, 90
Informal Word Recognition
    Inventory (IWRI), 142,
    145–146
Information-processing theory
    of intelligence, 103
    of learning disabled, 45, 60, 173
Information Subscale, of
    WISC/WISC-R, 128, 129,
    130, 131, 136
Inner shouting, in parent
    intervention programs,
    255–257
Instruction, *see* Teaching programs
Instructional groupings, in teaching
    learning-disabled/gifted,
    165–166
Intellectualization, as defense used
    by learning-disabled/gifted
    child, 86–87
Intelligence
    case-typing and, 142, 144–145
    information processing theory
        of, 103
    of learning-disabled children, 29,
        58, 68–69, 71
Intelligence tests, 46, 105–108
    Abbreviated Binet for the
        Disadvantaged, 108

Bender-Gestalt, 90
    criticisms of, 108
    for culturally diverse children,
        107–108
    gifted and, 14–15, 101–102
    group tests of, 108
    for learning-disabled/gifted, 105,
        107, 108
    Otis Quick-Scoring Mental Ability
        Test, 108
    Stanford-Binet Intelligence Test, 14,
        77, 102, 104, 105, 107,
        110, 159
    Structure of Intellect-Learning
        Abilities Test, 107
    System of Multicultural Pluralistic
        Assessment, 107–108
    Wechsler Adult Intelligence Scale
        (WAIS), 89–90
    Wechsler Intelligence Scales for
        Children and Wechsler
        Intelligence Scales for
        Children-Revised (WISC and
        WISC-R), 29–30, 83–84, 104,
        105–108, 159
        Arithmetic Subscale, 119, 120,
            121, 122, 123, 128
        Bannatyne recategorization of,
            124
        Block Design Subscale, 120, 121,
            122, 123, 128, 129
        for BOCES model program, 209
        in case-typing, 142, 144–145
        Coding Subscale, 120, 121, 122,
            123, 128, 129
        Comprehension Subscale, 119,
            120, 121, 122, 123, 127, 128
        as diagnostic measure, 269
        Digit Span Subscale, 119, 120,
            121, 122, 123, 125, 128, 129
        Full-Scale, 111, 114, 115, 117,
            118, 119, 121, 124, 127,
            128, 129
        gifted identified with, 113–118
        Information Subscale, 120, 121,
            122, 123, 128
        learning-disabled diagnosed with,
            106–107
        learning-disabled/gifted identified
            with, 44, 126–129

Object Assembly Subscale, 120, 121, 122, 123, 128
Performance Scale, 111, 112, 113, 114, 115, 116, 117, 118, 119, 124, 125, 127, 128, 129
Picture Arrangement Subscale, 120, 121, 122, 123, 128
Picture Completion Subscale, 120, 121, 122, 123, 128, 129
for pilot program, 231
reading problems identified with, 118–125
Similarities Subscale, 119, 120, 121, 122, 123, 125, 127, 128, 129
usefulness, 111
Verbal-Performance discrepancy on, 105–106
Verbal Scale, 111, 112, 114–115, 116, 117, 118, 119, 124, 125, 127, 128, 129
Vocabulary Subscale, 120, 121, 122, 123, 128
Interdisciplinary clinical setting *see* Clinical teacher
Interdisciplinary perspectives, for learning disabilities, 40
IRI, *see* Informal reading inventory

Johns Hopkins University, 80–81
research for identification with Temple University Reading Clinic, 118–138
Talent Search, 109

Kennedy School for Learning Disabled Children, clinical method for teacher training from, 262–273
Key Math Diagnostic Test, 269

Language development
in case-typing, 148, 149
within family, 246–247
Language experience approach, in teaching learning-disabled children, 163–164
Learning centers, for independent study, 218

Learning-disabled
assessment of the, 45–48
brain and, 56, 172–173, 179
clinic and, 42
curriculum for, 216
definition, 2–3, 38, 64–66, 79–81, 172–174, *see also* federal definition, *below*
behavioral, 48–49
as biological disorder, 38
common elements in, 49–54
historical development, 43–49
information processing model of, 173
intraindividual differences and, 173–174
medical, 48
operational, 81
reading-based, 79
in research, 60–62
state, 62–64
theoretical versus operational, 58–59, 65
underachievement, 58–59, 73, 174
federal definition, 39–40, 173
as academic disorder, 59, 69, 70, 71
ambiguity, 55
Children with Specific Learning Disabilities Act, 54, 57, 62, 63, 64, 71, 72
criticisms of, 55–58
Education for All Handicapped Children Act, 3, 8, 39–40, 54, 55, 57, 58, 62, 63, 65, 66, 71, 73
exclusion clause in, 57, 60–62, 65, 69, 70, 71
National Joint Committee for Learning Disabilities and, 65–66, 73
normal intelligence, 68–69, 71
in practice, 70–72
Procedures for Evaluating Specific Learning Disabilities, 50–51, 52, 53, 56, 58, 59, 61, 62, 63, 64, 65, 66
professional consensus regarding, 55–57
as psychological process disorder, 59–60, 69–70, 71

Subject Index

Learning-disabled—*continued*
  purposes and functions, 54
  underachievement, 68–69, 73
  federalization of, 38
  high IQ, highly motivated versus
    high IQ, 25, 26, 28
  historical perspective, 39–43
  identification, 159
    in case-typing, 120
    criteria for, 120–121
  information processing deficiency
    in, 45, 60, 173
  intelligence tests for, 29
  interdisciplinary approach to, 40
  peer status of, 45
  public school approach to, 40–41
  remedial approaches to,
    177–178, 180
  self-esteem of, 45
  teaching programs for, 174–175
Least restrictive environment, for
  learning-disabled/gifted child,
  154–155
Local educational agency (LEA),
  learning-disabled child
  assessed by, 73
LOGO programs, 203

Mainstreaming
  as BOCES model program goal,
    214–215
  for gifted child, 176
Management programs, computers
  for, 198–199
Marland Report, 172
Maryland State Department of
  Education, 80–81
Mathematics, adaptive methods for
  teaching, 188–190
Medical definitions, of learning
  disability, 56
Memory Span battery, in case-
  typing, 147
Mentor program, for gifted
  students, 177
Metaanalysis, of remedial programs,
  180
Microcomputers, *see* Computers

Minimal brain damage, 52, 56, 80,
  172
Modified Fernald approach, for
  visual/auditory learning
  problems, 165–166
Motor skills improvement, in
  teaching learning-disabled,
  178
Mourning process, in parent
  intervention programs,
  255–257
Multisensory teaching approach,
  163–164
  in clinical setting, 267
  computers for, 201–202
Myklebust expectancy formula, *see*
  Expectancy formula

National Advisory Committee on
  Handicapped Children,
  54, 57
National Joint Committee for
  Learning Disabilities, 55,
  65–66
  learning disability defined in, 73
Nature-nurture, intellectual
  development and, 78–79
Negativity, 87
  in adolescence, 93–95
Neurological impairment, in
  learning-disabled/gifted
  child, 87
Noncognitive traits, for screening,
  30–31
Nonintellective factors, in
  giftedness, 18

Observation, by classroom teacher,
  25, 26–28, 160
Ongoing diagnosis, 160–161
Operational definition, of learning
  disabilities, 67
Organization skills, teaching
  children with problems in,
  166
Orton-Gillingham method, as
  multisensory approach, 267

Otis Quick-Scoring Mental Ability Test, 108

Paraprofessionals, in teaching programs for learning-disabled/gifted child, 158
Parents, 240–260
  awareness factors for, 243–244
  checklists filled out by, 210
  clinical teacher involved with, 270
  communication and, 246
  counseling services to, 168–169, 178–179
  evaluation of, 248–249
  of excellent intellectual endowment with learning-disabled/gifted child, 84–85
  experiences and, 246
  family strength and, 244–245
  increasing awareness of, 280
  intellectual development of child and, 78–79
  intervention with, 251–259
    communication skills in, 257
  family strengthened by, 257–258
    inner shouting for, 255–257
  language development and, 246–247
  professional communication with, 249–250
  readiness to parent and, 245–246
  referrals initiated by, 82–83, 92
  reports of for screening, 25, 28
  school and achievement attitudes and, 247–248
  self-concept and, 246–248
Part-time special educational placement, for learning-disabled/gifted children, 154–155
Peer tutors, in teaching programs for learning-disabled/gifted child, 158–159
Performance Scale, of WISC/WISC-R, 119, 120, 121, 122, 123, 124, 125, 126, 127, 132, 135, 137
Perplexity, in learning-disabled/gifted child, 85

Personal adjustment, in case-typing, 142, 148
Personal Computing to Aid the Handicapped, 201
Personality
  of learning-disabled/gifted child, 43
  school psychologist assessing, 157
  see also Emotional and social development; Self-esteem
Personality tests, for reading problems, 134
Physical development, evaluation of, 159
Picture Arrangement Subscale, of WISC/WISC-R, 128, 129, 130, 131, 136
Picture Comprehension Subscale, of WISC/WISC-R, 128, 129, 130, 131, 136
Placement
  in BOCES model program, 210–211
  diagnostic teaching prior to, 160
  of learning-disabled/gifted child, 154–155
PL 91-230, see Children with Specific Learning Disabilities Act of 1969
PL 93-380, see Education of the Handicapped Amendments
PL 94-142, see Education for All Handicapped Children Act of 1975
Pre-/post-testing, for standardized tests, 161–162
Problem-solving activities, self-esteem fostered with, 213, 214
Procedures for Evaluating Specific Learning Disabilities,
  learning disability defined in, 58–59, 60, 61, 64, 66, 70, 71, 73
Process disorders, in learning-disabled child, 59–60, 69–70, 71
Productivity, evidence of in screening, 31

294   *Subject Index*

Program planning, 4–5, 92–93
  see also Teaching programs
Psycholinguistic model, of learning
    disabilities, 60
Psychological defenses, of learning-
    disabled/gifted child, 84–88
Psychological process disorder, in
    learning-disabled child,
    59–60, 69–70, 71
Psychologist, *see* School
    psychologist
Psychometrics, 44
  assessment and, 45–48, 72
Psychosocial problems, *see*
    Emotional and social
    development
Public awareness, increasing,
    279–280
Public schools
  assessment in, 46–48
  family and attitude toward,
    247–248
  learning disabilities approached
    by, 40–41
  learning-disabled/gifted child and,
    41–43
  see also Teacher; Teaching
    programs

Quota, as criteria for giftedness, 13

Raven's Progressive Matrices, 137
Readiness, in case-typing, 142, 146
Reading
  adaptive methods in teaching,
    184–187
    auditory mode, 185
    critical and creative thinking
      skills in, 186
    for mathematically gifted child,
      186
  case reports of, 133, 134
  in case-typing, 142, 146
  clinician judging, 126–134
  goals of
    information acquisition, 185
    language flow, 185
    literacy attainment, 184–185

  individual preferences considered
    in teaching, 185
  personality tests for, 134
  in teaching learning-
    disabled/gifted, 165
  see also Informal reading
    inventory
Referral, 82–83
  by classroom teacher, 83
  criterion for, 46
  delay in, 88
  lack of necessary, 95
  by parents, 82–83, 92
  to pilot program, 227–229
Related services, Education for All
    Handicapped Children Act
    and, 48
  see also Teaching programs
Remedial approaches
  to learning disabilities, 177–178
  metaanalysis of, 180
Repetition, in teaching learning-
    disabled/gifted, 165
Researchers
  Education for All Handicapped
    Children Act and, 41
  learning disabilities approached
    by, 40–41
Research studies of learning-
    disabled child, definitional
    criteria used in, 69
Resource rooms
  for gifted, 177
  for learning-disabled, 32

Scale for Rating Behavioral
    Characteristics of Superior
    Students, 210
Scarcity, as criteria for giftedness,
    12–13
Scholastic Aptitude Test (SAT), 109
School, *see* Public schools; Teaching
    programs
School psychologist
  functions of, 157
  screening ability of, 46–47
Screening, 24–28, 45–46
  in case-typing, 142, 148
  checklist for, 111

creativity measures for, 30
general ability evidence, 28–30
general assessment battery for, 47
of learning-disabled/gifted
  children checklists, 111
  intelligence tests for, 105–107,
    108
  methods for, 112–113
  teacher recommendations, 111
need for more effective methods
  of, 278–279
noncognitive tracts for, 30–31
parental reports of, 25, 28
performance for, 31
productivity for, 31
by school psychologist, 46–47
teacher observation for, 25, 26–28
see also Aptitude and
  achievement tests; Gifted;
  Identification; Intelligence
  tests
Selection, of learning-disabled/gifted
  child, 31–33
Self-contained class, see BOCES
  model program
Self-esteem
BOCES model program fostering,
  212–214
computers providing sense of, 200
counseling in pilot programs
  for, 234
counseling program fostering,
  167, 175–176
curriculum fostering, 267
family influence on, 246–248
of learning disabled, 45
of learning-disabled/gifted, 21, 33,
  162–163
low, 94–95
mainstreaming and, 214
Short-term memory problem,
  multisensory learning
  approach for, 164
Similarities Subscale, of
  WISC/WISC-R, 127, 128,
  129, 130, 131, 133, 135,
  136, 137
Simulation, computers for, 202–203
Small group instructional sessions,
  for counseling purposes,
  167–168

SMPY, see Study of Mathematically
  Precocious Youth, The
Social skills, see Emotional and
  social development
Social worker, in teaching programs
  for learning-disabled/gifted
  child, 158
Socioeconomic status, gifted
  and, 78
Sociopsychological approach, to
  gifted, 103
Special class, for gifted, 177
Special education placement,
  part-time, 154–155
Specialization, in learning-
  disabled/gifted child, 87
Specialized clinical instruction, in
  instruction for learning-
  disabled students, 177–178
Special school, for gifted, 177
Stanford-Binet Intelligence Test, 14,
  77, 102, 104, 105, 107,
  110, 159
States
  giftedness defined by, 79, 103–104
  learning disabilities defined by,
    70–72
Structure of Intellect-Learning
  Abilities Test, 107
Structure of Intellect (SOI)
  model, 107
  for pilot program, 240
Student committees, in teaching
  programs for learning-
  disabled/gifted child, 159
Study of Mathematically Precocious
  Youth, The (SMPY), 3,
  102–103, 104
Subgroups, of learning-
  disabled/gifted students,
  117–118
Surplus, as criteria for giftedness, 13
System of Multicultural Pluralistic
  Assessment (SOMPA),
  107–108

Taba's discussion model, in pilot
  program, 234

Subject Index

Taylor's Multiple Talents model, in
pilot program, 234
Teacher
of learning-disabled/gifted
students, 155–157
observations by, 25, 26–28, 160
recommendations of for
giftedness, 104, 110–111
referrals by, 83
screening and, 25, 26–28, 45
see also Clinical teacher; Teaching
programs
Teaching programs, 4–5, 92–93,
277–278
acquisition of knowledge in, 184
adaptive methods in
evaluation of, 190–191
for life, 190–191
in mathematics, 189–190
in reading, 184–187
administrative considerations,
153–154
placement, 154–155, 160
teacher characteristics, 155–157
counseling in, 167–169, 178–179
critical thinking in, 218–219
demonstration of knowledge
in, 184
diagnosis in, 159–161
multisensory approach for, 164
evaluation in, 161–162
independent study, 166–167, 218
individualized education programs
in, 179–180
for learning disabled, 174–175
model program, *see* BOCES
model program
pilot, *see* Gifted and Talented
Education Program
programming
for concentration problems,
163–164
concept and skill variability in,
165
content units for, 165, 167
independence acquired from,
166–167
instructional groupings for,
165–166

interests of children considered
for, 162–163
language experience approach,
163
multisensory approach to,
163–164
for organizational skill
problems, 166
reading in, 165
for recall problems, 164
for short-term memory
problem, 164
time needed for repetition in,
164–165
for verbalizers, 166
for visual/auditory learning
problems, 165–166
related services for, 157–159
aides, 158
paraprofessionals, 158
peer tutors, 158–159
school psychologist, 46–47, 157
social worker, 158
student committees, 159
self-esteem fostered by, 175–176
specialized clinical instruction in,
177–178
team approach in, 161
see also BOCES model program;
Clinical teacher; Computers;
Gifted and Talented
Education Program; Teacher
Team approach, for teaching
learning-disabled/gifted, 161
Temple University Reading Clinic,
The Johns Hopkins
University identification
research with, 118–138
Tests, *see* Aptitude and achievement
tests; Creativity; Informal
reading inventory;
Intelligence tests;
Specific tests
Test of Written Spelling (TWS),
microcomputer version of
the, 198
Theoretical definition, of learning
disabilities, 66, 67
Thinking skills, in teaching reading,
185–186

Subject Index 297

Time, for repetition needed in teaching, 164–165

Torrance Tests of Creative Thinking, 111–112

Underachievement, 19
eliminating, 39
in gifted, 102
in learning-disabled child, 58–59, 68, 69, 71, 73, 174
Un Game, as counseling activity, 234
University of Chicago Development of Talent Project, 243

Value clarification exercises, 234
self-esteem fostered by, 213
Verbalizers, teaching methods for, 166
Verbal Scale, of WISC/WISC-R, 119, 120, 122–123, 124, 125, 126, 127, 132, 133, 135, 137

Visual/auditory learning problems, teaching children with, 165–166
Visual perception improvement, in teaching learning-disabled, 178
Vocabulary Subscale, of WISC/WISC-R, 128, 129, 130, 131, 136

Wechsler Adult Intelligence Scale (WAIS), 89, 90
Wechsler Intelligence Scales for Children and Wechsler Intelligence Scales for Children-Revised, *see* Intelligence tests
Word processor, computers as a, 203
Word recognition, in case-typing, 142, 145–146
Word Recognition Inventory, 90
Writing, adaptive methods in teaching, 187–189